PageMaker® 4

PC/Windows

The Basics

Tony Bove
Cheryl Rhodes

John Wiley & Sons, Inc.

New York • Chichester • Brisbane • Toronto • Singapore

Publisher: Therese A. Zak
Editor: Katherine Schowalter
Managing Editor: Ruth Greif

Recognizing the importance of preserving what has been written, it is a policy of John Wiley & Sons, Inc. to have books of enduring value published in the United States printed on acid-free paper, and we exert our best efforts to that end.

This publication is designed to provide accurate and authoritative information in regard to the subject matter covered. It is sold with the understanding that the publisher is not engaged in rendering legal, accounting, or other professional service. If legal advice or other expert assistance is required, the services of a competent professional person should be sought. FROM A DECLARATION OF PRINCIPLES JOINTLY ADOPTED BY A COMMITTEE OF THE AMERICAN BAR ASSO-CIATION AND A COMMITTEE OF PUBLISHERS.

Library of Congress Cataloging-in-Publication Data

Bove, Tony, 1955-
    PageMaker 4 PC/Windows: the Basics / Tony Bove, Cheryl Rhodes.
      p.   cm.
    Includes bibliographical references and index.
    ISBN 0-471-52883-8 (paper)
    1. Desktop publishing—Computer programs. 2. PageMaker (Computer pro-
      gram) 3. IBM computers—Programming. I. Rhodes, Cheryl. II.Title.
Z286.D47B684 1991
686.2'2544536--dc20   91-17232

Printed in the United States of America

91 92 10 9 8 7 6 5 4 3 2 1

Acknowledgments

We would like to thank the following people for their support:

Paul Brainerd, Laury Bryant, Steven Carlsen, Jeff Halpern, Elaine Rickman, Gail Rice, and Freda Stephen (Aldus), Doedy Hunter, Ric Jones, and Keri Walker (Apple), Sara Scharf and Marty Taucher (Microsoft), and Bill Gladstone (Waterside Productions).

This book stayed on schedule thanks to the efforts of Diane Hume and Pinnacle Type (San Francisco, CA), who provided quick and accurate typesetting.

Dedicated to John Paul Bove.

Trademarks

Adobe Illustrator is a trademark of Adobe Systems, Inc.
Aldus FreeHand is a trademark of Aldus Corp.
Apple, LaserWriter, LaserWriter Plus, Apple LaserWriter II, and AppleTalk are trademarks of Apple Computer Inc.
AST and TurboLaser are registered trademarks of AST Research, Inc.
AST Premium 286, AST Rampage, AST TurboScan, and AST TurboLaser/PS are trademarks of AST Research, Inc.
AutoCAD is a registered trademark of Autodesk, Inc.
ConoVision 2800 is a trademark of Conographic Corp.
Crosstalk is a registered trademark of Digital Communications Associates, Inc.
dBASE II and dBASE III are registered trademarks of Ashton-Tate Corp.
Dataproducts LZR-2665 is a trademark of Dataproducts
DisplayWrite 3 is a trademark of International Business Machines Corp.
Document Content Architecture (DCA, also known as the IBM Revisable-Form Text) was developed by International Business Machines Corp.
Epson FX-80 is a trademark of Epson America Inc.
Ethernet is a trademark of Xerox Corp.
Gallery Collection is a trademark of Hewlett-Packard Corp.
GEM Paint is a trademark of Digital Research, Inc.
The Genius is a registered trademark of Micro Display Systems, Inc.
HALO DPE is a trademark of Media Cybernetics Inc.
Hercules is a trademark of Hercules Computer Technology
Hewlett-Packard, H-P LaserJet, H-P LaserJet Plus, and H-P Vectra are registered trademarks of Hewlett-Packard Corp.
HPGL is a trademark of Hewlett-Packard Corp.
HotShot is a trademark of SymSoft
IBM, PS/2, and Proprinter are registered trademarks of International Business Machines Corp.
IBM DisplayWrite 3 is a trademark of International Business Machines Corp.
In*a*Vision is a trademark of Micrografx, Inc.
InBox is a trademark of Symantec
INTEL and Intel Above Board are registered trademarks of Intel Corp.
Linotronic is a trademark of Linotype Corp.
Lotus, Freelance, Freelance Plus, Symphony, and 1-2-3 are registered trademarks of Lotus Development Corp.
MacDraw, MacPaint and MacWrite are trademarks of Apple Computer, Inc.
Macintosh is a trademark of McIntosh Laboratories, Inc. and is licensed to Apple Computer, Inc.
MacLink Plus is a trademark of DataViz, Inc.
MacMemories is a trademark of ImageWorld, Inc.
MacPaint is a trademark of Claris
MaxiMITE is a trademark of Mycroft Labs
Micrografx Windows "Draw!", Micrografx Windows "Graph!", and Micrografx Graph Plus are trademarks of Micrografx, Inc.
Micrografx Designer is a trademark of Micrografx, Inc.
Microsoft is a registered trademark of Microsoft Corp.
Microsoft Chart, Microsoft Excel, Microsoft Windows, Microsoft Windows Paint, Microsoft Windows Write and Microsoft Word are trademarks of Microsoft Corp.
Mirage is a trademark of Zenographics
The Missing Link is a trademark of PC Quik-Art, Inc.
MS-DOS is a registered trademark of Microsoft Corp.
MultiMate is a registered trademark of MultiMate International Corp., an Ashton-Tate Company
MultiMate Advantage is a trademark of Ashton-Tate Corp.
Multiplan is a registered trademark of Microsoft Corp.
NetWare is a registered trademark of Novell, Inc.
Olitext Plus is a trademark of Olivetti
PageMaker is a registered trademark of Aldus Corp.
PC AT and IBM PagePrinter 3812 are trademarks of International Business Machines Corp.
PC Mouse and PC Paint are trademarks of Mouse Systems
PC Paintbrush is a registered trademark of ZSoft Corp.
PC Talk III is a trademark of Headlands Press
PC Write is a trademark of Buttonware
PostScript is a registered trademark of Adobe Systems, Inc.
ProComm is a trademark of PIL Software Systems
ProIndex is a trademark of Elfring Consulting
PublishPac is a trademark of Dest Corp.
Publisher's Paintbrush is a trademark of ZSoft Corp.
Relay is a trademark of VMPC
Samna Word and Samna Word III are trademarks of SAMNA Corp.
Scan-Do is a trademark of Hammerlab Corp.
SideKick is a registered trademark of Borland, International
Symphony is a registered trademark of Lotus Development Corp.
Timeline is a trademark of Symantec
TOPS is a registered trademark of TOPS, a division of Sun Microsystems
TOPS Network, TOPS PRINT, and TOPS Translators are trademarks of TOPS, a division of Sun Microsystems
Turbo Lightning is a registered trademark of Borland, International
Varityper VT-600 is a registered trademark of AM International
Viking 1 is a trademark of Moniterm Corp.
Volkswriter is a registered trademark and Volkswriter 3 is a trademark of Lifetree Software, Inc.
Webster's NewWorld Spelling Checker is a trademark of Simon & Schuster, Inc.
Word Finder is a trademark of Writing Consultants
WordPerfect is a trademark of WordPerfect Corp. (formerly Satellite Software International)
WordStar, WordStar 3.3, WordStar 2000, and MicroPro are registered trademarks of MicroPro International Corp.
XyWrite III is a trademark of XyQuest, Inc.

Contents

Preface

This book provides a step-by-step approach to setting up publication files and templates for typical office documents, technical manuals, marketing literature, books, newsletters, and magazines. It assumes only a basic knowledge of word processing, so that anyone with a need to publish documents (but without training in page makeup or production) can use the book to produce the documents.

Each chapter introduces a different type of publication. This book also introduces the most basic concepts of design and typography. The intent is not to bog you down in details, but to show you some of the tried and true elements of good design. In some cases, examples of real publications are used. Other cases use simulated publications.

The following is a breakdown of the chapters and what you can expect to find in them.

Chapter One: Preparing for Desktop Publishing

The first chapter provides a brief description of the desktop publishing process, including word processing, graphics creation, text and graphics scanning, page makeup, laser printing, and typesetting. It provides a brief overview of Microsoft Windows and the use of a mouse and keyboard controls, plus how to perform simple file and window operations.

This chapter also explains in detail why certain word processing and graphics programs are better than others for working in conjunction with PageMaker. It also explains nearly all of PageMaker's features.

The chapter concludes with descriptions of the similarities and differences between the various laser printers, scanners, typesetters, and other output devices that work with PageMaker.

Chapter Two: A Newsletter Tutorial

This chapter takes you step-by-step through the process of producing a four-page newsletter, from starting PageMaker and designing a publication file from scratch, to producing and printing a sophisticated newsletter and saving templates for future issues. The instructions are suitable for starting up any design and production effort, and serve as a basis for understanding techniques used in subsequent chapters. This chapter can also serve as an impatient user's tutorial because it covers nearly everything that PageMaker can do.

Some highlights are step-by-step instructions for creating a newsletter title, placing formatted and unformatted text, using graphics with text, scaling and cropping graphics, sizing and resizing text, changing type styles, placing formatted and unformatted text files, changing column widths, changing the entire layout, editing text in the Story Editor, and setting up automatic page numbers.

Chapter Three: Reports, Manuals, and Books

This chapter discusses how to put together a company annual report that features spreadsheets, charts, graphs, the company logo on the cover, and a designed interior. Special effects include a custom column layout, pouring text with the Autoflow option, adjusting hyphenation, adjusting word spacing to fix any widows or orphans, wrapping text around images, creating master page elements, and creating templates. Spreadsheets and graphs are enhanced with boxes and drop shadow effects. The Story Editor is used extensively to edit text, search and replace text, and check spelling.

The chapter applies the steps presented earlier in the book to produce a typical technical manual and a book (using the page design for this book). It also explains how to set up style sheets so that global changes can be made automatically. The use of templates, master pages, and style sheets allows a production group to work efficiently, sharing master page designs and graphic elements.

Chapter Four: Graphic Design

This chapter offers techniques for customizing pages and adding design touches and special effects. It shows how to mix column layouts, wrap text around irregularly shaped graphics, spread headlines and titles, control word spacing and letterspacing, and perform manual and automatic kerning. The examples illustrate the use of special effects, such as reverse type, boxes, rules, and borders.

The examples include pages from magazines, newsletters, manuals, and books. This chapter also discusses how to prepare electronic pages with separate color overlays for handling spot color and four-color separations.

Chapter Five: Tips and Techniques

This chapter is a summary of the tips and techniques that can shorten your production time. You could use this chapter as an impatient user's summary, together with the PageMaker manuals from Aldus.

Appendixes

The appendixes include information on importing text from word processing programs exporting to word processing programs, and importing graphics from painting and drawing programs. The appendixes also contain a list of special characters that can be produced, plus hints about how to transfer PageMaker publication files between PCs and Macintosh computers. Appendix E is a bibliography, and the book concludes with an index.

*   *   *

This book has been fun to produce, thanks to PageMaker. After writing a book about the Macintosh version of PageMaker, we took the same examples and tried them on PCs, with excellent results. This entire book was written and edited on several PCs (an IBM PS/2 Model 70, a Turbo 386 PC, and a Sun Moon Star) and placed onto PageMaker pages. The PageMaker pages were printed first with an AST Research Turbolaser/PS or an Apple Personal LaserWriter NT, and then printed with a Linotype Linotronic 300 typesetter (all are PostScript devices). Microsoft Word was used (on both PC AT computers and Macintosh computers) to prepare text files. Tiffany Plus (Anderson Consulting and Software) was used to capture images of the screen activity, which were used throughout the book for examples. Tiffany can save images as TIFF (Tag Image File Format) files, which are universally recognized.

The entire project took less than three months for writing, editing, and production. This book is an example of what can be accomplished in a relatively short time and with little cost by using a desktop publishing system and PageMaker.

Aldus Manutius, the "patron saint" of publishing, would be proud of Aldus Corporation for its efforts to advance the state of the art.

Tony Bove and Cheryl Rhodes
Gualala, California
April 1, 1991

Introduction

Talk of nothing but business, and dispatch that business quickly.
—Aldus Manutius (placard on the door of the Aldine Press, Venice, Italy established about 1490)

What do Northwestern Mutual Life Insurance, Boeing, 3Com Corporation, the U.S. Congress, Hesston Corporation, Lawrence Livermore Laboratory, RTE Deltec Corporation, and the Queen Elizabeth II have in common? These organizations use PageMaker to produce publications. Hundreds of small- and medium-sized commercial publishers use PageMaker (which is to be expected), but it is significant that *companies that are not commercial publishers* are doing desktop publishing.

Many people are involved with publishing, whether or not they see themselves as publishers. If you produce sales literature, marketing brochures, flyers, newsletters, advertisements, operating manuals, or other business communications, you may be able to save time and money—and have a great deal of control over the production process—if you use a desktop publishing system. A page-makeup program, such as Aldus's PageMaker, plays the central role in any desktop publishing system.

For example, Northwestern Mutual switched from conventional methods of production to PageMaker for an in-house technical newsletter, and cut the production time in half. The company also found PageMaker useful for producing advertising flyers and transparencies for speeches.

3Com Corporation, Lawrence Livermore Laboratory, and Hesston Corporation all use PageMaker to produce large manuals. Livermore Lab also uses PageMaker to produce research reports and papers for publication in scientific journals. Hesston also uses PageMaker to produce parts catalogs, department forms, and other instructional material.

The Queen Elizabeth II uses PageMaker to produce a daily world-news bulletin. The news pages are put together into a PageMaker publication file in London and then transmitted by satellite to the luxury liner, where a laser printer prints 1,200 copies for the ship's passengers.

Newspapers such as *The State Journal* (Charleston, West Virginia), *Behind the Times* (Corinth, Vermont), and *Roll Call* (weekly newspaper for the U.S. Congress), and magazines such as *Publish, MacUser, Macworld, Chartering Magazine*, and *Balloon Life* use PageMaker because the desktop publishing equipment shortens the production cycle and saves money.

Graphics experts and consultants can now focus on the design task and perform that work much more quickly and inexpensively with desktop publishing equipment, or else let their clients do their own production work. Small publishers have the ability to produce commercial publications that have the same quality look and feel as publications from large publishers. Corporations can cut down on the cost of designing forms, brochures, and marketing literature. Technical publications departments can now produce manuals and data sheets very quickly.

The desktop-publishing phenomenon started when laser printers, which offer near-typeset-quality text and graphics printing, were introduced to work with personal computers. As a result, inexpensive publishing tools became available, which made it easier for people to do publishing production tasks without resorting to typesetting services and graphic design houses.

Desktop publishing tools became useful for commercial and corporate publishing when they were made compatible with typesetters and higher-resolution devices (such as film recorders and plate makers). The industry-wide acceptance of a common language of typesetting, called PostScript (developed by Adobe Systems and first used in printers by Apple, then by

Digital Equipment Corporation, IBM, Sun Microsystems, Texas Instruments, QMS, AST Research, and Wang) made it possible for desktop publishing software to produce typeset-quality text and high-quality photographs.

A page-makeup program plays a central role in a desktop publishing system, and is used as a finishing tool for preparing text and graphics for presentation and publication. A word processing program and a graphics program are used to create the text and graphics, and a page-makeup program brings the elements together on a page. The page-makeup program lets you adjust the design of the page at the same time that you place the elements.

Electronic page makeup offers many benefits over conventional manual page makeup and design methods. Because the electronic elements can be easily moved, cut, copied, resized, edited, and repasted on the page, the elements do not get lost. There are no cut marks where a sharp knife has slipped. You do not have to wait for images or type to be repro-duced at a new size, or for the production of new typesetting galleys to replace a misspelled word found in a typeset galley.

PageMaker is the quintessential electronic page-makeup program because it simulates the procedures that artists and designers use in conventional page makeup. Text and graphic images are pasted onto an electronic page and cropped with an electronic "knife." Master page elements are created and duplicated automatically for all or some of the pages. Blocks of text can be moved on the page to fit around graphics, and you can wrap text around irregular shapes automatically. Columns of text are linked so that changes made to a column cause a ripple of reformatting to occur automatically. You can experiment with minor editing changes to shorten or lengthen a block of text, or change the size of the text block itself. You can even pour text onto multiple pages automatically and quickly, to see how many pages the text will fill.

With this metaphor in action on the screen, designers, artists, and graphics-oriented people can feel the power of the computer and relate immediately to its use in desktop publishing. The metaphor of text threading is very close to the physical task of threading typeset galleys through a layout. Designers and graphic artists have no trouble understanding how PageMaker works; the precision of its rulers and various page displays make it very easy to line things up (without the need for a T-square and a fluorescent light table).

The metaphor works with beginners as well, providing a real-world model for the activity of mixing text and graphics on pages. Coupled with Microsoft Windows 3, which handles file and disk management as well as program execution on DOS computers, PageMaker fits neatly into the desktop environment and is therefore easy to learn. The menus from which you select options look just like the menus in Windows and in other Windows applications. This is also true of the OS/2 Presentation Manager (PM) version of PageMaker: it fits neatly into the Presentation Manager environment, which handles the file and disk management tasks for computers running OS/2.

The Windows and OS/2 PM versions of PageMaker have been used for many applications, including the production of magazines and books, even though PageMaker was originally designed for newsletters. The authors of this book used PageMaker to produce a magazine *(Desktop Publishing,* now called *Publish)*, and now use both Windows and OS/2 versions of PageMaker to produce books, a monthly newsletter, and a variety of other publishing tasks. The authors also use PageMaker to produce tabloids and oversized brochures and flyers, even though the program supports only A4, 8 1/2 by 11-inch, and 8 1/2 by 14-inch pages on the laser printer. (To produce a page wider than 8 1/2 inches, use PageMaker's *tiling* techniques, which allow the printing of tabloid size pages in sections. You paste the pieces together to match up the elements. If you use a typesetter such as the Linotype Linotronic 100 or 300 imagesetter, or a printer such as the DataProducts LZR 2665, all of which support a larger page size (11 by 17 inches), you can print the tabloid page in one piece without tiling.)

A sure sign that desktop publishing has grown past the adolescent stage is the emergence of a program like PageMaker that can do practically everything a word processor can do, as well as provide a level of precision to accommodate the professional graphic artist and publisher. It was once predicted that word processing programs would take over the turf held by the page makeup programs, but the opposite may well come true: that page makeup will swallow word processing.

You can now expect a page makeup program to provide full kerning, word spacing, and letterspacing, and in fine-enough increments to satisfy a professional. You can expect word processing features, including search and replace, spell checking, and indexing. You can use any type of graphic image and perhaps even anchor the image to a reference point in the story. You can also expect a page makeup program to handle multiple stories over multiple pages, and provide an accurate depiction of the page on the screen at different viewing percentages, with rulers and guides available to align objects.

PageMaker version 4 for Windows and OS/2 not only satisfies these requirements; it does much more, and is also easy to learn and use. PageMaker 4 is effective as a word processing program as well as a complete document publishing system. You may well decide to switch to PageMaker 4 as their complete document production system, foregoing the use of separate word processing programs. No other program provides such an extensive set of typographic, layout, and file management features.

PageMaker 4 offers 75 new features including a fully-integrated Story Editor for editing text in a window at faster speed. A sophisticated search and replace facility that can search for and replace text based on font or style attributes, and a spelling checker, are both provided. The import and export features make it easy to create, edit and manage text files for use with other applications. Optional foreign language dictionaries allow hyphenation and spell checking of up to six languages at once, with the selection of a dictionary recorded as a paragraph style, so that different paragraphs can be checked by different dictionaries. A separate Table Editor is provided for creating and editing tables that can be imported into PageMaker.

Features for publishing lengthy documents include table of contents and index generation capabilities, as well as the ability to link graphics to move with associated text, and widow/orphan control. File management facilities include the ability to track revisions of text and graphics files used by PageMaker files, and the ability to chain separate PageMaker files into a "book" for printing, and for table of contents and index generation. The maximum file size has been increased from 128 to 999 pages (or available disk space).

New color features include PANTONE Matching System color charts, and the ability to import, display and print color images. Color separations can be printed using the Aldus PrePrint option, sold separately. Thirty custom-designed templates and an on-line help system (as well as greatly improved manuals) are also provided.

If you are new to the program, or if you never used version 3, you will appreciate the basic features that were provided then and are now enhanced in version 4, including automatic pair kerning (as supported by the different font manufacturers) and manual kerning, as well as automatic letter spacing and word spacing (for justified text only). PageMaker offers paragraph spacing, typographic fixed spaces, leader tabs, additional line styles, the ability to size and resize columns at will, and hand-scrolling of an image within the space reserved for it on the page. The program also offers automatic hyphenation based on a 110,000-word dictionary from Houghton Mifflin as well as a 1,300-word supplementary dictionary, prompted hyphenation (the program displays words not found in the dictionary and lets you hyphenate them and add them to the supplementary dictionary), and manual hyphenation (discretionary hyphens).

With these features, Aldus improved PageMaker so much that it is now an excellent tool for producing books, manuals, reports, and commercial publications, as well as newsletters and marketing literature. The program is now capable of producing so many different publications that entire books about using PageMaker (such as this one) are needed.

*   *   *

Will desktop publishing foster a renaissance in the printed word and image? Some believe that poorly designed results from desktop publishing will prove that publishing should be left to the experts who have design skills. But the enthusiasm for desktop publishing is infectious, and people can learn design skills by reading books, consulting with experts, and taking design courses.

In an era when automation is making information workers more productive, the ability to self-publish is a valuable asset for the smallest communications service company to the largest corporation, from the individual writer to working partnerships and government organizations. If you can present information in a professional style and publish it without incurring variable costs or costly delays, you are using desktop publishing for what it was intended—to make you more productive in your business.

1 | Preparing for Desktop Publishing

To produce a publication, even a very small one, you invariably have to go through four major steps: (1) designing the publication, (2) creating the text, photographs, and graphics, (3) making up the pages by combining the text, photos, and graphics with design elements, and (4) using a prepress shop or print shop to prepare film negatives, from which plates for the pages are made. The plates are then used with a printing press.

The goal of desktop publishing is to automate as many of the repetitive tasks in the production cycle as possible. A major advantage of desktop publishing is greater flexibility in design and layout. Changes are not only possible, but easy to accommodate, right up to press time. Page design can easily be performed on personal computers, and sample pages can be printed with laser printers. Comments and editing changes are more easily incorporated when the manuscript is stored in electronic form. Line art that is stored in electronic form can be precise and revisable, and electronic page makeup is faster and easier than the process of manual paste-up.

Text and graphics should be stored in electronic form as early in the process as possible. They may either be created electronically with a personal computer, or else the information may be converted into electronic form by using a scanner. Text and graphics can be created on any type of computer from a mainframe to a portable, and then stored in files on floppy disks, hard disks, erasable optical discs, magnetic tape cartridges, and other digital storage devices. To convert paper-based information, you can scan typewritten text and hand-drawn line art with a desktop scanner that costs less than $4000 (and perhaps as low as $1500).

Why is it so useful to store text and graphics in electronic form? For one thing, text stored in electronic form can be sent to a typesetter or imagesetter without having to retype it or scan it. For another, graphics can be included with the text without the need to perform manual paste-up, and pieces of graphic elements can be used again in other illustrations without having to draw them or use photographic methods to copy them.

The PageMaker screen closely displays the same image you can expect on paper, so carefully check the screen for any errors before printing. When you finish making all of the changes that you want, entire pages can roll out of the typesetter, imagesetter, or laser printer. The pages are ready to be used as camera copy for volume printing, with no need for further mechanical processes (wax, glue, etc.). You can take advantage of other options with imagesetters, such as printing directly to film-based materials or directly onto printing plates.

Where to Start

If you're new to publishing or production work, you may be surprised to find that there are many steps to climb before you reach the finished, published work. At the top of the stairs is the volume printing process—the method by which you print mass quantities of the publication.

Even if you need only 10 copies of the publication, you must start with an idea about what the final printing process will entail. Will you use a copier or a laser printer to produce 10 or 20 copies? Will you need more than 200 but less than 500 copies? More than 1000? More than 10,000? You must answer this basic question first, and then plan the publication's production effort.

For example, a newsletter or business report may require a clean, polished look. Because this type of publication is inexpensively printed in small quantities (less than 500), the extra expense of production on a 1000 dots-per-inch (dpi) typesetter is not required—a laser printer could do the job. For these applications, you can use almost any desktop laser printer (at 300 or 150 dpi), and not worry about compatibility with a typesetter.

However, a book, a magazine, a piece of marketing literature (such as a page advertisement, flyer, or brochure), or an instruction manual might require typeset-quality text and photographic-quality images. For such production efforts, compatibility with a typesetter is critical. The surest way to maintain compatibility between your laser printer and higher-resolution typesetters is to use a PostScript-compatible laser printer. PostScript is the most popular page-description language used in both printers and typesetters, as well as in high-resolution film recorders and display systems.

For some production efforts, a desktop publishing system needs to have the speed of laser printing, plus flexibility and compatibility with typesetters. PageMaker offers the best of both worlds because it supports virtually every type of printer for PCs, as well as every PostScript typesetter and printer. You can proof the file on a laser printer, and then provide your file on disk (or via modem) to a PostScript typesetting service bureau that produces final typeset pages.

Consider also the type of system that you will use: Are all of the pieces available now; is retraining necessary; and can you purchase enough systems to handle the project? Will the same computer be used to write, edit, create graphics, and compose pages? How much time should you allocate for volume printing? All of these factors contribute to the development of a timetable for production efforts.

An AST Premium 286 (Figure 1-1) and a Sun Moon Star System 286-12/CD were used to create examples for this book as well as to write and edit text. An IBM PS/2 Model 70 (Figure 1-2), with two megabytes of RAM and an 80-megabyte hard disk, was used to produce this book with PC PageMaker 4.0. (A Macintosh was also used to test compatibility with the Macintosh version of PageMaker.)

The Hewlett-Packard LaserJet IIP and LaserJet III printers, both in native (PCL) mode and with the Adobe Systems' PostScript cartridge,

Figure 1-1. The Premium 286 Publishing System from AST Research.

of the book, we used PostScript as the target printer, proofed the pages on
the Apple LaserWriter, and typeset the final pages on an Allied Linotype
Linotronic 100 typesetter.

If you are familiar with the PC's operating system, you already know
how to use system commands to format disks, copy or delete disk files,
add or remove printers and other devices, print files, and run programs.
Microsoft Windows (the full version) is a level of software that lets you
use the operating system without knowing specific commands. You can
format disks, copy or delete files, add or remove printer control software,

Figure 1-2. The IBM PS/2 Model 70, which offers built-in support for a VGA color monitor.

Datacopy card interface.

To produce the final camera-ready pages of the book, the PostScript-based Linotype Linotronic 100/300 imagesetter was chosen as the printer before resizing the screen examples. The screen examples, captured with Tiffany Plus (Anderson Consulting & Software, N. Bonneville, WA) and saved as ".TIF" (Tag Image Format) files, were resized for the imagesetter's resolution using PageMaker's built-in scaling sizes, and the publication files were saved with the Linotronic set as the printer.

For proof printing, the printer was changed to the AST TurboLaser/ PS or the Personal LaserWriter NT (both PostScript), and test pages were printed. The original publication files were sent (after final editing) to the service bureau for output to photograph paper using a Linotronic 300. There was never any need to obtain the high-resolution imagesetter in-house because the service bureau was capable of fast turnaround (without having to perform any typing or editing on the book's files), and the PostScript laser printer produced more-than-adequate proof pages. (For some publishing efforts, the laser printer pages are fine for use as camera-ready pages.)

PageMaker (version 4) requires a computer that uses the 80286, 80386, or 80486 processor. The computer must have at least two mega-bytes of RAM (random access memory) and be able to run Windows 3, which is required for running PageMaker. Aldus recommends that you have more than two megabytes of RAM for faster performance, although the authors were able to produce this book with a two-megabyte machine.

A color VGA (Video Graphics Adapter) display monitor is recom-mended, but you can also use PageMaker 4 with any display adapter and monitor that can be used with Windows 3. For example, you can use a Hercules monochrome adapter and display. You also need a mouse device compatible with Windows 3. A color monitor is recommended so that you can see text, graphics, and images in color as they would appear when printed in color, and so that you can easily distinguish between the active and inactive windows in Windows 3. (The authors used color VGA displays.)

It is recommended that you have at least 20 megabytes of hard disk space for storing the program's files and your publication files, and a floppy disk drive that reads 1.2-megabyte 5.25-inch disks or 720-kilobyte 3.5-inch disks. The authors used an 80-megabyte disk in order to have enough space to accommodate the publication files and images for this book.

PageMaker requires a hard disk or similar high-capacity random access storage device because it is impossible to use the program and manage publication files without the capacity and speed of a hard disk, especially if you use scanned images or produce multiple-page publications. You gain faster program interaction and additional work space by adding a hard disk to your system.

Learning Windows

If you and your production staff have no experience with Windows 3 and DOS computers, set aside time to become familiar with them. Start with the "Getting Started" and "Basic Skills" section of the *Microsoft Windows User's Guide* supplied with your copy of Windows 3.

You should become familiar with DOS (Disk Operating System) and Windows to the point where you know how to prepare formatted floppy disks, copy or delete disk files, add or remove printers and other devices, print files, and run programs.

Windows lets you perform most if not all of your DOS operations so that you don't have to learn the DOS commands. You can perform all of the steps just listed—in short, you can do almost everything the operating system lets you do, but without having to learn commands.

You operate Windows by dragging downward from a menu topic with a mouse and highlighting the commands and options in the menu until you reach the one you want, then letting go of the mouse button to select the command or option. You may then have to type a file's name or *path*. A path is a list of the directory names, separated by backslashes, starting with the drive name and ending with the actual file name, as in C:\PROJECTS\TEXT\MYWORK.TXT (the file MYWORK.TXT is in directory TEXT, which is inside directory PROJECTS, which is a directory on the C: disk).

DOS controls all operations in your computer, such as executing programs, copying files from one disk to another, and copying data to printing devices. However, DOS offers only the lowest level of operational control, and you must learn various DOS commands and run various programs to actually control operations.

Microsoft Windows is a graphical operating environment that runs on top of DOS, providing access to DOS operations through the use of windows, icons, menu selections, and buttons. Windows provides an environment for using a mouse or other pointing device to perform operations and execute programs. It also provides a consistent interface for controlling any devices (printers, displays, disk drives, etc.) connected to your computer. (If you prefer not to use a mouse, Windows offers keyboard-style shortcuts for executing commands, selecting options, and running programs.)

After starting up Windows by typing **WIN** as a DOS command, you are presented with windows and icons (the arrangement depends on how you've installed Windows). In a typical installation, Windows displays the Program Manager window, and inside this window are displayed the Main window, the Windows Applications window, and the Aldus window (see Figure 1-3). Other windows are represented by icons along the bottom of the screen, such as Games, Non-Windows Applications, and Accessories (your screen may differ depending on your installation). To

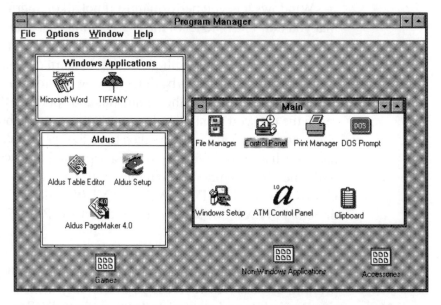

Figure 1-3. Microsoft Windows displays windows containing icons and menus, which are used to perform DOS operations and to execute Windows-compatible programs and other DOS programs.

open these windows, use the mouse to move the pointer cursor over the icon, and click twice. This is called *double-clicking* the mouse, and it is the action you will perform most often when using Windows.

After you learn the basics, you can quickly learn any new Windows-compatible program because you can apply what you know. Windows provides basic actions that are the same from one well-designed Windows-compatible program to another. You can also execute DOS programs from within Windows. However, DOS programs that know nothing of Windows do not change when you run them—they still look and act the same as when you are not running Windows.

Using a Mouse

PageMaker is a Windows-compatible program that fits nicely in the Windows environment of menus, icons, and windows. To use PageMaker and other Windows applications, and to perform Windows operations, you should become familiar with the mouse. All of PageMaker's and Windows' functions can be used with a mouse or other pointing device. You must install Windows with the proper selection for the mouse or pointing device (in some computers, Windows is preinstalled for the mouse). The most popular mouse devices are from Microsoft, Logitech, and Mouse Systems.

Basically, six actions are performed with a mouse:

1. *Point.* When you move the mouse, a pointer (shaped like an arrow in most cases) moves across the display. The pointer may turn into a symbol of an hourglass when the program or the System is busy, or into an I-beam symbol when you move it over text after selecting the "A" text tool in PageMaker. Some application programs (such as PageMaker) display a toolbox for changing the pointer into a crosshair for use in drawing lines or polygons, or for changing the pointer into symbols for other tools supplied by that program. To point, you move the tip of the pointer to the desired area on the display. The mouse tracking speed can be set in the Control Panel, described on page 14.

2. *Click.* To click, quickly press and release the mouse button (usually the left button, but you can switch to another button in the Control Panel, described on page 14). Click to select an icon, a starting point in text, or

a button (such as the OK button). Buttons are highlighted when selected.

3. *Double-click.* To double-click, quickly press and release the mouse button twice. The double-click setting can be changed in the Control Panel, described on page 14.

4. *Drag.* To drag something (such as a graphic object, block of text, or icon), point the mouse, hold down the main mouse button (usually the left-most button), and move the mouse so that the pointer (or object) moves to a new position. Next, release the button.

5. *Select.* To select a menu option or command, drag down a menu (which drops down to show you the options or commands) until the command or option that you want is highlighted. Release the mouse button. (Keyboard shortcuts are available for many commands.) To select text, double-click a word or drag across one or more words or paragraphs.

6. *Flow (Place).* This is a PageMaker variation of click, in which you point and click a text flow icon to pour the text down the column.

The Program Manager

The Program Manager window is the first large window you see when you start Windows. This window has a menu bar along the top with menus labeled File, Options, Window, and Help. The commands and options in these menus let you create new group windows containing icons for programs, and let you manipulate those windows to display them for convenience in running programs. These are the basic operations you can perform with the Program Manager.

You can run any program from the Program Manager window. For example, to run PageMaker, simply double-click the program's icon in the Aldus window. (As an alternative you can use the File Manager application to select a PageMaker publication file, and then double-click that file to launch the program, as described on page 18.)

The windows opened within the Program Manager, such as the Main window, the Accessories window, and the Aldus window, represent *groups* of programs. The Aldus group window is created automatically when you install PageMaker. The Aldus group window contains an icon representing the PageMaker program. Each group window contains a collection of icons representing programs. The Main window contains programs such as the Control Panel, which is used to modify the Windows environment.

Group windows that are not open are represented by group icons. To open a group window, double-click its icon, or press the Control and Tab keys simultaneously (or Control and F6) and press the Enter key.

When you run PageMaker (or any other Windows-compatible program) by double-clicking its icon, the program creates another window with its own menu bar and menus.

Using the Windows Control Menu

All windows have a title bar with the name of the window, and most windows have a window-specific menu bar with menu labels.

To use the menus, move the pointer to a menu label in the menu bar and hold down the mouse button. The menu opens. Hold down the mouse button and drag the mouse down the menu to the desired command, which is highlighted when it is selected. To activate the command, release the mouse button. An alternative is to click the menu label once, then move the pointer down to the command or option in the menu, and click that command or option once.

Special window controls are attached to the top of each window. Two arrow buttons appear on the right side of the title bar, and a special box button appears on the left side of the title bar. This box button is called the Control-menu box; when you click this box, the window's Control menu appears (Figure 1-4).

The Control menu contains the following commands:

Restore—restores the window to its former size from an icon.

Move—lets you move the window around the screen.

Size—lets you resize the window from any corner or edge.

Minimize—turns the window into an icon.

Maximize—turns the window or icon into a full-screen window.

Close—closes the window.

The Control menu for the Program Manager window also contains the Switch To command, for switching from one program to another.

Use the Control menu for each window to perform operations such as resizing the window, maximizing (full screen) or minimizing the window into an icon, and restoring the window from an icon to its full size. You can close the window by choosing Close, or just by double-clicking the Control-menu box. The Control menu is also available when you click a window that has been minimized into an icon—use Restore to restore it

 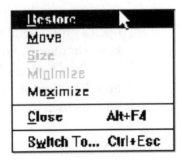

Figure 1-4. The Control menu for each window lets you resize or move the window, change the window into an icon, and restore the window to its full size. When a window is minimized into an icon, click the icon once to display its Control menu.

to window size.

The arrow buttons on the right side of the title bar correspond to Control menu options: the down arrow button performs a Minimize to turn a window into an icon, and the up arrow button performs a Maximize to make the window fill the screen.

Nearly all Windows-compatible programs work in this fashion, with pull-down menus that contain all commands and options. Some programs display documents in separate windows with their own Control menus. PageMaker displays itself in a window and also creates a separate, *child* window (with PageMaker as the *parent* window) to display a publication. The child window always disappears with the parent window when you close the parent window or turn the parent window into an icon. In addition, a child window can be turned into an icon within a parent window.

The Main Window

The Windows Main window displays a group of programs that are a standard part of the Windows environment. These include the File Manager, the Print Manager, the Windows Setup program, the Clipboard, and the Control Panel. The Main window may also include other Windows options, such as Adobe Type Manager (ATM) from Adobe Systems, which provides outline font display and printing.

The Control Panel (Figure 1-5) provides access to system functions

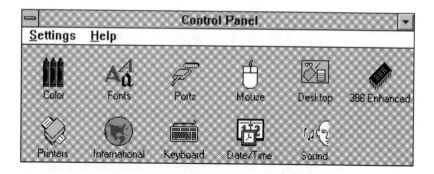

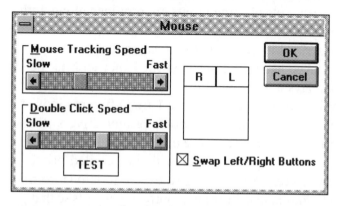

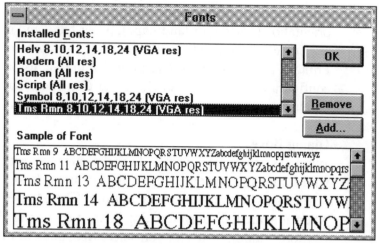

Figure 1-5. The Windows Control Panel icon lets you set the time and date, set up printers, install fonts, adjust the mouse controls, and other Windows options. The icons in the Panel represent devices and system functions. Click the Mouse icon to adjust the mouse settings, or the Fonts icon to install screen fonts.

such as the time and date, the desktop colors, network connections, printer configuration, font installation, keyboard setup, mouse setting adjustments, and the volume of the computer's internal speaker.

For example, you can change the way the mouse works, such as switching the functions of the left and right buttons, changing the speed for double-clicking, and changing the tracking speed (at which the mouse moves the pointer).

Another popular adjustment for PageMaker users is to add or delete sets of screen fonts. Screen fonts determine how characters look on the screen. Sets of screen fonts are provided along with printer fonts for the purpose of assigning fonts to text in PageMaker before printing. Fonts are described in more detail in Chapter 2.

Another important Control Panel icon is the Printers icon, which displays a window of dialog box that lets you configure printers for all Windows programs (Figure 1-6). Different kinds of printers can be used with your installed Windows printer drivers (the software for driving printers), and the purpose of the Printers dialog box is to let you associate a specific type of printer with an installed printer driver. The Printers dialog box lets you change the configuration information for printers, and lets you change the printer-port assignments so that you can add or remove a printer. For each printer, you can set print options such as page orientation (portrait or landscape), paper feed, and graphics resolution.

To select an installed printer, click a printer in the list of Installed Printers, and click the Active button in the Status box. You can change configuration details by clicking the Configure button. Click the OK button to save your changes, or the Cancel button to cancel the changes.

Dialog Boxes
Windows programs generally look the same, offering pull-down menus with commands and options that display dialog boxes which contain lists of files and buttons for setting options. The Mouse and Printers icons, when activated, displayed dialog boxes for making choices.

Some dialog boxes let you select filenames from a displayed list. If there are scroll bars, you can scroll the items in the list window.

For example, you can use PageMaker to open a publication file by selecting the Open command from the File menu (Figure 1-7). Open command displays a dialog box that includes a list of publication files,

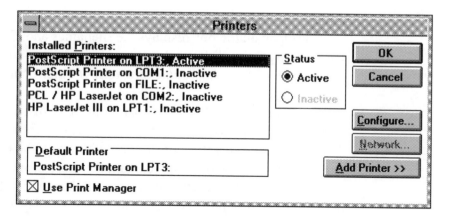

Figure 1-6. With the Printers icon in the Control Panel, you can set up several
different printers to use with all Windows programs (a PostScript printer is chosen
on the left). You can also configure the printer ports on your computer to match
specific printers, and define a default printer.

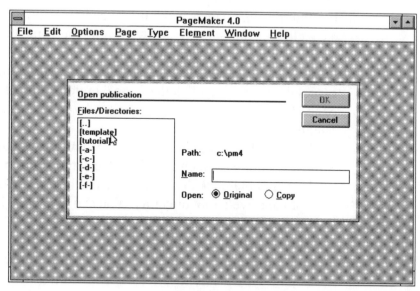

Figure 1-7. The File menu's Open command displays a dialog box with a list of
directories and disks (names in brackets). Double-click a directory to see its contents;
if it contains more directories, double-click one to see its contents.

directories, and drives.

The Open dialog box displays the filenames and directory names for the currently active disk and directory. A directory is an area of a disk that contains files and perhaps more directories (which contain more files and directories, etc.).

Often the Open dialog box displays only a list of directories and drives rather than files. Directories and drives have brackets around their names. To look inside a directory or drive, double-click the directory or drive name. A drive will most likely contain directories, and many directories also contain directories (sometimes called subdirectories). You can double-click a subdirectory's name in order to display its contents. As you open a subdirectory that is contained within another directory, you are moving down through an organized set of directories (as if you were going up a tree from the root) until you reach the file that you want.

If the list of names is longer than the dialog box window, scroll bars appear for scrolling up and down the list (Figure 1-8). To operate the scroll bar and see more names in the list, click below the white box in the gray area, click the up or down arrow, or drag the white box up or down.

If the directory contains PageMaker publication files, you can select them by clicking the file's name, and then clicking the OK button. To cancel the command, click the Cancel button. All dialog boxes have the equivalent of an OK button (to proceed with the action) and a Cancel button (to cancel an action).

You may have to switch back to the disk (the root of the tree) in order to move to another branch of the tree that contains one or more directories. To do so, double-click the drive name (such as **[c]** or **[d]**) to see the contents of the drive's root directory. You can then open files or directories on that disk.

The Open command in PageMaker displays the names of all drives and directories as you move through the tree structure of a disk, but it does *not* display the names of files that it does not recognize as publication files. If your file is not a PageMaker publication file, you will not see it listed in the Open dialog box. This prevents you from trying to open an inappropriate file and causing the program to crash.

PageMaker can, however, open other types of files for *placement* into a PageMaker publication file. For this purpose, PageMaker provides the

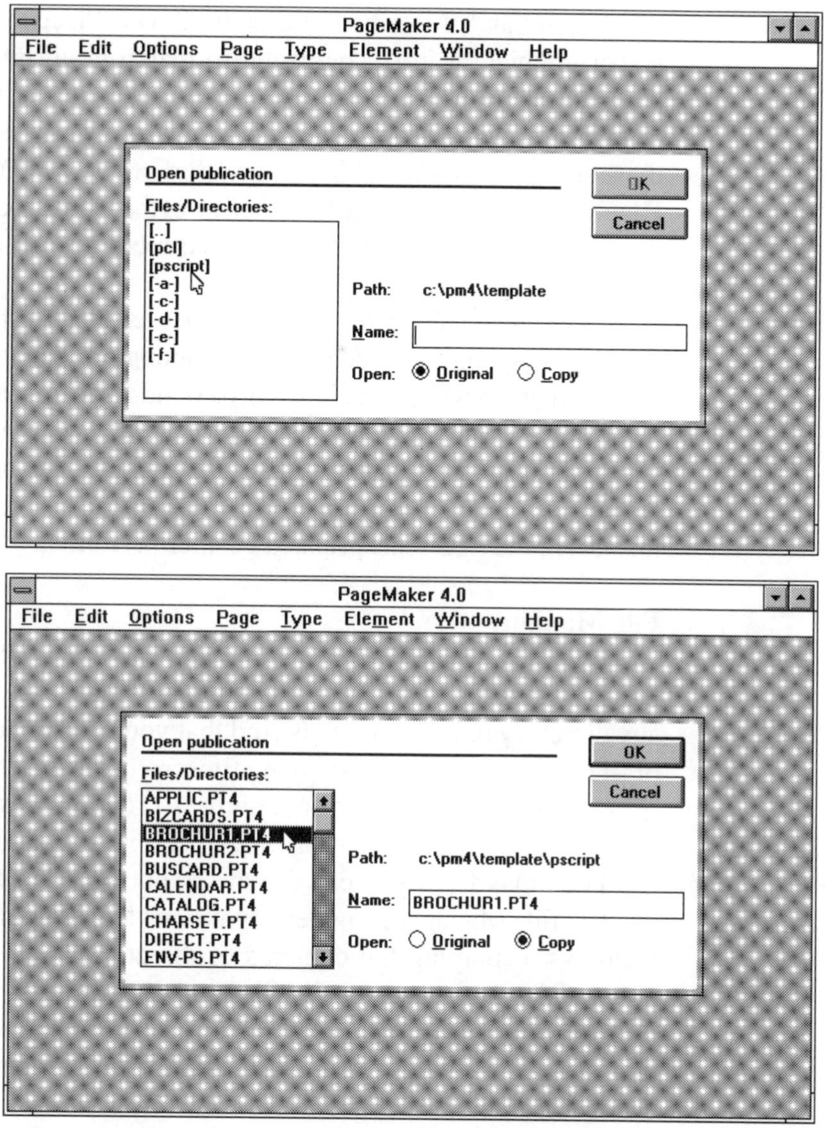

PageMaker 4.0

File   Edit   Options   Page   Type   Element   Window   Help

Open publication

[OK]

Files/Directories:

[..]
[pcl]
[pscript]
[-a-]
[-c-]
[-d-]
[-e-]
[-f-]

[Cancel]

Path: c:\pm4\template

Name: [   ]

Open: ⦿ Original   ○ Copy

PageMaker 4.0

File   Edit   Options   Page   Type   Element   Window   Help

Open publication

[OK]

Files/Directories:

APPLIC.PT4
BIZCARDS.PT4
BROCHUR1.PT4
BROCHUR2.PT4
BUSCARD.PT4
CALENDAR.PT4
CATALOG.PT4
CHARSET.PT4
DIRECT.PT4
ENV-PS.PT4

[Cancel]

Path: c:\pm4\template\pscript

Name: [BROCHUR1.PT4]

Open: ○ Original   ⦿ Copy

Figure 1-8. If the active directory in the Open dialog box contains PageMaker publication files, a list appears (including scroll bars if the list is long), and you can select a publication file by clicking its name and clicking OK (or double-clicking its name).

Place command, described in Chapter 2. Use Place to select any type of text or graphics file in a recognizable format from any program. PageMaker recognizes any ASCII (American Standard Code for Information Interchange) text-only file plus several formatted word processor files, including those created with Word (Microsoft), Works (Microsoft), and WordPerfect. PageMaker recognizes some, but not all, of the word processor's formatting commands. Appendix A describes the word processor formatting that PageMaker uses.

PageMaker recognizes graphics files created with several different painting programs, provided that the painting program saves the file in the PCX format, TARGA (TrueVision), or Windows Clipboard or BMP formats (nearly all PC paint programs save one of these). PageMaker also recognizes standard Macintosh MacPaint and CGM graphics files, and files in the TIFF format (Tag Image File Format, which offers the best results with scanned images) or the EPS (encapsulated PostScript) format.

File Manager

Although PageMaker's Open command can open publication files, and PageMaker's Save and Save As commands can save publication files in any directory or disk, you may find that you need to perform other kinds of file operations, such as copying files from one disk to another, moving files from one directory to another, creating new directories and subdirectories, and formatting disks. These tasks can be performed with DOS commands, or you can use the Windows File Manager program.

The File Manager provides a window view of your directory tree and windows displaying the contents of directories and disks. With menu commands you can search for files and directories by name, create new directories, move or copy files and directories, rename files and directories, set file attributes (such as "read only" to prevent a file from being changed), associate document files with programs so that you can launch the appropriate program by double-clicking the document, and start running any program.

When you start Windows, the File Manager icon appears in the Main group window, and you can start the File Manager program by double-clicking this icon. The File Manager starts by displaying the Directory Tree window (Figure 1-9), which contains the directory tree structure of

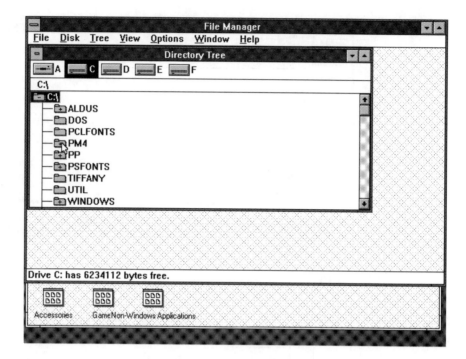

Figure 1-9. The Directory Tree window, displayed by the File Manager, shows the overall organization of directories and subdirectories on any disk drive. Directories appear as branches connected to the top-level "root" directory of each disk. Disks are represented by disk drive letters (A, B, C, etc.).

the currently selected disk (usually disk drive C, where PageMaker and Windows are often installed). The directory tree starts with the *root* directory, represented by a single backslash (\) following the drive letter (as in **C:**), which contains all directories on a particular disk (including subdirectories). Each directory name is accompanied by a folder icon. The window has scroll bars for scrolling the list up and down, and a status bar displays the amount of disk space available on the currently-selected disk. The currently selected disk and root directory is highlighted.

A folder icon with a plus sign indicates that the directory contains one or more subdirectories. To open such a directory and see its subdirectories, click the directory name once (Figure 1-10). You can repeat this procedure if any subdirectory has a plus sign in its folder (indicating that it, too,

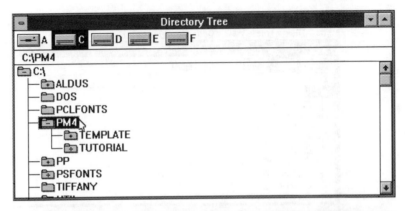

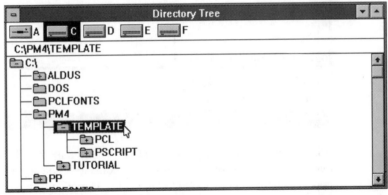

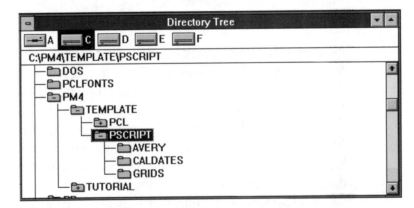

Figure 1-10. Click on a directory's name to see its subdirectories, and click on one of these subdirectories to see any subdirectories within it (a plus sign in the folder icon indicates a subdirectory exists within the directory).

contains one or more subdirectories).

To see the contents of any directory (Figure 1-11), double-click the directory name. The File Manager displays another window (a child window) showing the files in that directory (any subdirectory names are enclosed in brackets). Included in the list of files is an entry showing two periods enclosed in brackets. This is a special entry you can use to move backward in the tree back to the directory containing the directory shown in the window. Double-click the entry to move back one directory toward the root directory.

A file can be selected by clicking once on the file name. Multiple files listed in sequence can be selected by clicking the first file name once, then holding down the Shift key while clicking the last file name in the sequence. Multiple files not listed in sequence can be selected by clicking the first file name once, then holding down the Control (Ctrl) key while clicking each subsequent file.

You can move or copy one or more files that have been selected. One way is to use the Copy or Move commands in the File menu, and specifying the path for the *destination* (a drive letter, followed by a colon and a backslash, followed by the directory names separated by backslashes; as in **C:\PM4\TEMPLATE**). The Copy and Move commands assume that the selected files are the *source*.

Another way is to open another window for the destination (or make visible the folder icon for the destination directory). You can have more than one window open at a time, and you can move the windows around, or resize the windows, in order to view them together. You can also use the Tile or Cascade commands in the Window menu to change the way the windows are displayed. With both windows (the source, with the selected files, and the destination) open, you can use the mouse to drag the selected files into the destination window.

If the destination directory is on a *different disk* than the source directory, you must hold down the ALT key while dragging in order to move the files to the destination directory (and remove from the source directory). Otherwise, the files are copied to the other directory. However, if the destination directory is on the *same disk* as the source directory, the files are moved with or without the ALT key. In the latter case, you must hold down the Control (Ctrl) key in order to copy the files rather than

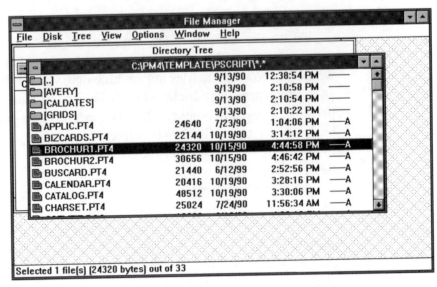

Figure 1-11. When you double-click a directory or subdirectory name, another window appears presenting the files in that directory (plus other directory names in brackets). You can select any file by clicking its name; some files will launch programs if you double-click their names.

move them.

An entire directory can be moved or copied the same way as a file. Multiple directories can be selected in the same way as files (in a directory window, but not in the Tree Directory window), and then moved or copied as files. The entire contents of each directory is moved or copied as well.

You can delete the selected files by choosing the Delete command in the File menu. Entire directories can also be deleted this way (including the contents of the directories). Files are not recoverable after they are deleted unless you use a file/disk recovery program, such as the Norton Utilities. In normal Windows installations, confirmation messages appear before deletions actually occur, so that you can confirm or cancel the operation for each selected file or directory.

You can also rename any selected file or directory with the Rename command in the File menu. Valid file names can have up to eight characters, followed by a period and three characters called the *extension*. The file name extension is usually fixed by the program that creates the file; for example, PageMaker publication files use the extension ".PM4" and PageMaker template files use ".PT4" (these extensions are automatically appended to the eight-character name you assign when you save the file).

Switching Among Windows Programs

You can run several programs at once with Windows. It is often the case that different windows can fill up the screen, making it difficult to find a particular window.

You can display windows in a cascading fashion, or side-by-side in a tile fashion. You can move any window by dragging the window's title bar. To resize a window, drag any edge or corner to the desired size.

The active window always appears in the foreground, in front of other windows. You can switch to another window by clicking anywhere within it. If the other window is obscured, press the ALT and ESC (Escape) keys simultaneously to make another window appear; repeat the sequence to make other windows appear.

An alternate way to switch from one program window to another is to choose Switch To from the active window's Control menu (described earlier), or to double-click anywhere in the desktop area. Either action displays the Task List (Figure 1-12), in which you select a program and click the Switch To button.

If you've minimized several programs into icons, you can arrange the icons along the bottom of the desktop with the Arrange Icons button in the Task List.

Consistent Features of Windows Programs

Although mouse operation is part of the Windows look and feel, some users prefer to issue commands by typing keyboard shortcuts. Nearly every PageMaker menu command can be activated by typing a key while holding down the *Control key* (sometimes marked Ctrl). For example, to use the Open command, which is in the File menu, you can drag down the File menu and release the mouse on the Open command. You can also quickly select this command by typing a shortcut: Hold down the Control key and type an **O**. This book refers to a key sequence of this type as "Control O."

Another method common to all Windows-compatible applications is

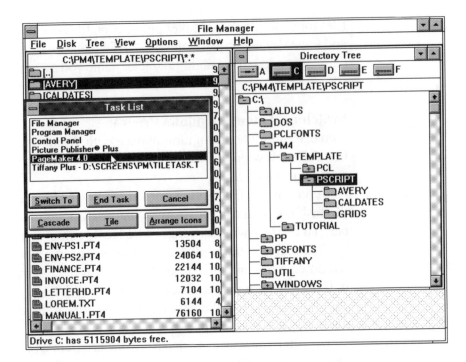

Figure 1-12. Windows can display program windows in a Cascade design (as in earlier figures) or in the Tile design shown above. The Task List window, for switching among different open program windows, appears when you choose Switch To in the Control menu, or double-click anywhere in the desktop area.

to press the Alt key, then the underlined letter of the menu (**F** for the File menu), then the underlined letter of the command or option in the menu (**O** for the Open command). You can also use the cursor movement keys to move down selections in the menu one by one, and then press Enter (Return on some keyboards) for the selection you want.

The Control key and Alt key combinations make it possible to run programs entirely from the keyboard without using a mouse.

PageMaker, like every other Windows-compatible program, displays a menu bar and a window that you can move, close, or resize at any time. It also displays windows within the main window. Windows can overlap each other, but there is only one active window at a time.

When working with different Windows-compatible programs, the operations you will use most often are the Cut, Copy, and Paste commands (found in the Edit menu of most programs). You can use these commands to transfer text and graphics within a program's window (from one document to another, or within the same document), and from one program to another. For example, you can use this feature to transfer a graphic image (or a piece of a graphic image) from a program such as Paintbrush (included with Windows and created by ZSoft) to a PageMaker publication.

Part of nearly every Windows program (including PageMaker) is the ability to undo an action that you've just performed. The Undo command is usually found in the Edit menu, and only undoes the results of the most recent operation. You must use it immediately, before doing anything else, if you are not sure about something that you did. If, after using Undo, you decide that the original operation was correct, you can re-do the operation. (After selecting Undo, Undo is replaced by the Redo command in the Edit menu.)

Most programs (including PageMaker) also offer a Revert command in the File menu that reverts back to the last saved version of your publication file. This command lets you return to a previous version, throwing away the current version of the file. You would only do this if you really did not want to save the current version.

Every dialog box has a Cancel button, so you can always back out of a command. Even when the power fails, PageMaker can usually recover the file. You should cultivate good computer operation habits, such as regularly copying your important work to a backup floppy disk for safekeeping.

This book does not attempt to provide a complete description of the process of operating a PC with Windows, because a complete description is available in the manuals shipped with your computer. The *PageMaker Reference Manual* from Aldus also provides a summary of the process of operating PageMaker with Windows. You will likely have an easy time learning to use Windows—it usually takes considerably less time than learning to operate DOS by itself.

Enough information is provided in this book to get you started in desktop publishing with PageMaker, including a step-by-step tutorial in Chapter 2 (which uses a newsletter as an example). In addition, it is wise to read all of the manuals supplied with PageMaker.

Online Help

Included in the PageMaker package is an online "help" system you access by choosing options from the Help menu (Figure 1-13).

The Help dialog box displays a series of interactive help screens for PageMaker so that online help is available while you use the program. You can choose to see a list of topics or an index. With the context-sensitive help feature, you can get help for any menu option and tool in PageMaker by first holding down the Control key and typing a slash (/), and then clicking on the menu option or tool. The help messages are designed to be brief and to-the-point; for more information, consult this book and the PageMaker manuals.

Plan to spend from a day to a week learning to operate Windows, and an additional day learning the basics of PageMaker. You may be able to learn how to use PageMaker in just a couple of hours, and then build on the basic skills as you explore the more advanced features of PageMaker.

Project Planning

The best tool you can use for scheduling the production of a publication is a project planner. You may either use paper and pencil, or a software package such as Timeline (from Symantec). A basic critical path chart or schedule that shows task completion dates would be useful. You can alternatively plan your project using a drawing program, a spreadsheet program, or an outlining program.

Think of the publishing process as consisting of these steps:
• Develop an idea into a written and edited manuscript.
• Create and gather together illustrations and photos.
• Design the overall look and the individual pages.
• Produce the master pages for printing.

Personal computers can be used in all of these steps. PageMaker plays an important role in the third step (design), and is responsible for the last step (production).

Figure 1-14 shows a project plan for producing a book or technical manual, and Figure 1-15 shows a plan for producing a newsletter (which

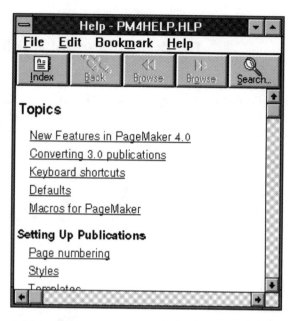

Figure 1-13. Using PageMaker's online help system to display help messages on topics and commands while using the program—click a topic or the Index or Search buttons.

could also be used as a general plan for producing a magazine or newspaper). In both cases, the step of page design occurs early in the project so that the writers and artists have an idea about how the final publication will look.

Page Design

Page design cannot be finalized until the designer knows the length of the manuscript and has information about the illustrations and photos. The manuscript stage for text and the rough stage for illustrations and photos (Figure 1-16) are the starting places for production. From there, manuscripts and roughs are turned into formatted text and final artwork, which are then combined in PageMaker to make the final pages.

A designer can start early by using PageMaker to plan the overall look

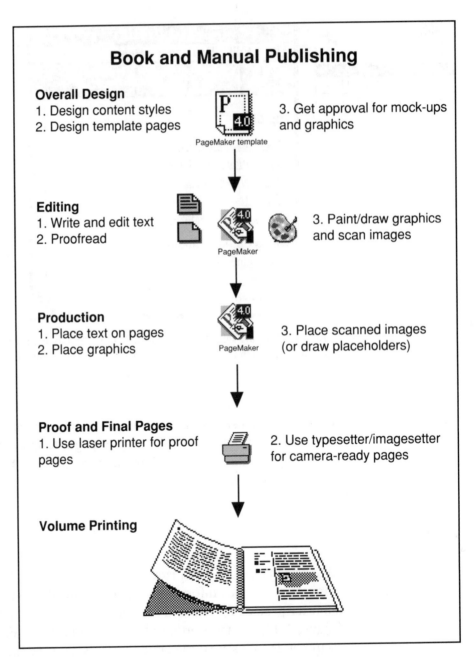

Figure 1-14. A project plan for producing a book or technical manual.

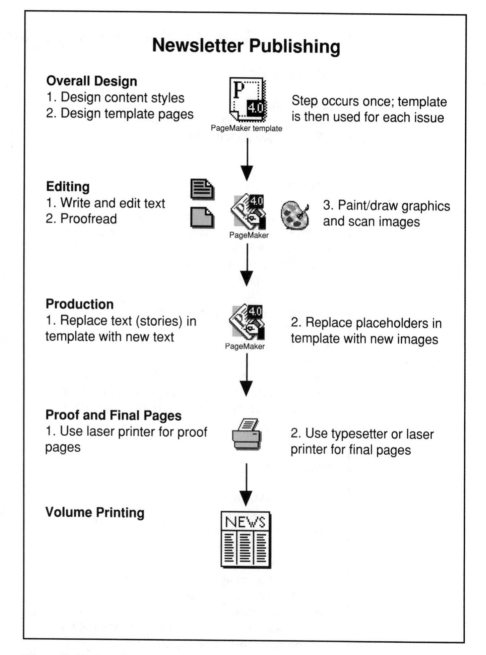

Figure 1-15. A project plan for producing a newsletter.

Steps for Desktop Publishing

Overall Design

Using PageMaker:
• Produce mock-up pages for approval
• Save pages as template

Editing

Using PageMaker or a word processor:
• With PageMaker, edit directly in publication file
• Write and edit text, import text from other programs
• Proofread, incorporate editing comments
• Check spelling

Using a painting/drawing program:
• Paint or draw graphics
• Edit and improve graphics

Using a scanner with image editing software:
• Scan photos (for placeholders or for imagesetting)
• Scan line art for tracing in a drawing program
• Retouch photos

Production

Using PageMaker:
• Replace existing text in template file or place
  new text in publication file
• Replace existing graphics or placeholders, or place
  new graphics
• Draw boxes, rules, and other page elements
• Assign colors for preparing color overlays
• Print proof pages on laser printer
• Print final pages on laser printer or typesetter/
  imagesetter with color separations

Figure 1-16. The stages of desktop publishing production.

of the publication. With an estimate of the number of pages, you can determine the page size, image area, page orientation, and perhaps even the number of columns per page. You can print *thumbnail sketches* of the pages, using gray boxes to represent text, black boxes to represent images, and white boxes for line art. Experiment with titles, headlines, logos, and rough graphics (scanned or created on the computer). You may even produce full-size sample pages before placing manuscript text and final graphics and images. PageMaker has line-drawing, box-drawing, and circle-drawing tools, with several different line styles (as well as reverse/none for each) and many patterns, plus the ability to use graphics from a variety of programs.

Writing and Editing a Manuscript

PageMaker offers complete word processing features so that you can write and edit the text as well as create the pages. The Story Editor lets you write and edit text without having to wait for the page to be reformatted.

However, recognizing that many people want to continue to use their favorite word processing programs, Aldus designed PageMaker to be able to import text from nearly every popular word processor for the PC. You can type and edit words in PageMaker's Story Editor, or import text from a word processing file. In addition, text created in PageMaker's Story Editor can be exported into a word processing file format for use with other programs.

Word processing programs are designed for writing and editing text, and formatting controls (which govern how the text appears on the page) were added almost as an afterthought. Sometimes it is very difficult to produce special effects with word processors, such as the use of a different font for page numbers (if you have a choice of fonts at all), or drawing boxes around text and vertical lines (called *column rules*) between columns.

Page makeup programs, however, specialize in formatting, even if they include word processing functions. PageMaker lets you edit text, but the program is also designed as a finishing tool, so it accepts text from a variety of word processors and gives you complete control over the page layout.

You can import or type large amounts of text directly into PageMaker's Story Editor, which is a text-only window that uses a generic font and size for the text, but can display different styles, such as italic and bold. The original font information in the story is not changed; the generic font is used only for fast display in this window, which is optimized for fast editing and for applying styles to paragraphs. Once you've completed working in the Story Editor, the text is automatically poured back into its original location on the page, or loaded into the Place icon for automatic, semiautomatic, or manual placement.

The Story Editor in PageMaker 4 offers the ability to search for and replace letters and phrases, fonts, point sizes, and paragraph styles. Therefore, you can make sweeping global formatting changes in a single operation.

You can use the word processor that you are already familiar with to prepare your text. The leading word processors for the PC are Microsoft Word, WordPerfect, DisplayWrite, XyWrite III, and Ami. The PC and Macintosh versions of Microsoft Word are completely compatible with PC PageMaker.

The files PageMaker can import (bring into the page) and export (send out to a file) depend on which *filters* you install for PageMaker (the import and export filters are described in PageMaker's *Reference Manual*). You can install some or all of the filters, including import and export filters for Microsoft Word, Microsoft Windows Write, Rich Text Format (RTF), and Document Content Architecture (DCA, also known as the IBM Revisable-Form Text). Filters are available for WordPerfect (WordPerfect Corp., Macintosh and PC versions), WordStar 3.3 (MicroPro International), XyWrite III (XyQuest, Inc.), and any word processor that can save a file in the DCA format, such as DisplayWrite 3 (IBM), Ami (Lotus), Volkswriter 3 (Lifetree Software, Inc.), and WordStar 2000 (MicroPro). Filters are also available for importing Lotus 1-2-3 and Microsoft Excel spreadsheets.

All of these programs can produce preformatted text for PageMaker—text that already has some of the characteristics (font, type style and size, tab settings, indents, and paragraph endings) needed for eventual appearance on the final pages. If your word processor can produce files in simple

ASCII (American Standard Code for Information Interchange) format, which is a standard among all personal computers, you can use the text with PageMaker.

PageMaker can also export the text on its pages into ASCII, RTF, DCA, Windows Write, or Word files. When PageMaker exports a Word file, it also exports style sheet definitions in the Microsoft Word format.

Aldus provides the Aldus Setup Utility program, ALDSETUP.EXE, to install PageMaker and the text import and export filters. All of the filters you install are copied to the ALDUS directory. You can delete filters you don't need to save disk space.

You don't have to know anything about PageMaker in order to write and edit text for PageMaker pages. Editors and writers may use different computers in different offices—or even in different countries—and still prepare text for someone who uses PageMaker. Large manuscripts can be sent from one computer to another over the telephone or through network connections, and PC disks are easy to exchange.

Writers and editors can prepare text for printing from their word processors without regard to PageMaker. Margins, footnotes, page numbers, headers, and footers created by word processors are not used by PageMaker. The settings for these functions can be changed at will, without any consequence to the PageMaker production effort.

Proofreading a Manuscript

Once in electronic form, a large manuscript can be checked for spelling in a few minutes. Words never have to be retyped, and editing changes can be added or deleted in an instant.

PageMaker's Story Editor offers spell checking with up to six different languages at once, with hyphenation rules applied in up to eleven languages at once (if you install the dictionaries).

Some word processors contain built-in spell checkers, such as Microsoft Word and WordPerfect, which can be used while putting together the draft text. Use PageMaker's spell checker any time you want to in the Story Editor, but also when you are finished making editing changes to the final version of the publication. PageMaker can automatically check the spelling of multiple stories in a publication, and you can add new words or ignore words that are correctly spelled (such as proper nouns that are not in the dictionary).

Formatting a Manuscript

You can change fonts (styles and sizes) as well as faces for the text at any time in PageMaker, but you can save time by selecting font styles and sizes while writing and editing the text in the Story Editor or in the word processor (if it is supported by PageMaker—see Appendix A). The text is then formatted for placement onto a PageMaker page, and you may place text on many pages at once without stopping to select fonts.

An example of this approach is outlined in Chapter 2. During the creation of the fourth page of a newsletter, a questionnaire is formatted in Microsoft Word for Windows (Figure 1-17). Some of the formatting that was performed in Word is carried over into PageMaker. Remember, PageMaker does not use the right margin setting, footnotes, page numbers, headers, footers, or special formatting features created by word processors. PageMaker does recognize the following features:

1. Fonts (type styles and type sizes), line spacing (also called *leading*), and upper- and lowercase letters. Special characters, if they can be typed, will be recognized.

2. You have the option to retain keyboard-style single and double quotes ('"), or to have PageMaker substitute open and closed typographic quotes ('' "").

Double hyphens (- -) can be converted into an em dash (—), and a line of hyphens can be turned into a thin rule (————) that comprises a row of em dashes.

3. The left margin is the basis for indents, but only if the word processor has a separate setting for the left indent. PageMaker breaks lines to fit its columns.

4. Left and right indents are measured from the corresponding edges of the PageMaker column. If your text file has a 1-inch indent from the left margin, PageMaker measures 1 inch from the left edge of the column when placing your text file.

5. The first line indents of a paragraph are recognized as either regular, indented to the right, or a hanging indent to the left of the left margin.

6. Carriage returns (produced by pressing the Enter key or Return key in most word processing programs) are recognized as paragraph endings

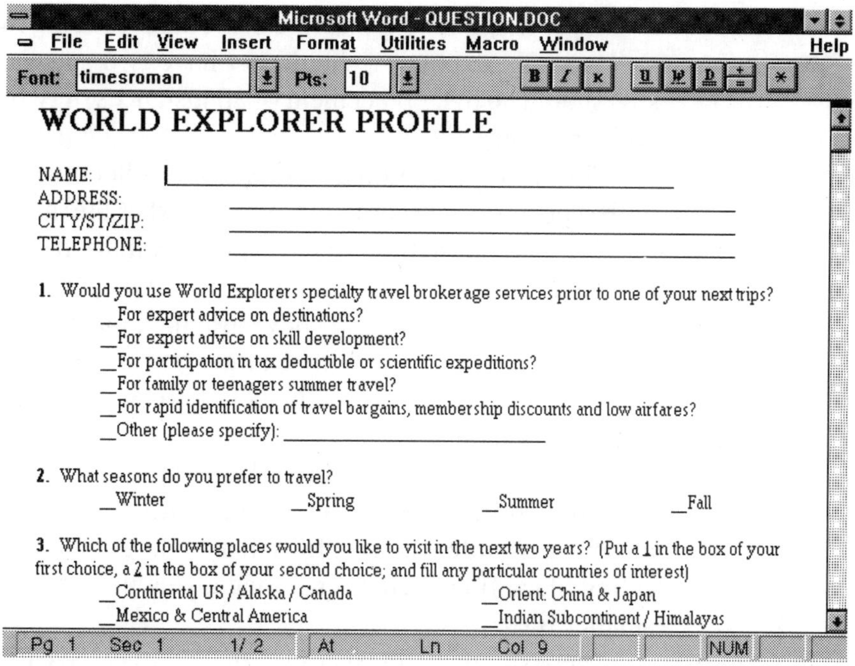

Figure 1-17. Microsoft Word for Windows creates files that are compatible with the other versions of Word and with the PC and Macintosh versions of PageMaker. Text formatting and style sheet information can be imported into PageMaker from all versions of Word, and exported from PageMaker into Word files.

and as a forced end of a short line.

7. Tabs are recognized and used to align text or numbers in tables. You can use PageMaker to change tab settings to fit the column width, and specify the position, alignment, and leader pattern (such as a dot or dash leader to fill the tab space). End each line of a table with a carriage return.

PageMaker will remember the font you chose, even if the printer selected as the default printer does not print that font. If you haven't installed the font in Windows, generic vector fonts are used to simulate the font on the screen. PageMaker substitutes the closest font printable by your printer and remembers the actual font when you switch to another printer that can print it.

Many writers and typists are in the habit of using two spaces after each sentence. Typeset copy should not have two spaces, so one formatting step should be the replacement of all instances of two consecutive spaces with one space.

Tip: Remove captions, footnotes, and other independent elements that will be positioned separately from the text of the manuscript. The authors of this book routinely store the captions and footnotes in one file and the body of the manuscript in another file. This saves time later when placing text on pages. If you already have graphic images in your word processor file, the publication file will be larger and slower to place than a text file without images. It is usually better to place images separately onto PageMaker pages.

Another tip: Break up very large text files into smaller files of less than 64K, so that PageMaker can quickly place them. Some word processors also have trouble with text files that are larger than 64K. PageMaker can safely place files well over 2 megabytes in size, but works faster with smaller files.

There are many instances where you may have preformatted text, but prefer to use PageMaker's formatting and thus would rather work with ASCII text. For example, you may want to use PageMaker default settings and override the word processor font and other settings. Or you may have records from a database that are in a text format. In such cases, you can choose to *not* retain the format of the word processor file, and import that text into PageMaker as ASCII-only text.

Tabs and carriage returns, as well as spaces, are recognized by PageMaker in ASCII-only files, but no formatting settings from the word processor are used. You can bring tables and paragraphs of text into PageMaker without retaining formatting settings (that is, as ASCII-only text), and still retain paragraph endings and table column positions—as long as each table row ends with a carriage return.

PageMaker offers a Smart ASCII text filter that provides several options for importing ASCII-only text. After you select a file to place without retaining formatting, PageMaker displays a Smart ASCII import filter dialog box. You can choose to remove extra carriage returns from the file, which is a useful option if your ASCII file has a carriage return at the end of each line (carriage returns are interpreted by PageMaker to be end-of-paragraph markers).

After choosing to remove extra carriage returns from the file, you can further refine your choice by selecting an option to remove carriage returns from the end of every line, from between paragraphs, or from both the ends of every line and from between paragraphs.

If you choose to remove carriage returns from every line, PageMaker can still recognize paragraph endings, if those paragraphs are separated by a blank line. (The paragraphs must be separated by two carriage returns; one to end the paragraph, plus a blank line between paragraphs. Only one carriage return is removed by the operation, leaving one to represent the paragraph ending.)

If you choose to remove the extra carriage returns from between paragraphs, the filter deletes one carriage return wherever it finds two in a row, thus deleting the extra line between paragraphs (but leaving a carriage return as a paragraph ending).

With either (or both) option that changes carriage returns, you can choose to leave indents, tables, and lists unchanged. PageMaker recognizes tables and lists if each line of text has one or more embedded tabs but does not start with a tab, or if each line of text is followed by a line starting with a space or a tab. In either case, the line must already end with a carriage return. For a complete description of importing ASCII text, see Appendix A.

If the text is transferred from another computer or through an electronic mail or videotex service (via modem), there may be line-feed characters at the end of each line. PageMaker can ignore the characters when it imports a word processor file that it recognizes (depending on the filters you installed). If PageMaker doesn't recognize the file, irregular line endings and boxes may appear in your text at the start of each line. Use a program that strips line-feed characters during the file transfer to save time.

If too many line breaks appear in the middle of lines after your file is placed, you have an unwanted carriage return at the end of each line. Choose the option to remove them from the end of each line as described above. An alternative method is to use a word processor to search for instances of two carriage returns (called "end of paragraph markers" in Word) and replace them with one carriage return, and then place the file into PageMaker.

PageMaker's paragraph default settings apply to ASCII-only files, unless you change the default values (by using the pointer tool, with no text selected). When you change the default values and then place your text, the new settings are applied. You can choose new settings before placing the text, and ignore any existing formatting in the text file, by placing the file as an ASCII-only file. If you don't change default settings, you will have the default font setting (usually Times) with default type specifications (usually 12 points), no left or right margin or first line of paragraph indents, no spacing between paragraphs, and left-justified alignment of text in columns with ragged-right margins.

PageMaker exports some text changes that you make on the page back to the word processor files. Any changes made during page makeup should be made to the text using the Story Editor and then exported back to overwrite the word processing file, so that the two versions (the text file and the PageMaker publication file) coincide. You can export the file, or any selected text, from PageMaker back to your word processor using PageMaker's export filters.

If there is no export filter for your word processing program, you can export the file as a text-only file, preserving the type specs, tabs, and indents used by PageMaker. Export filters are available from Aldus for Microsoft Word and many other word processors. (For details about how PageMaker deals with text files from popular word processors, see Appendix A.)

If you use Microsoft Word, be sure to turn off the fast save option before you save the file. If you leave the fast save option on when you save the Word file, PageMaker will place the file very slowly. Use Word's Save as command to turn off the fast save feature.

Special Characters
Although your chosen printer or font may not be able to print all of the special language characters and symbols in the PC character set, you can type all of these characters and symbols in PageMaker (and also in Windows-based word processors, such as Microsoft Windows Write). To type any character in the Windows ANSI character set, hold down the Alt key, type a zero on the numeric keypad, and type the ANSI code (with the

Alt key still depressed). To type the special language characters, hold down the Alt key and type the three-digit IBM PC character code on the numeric keypad.

Special symbols include trademarks, registered trademark and copyright notices, section and paragraph marks, bullets, and various nonbreaking spaces. Special characters also include a page number marker for automatic page numbering, open and closed quotes, and em and en dashes.

If you can't type these characters and symbols using your word processor, you may leave *place holders* (a character or a note to the production person) and then type the characters to replace the note using PageMaker. The Story Editor lets you incorporate graphics into the text, called *inline* graphics, which move with the text when you edit the text. This feature is described in Chapter 3.

Some characters are automatically placed by PageMaker on the page. For example, PageMaker automatically changes a double quote (") with a preceding space into an open quote ("), and changes a double quote with a following space into a closed quote ("). The program also changes a single quote (') in the same manner, so that contractions, possessives, and quotes-within-quotes have the properly slanted symbols. PageMaker changes a double hyphen (- -) into an em dash (—), and changes a series of hyphens (——)into half as many em dashes (creating a solid line).

Creating and Editing Graphics

There are two types of graphic images: *paint-type*, also called *bit-mapped*, and *draw-type*, also called *object-oriented*. Painted images consist of dots that correspond to screen pixels, and are limited in resolution to the display used to create the images. Drawn images consist of a series of drawing commands that describe the image, and are usually not limited in resolution except by the printer or typesetter.

Painting programs (Figure 1-18) are popular with freestyle painting and amateur artwork because the programs are easy to learn and very flexible. You can touch-up the dots to improve images, and paint intricate patterns and shapes.

Drawing programs (Figure 1-19) are popular with commercial artists,

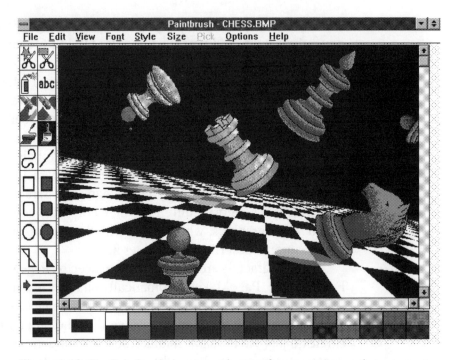

Figure 1-18. The Paintbrush Accessory is one of many programs that can create paint-type graphics.

designers, architects, and engineers. These programs offer precision tools, perfect geometric shapes, and graphic objects that can be moved, transformed, and cloned, as well as grouped with other objects.

Both types of programs are popular with desktop publishers, who tend to use draw-type programs for logos, line drawings, business charts, graphs, and schematics, and use painting programs to create intricate designs and freestyle artwork. The highest resolution can be achieved with PostScript-drawing programs, which permit the creation of resolution-independent PostScript graphics (described not by screen pixels, but by graphics commands).

Paint-Type Graphics

PageMaker places graphics saved in popular graphics file formats such as PCX (PC Paintbrush), BMP (Windows Paintbrush), MSP (Windows

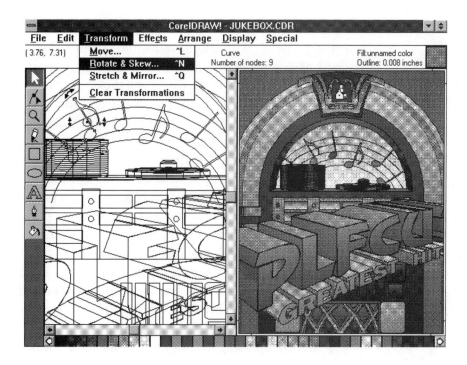

Figure 1-19. Corel Draw is one of several programs that create draw-type graphics in PostScript. Drawn objects can be independently moved, transformed, and grouped with other objects.

Paint), MacPaint, and TIFF (Tag Image File Format).

Pixel sizes in paint-type graphics are fixed in resolution. If you use one type of graphics display device on a PC when you create a graphic image, and you use another type of display with PageMaker, the graphic image will appear distorted on the PageMaker screen even though it will print properly. It is difficult to resize images by hand to proportions that print properly, because the resolution of the screen and the resolution of the printer do not match exactly—fine details and dot shading that appear clearly on the screen may appear distorted (muddy) when printed, or the image may contain moirés and other unwanted patterns.

PageMaker's built-in resizing feature automatically selects the best proportions for your printer when you hold down the Control (Ctrl) key while dragging to resize the image. PageMaker also offers the choice to resize the image with length and width equally proportioned (hold down the Shift key while dragging), or in unequal proportions for stretching, condensing, and otherwise distorting the image. To enlarge or reduce an image at an optimum size for your printer, and to resize its length and width in equal proportions, hold down both the Control (Ctrl) key and the Shift key while dragging the image.

The built-in sizes for Control-dragging depend on the printer you choose with the Target printer command. You should, therefore, choose a target printer for the publication before placing graphics, even if you are currently using a different printer than the target printer. If you want the images in your publication to be sized at the best sizes for the final printer, select that printer with the Target printer command in the File menu (as described in Chapter 2), and then begin placing images. You don't have to actually print the publication, nor does that printer need to be physically connected—PageMaker simply assumes that you will use that printer when you print the final version (and you can always change the printer selection after placing the graphics). Chapter 5 offers tips and techniques for placing and resizing graphics.

When you place a paint-type graphics file, you have the option to store the graphics inside the PageMaker publication file, or leave it outside the file and establish a link to the file. The links are managed in the Links dialog box, which lists each text and graphics file imported into a publication, indicating its file type and page in the layout. PageMaker forms a link to each imported text and graphics file so that changes to the original can optionally be passed automatically to the publication file.

Since the linked file can be stored outside the PageMaker publication, publication files can be smaller. With graphics files you have the choice to include the graphics within the publication file, or keep them stored externally. The Links dialog box is described in more detail in Chapter 2.

When you leave the graphics stored externally, PageMaker creates a lower-resolution version of the image for displaying on the page. At the same time, PageMaker establishes a link from the low-resolution display version of the image to the original, higher-resolution version, so that the program can use the higher-resolution version when printing. PageMaker uses the lower-resolution image for display purposes in order to increase the speed of the program.

In order for PageMaker's link to work automatically when printing graphics from external files, you have to leave the original graphics file in the directory that it was in when you placed it (that is, not move it or delete it); otherwise, you must select the directory and file in a dialog box when you open or print the publication, or re-establish the link in the Links dialog box (as described later in Chapters 2 and 5).

You can move, resize, and crop any type of graphic image, and PageMaker will apply those changes when printing, but will not change the original image file itself. You can't edit the pixels of a graphic image in PageMaker (except to enhance the contrast and brightness in a scanned image, as described in Chapter 4). Also, you can't erase parts of an image in PageMaker, although you can draw white boxes and ovals with no outlines to "white-out" areas of the page. You can also *crop* the image with the cropping tool in order to show only a portion of it, as described in Chapter 3. Use your painting program to clean up an image before placing the image in PageMaker.

If you don't like the printed result after enlarging or reducing the image, you can restore the image at any time to its original proportions. To do so, select the image, and then hold the Shift key down as you click on it. Also, if you change the target printer, you should resize all paint-type graphics. Select each paint-type graphic and resize it by holding down the Ctrl key, or by holding down the Ctrl key and the Shift key to resize the image in equal proportions.

Excellent printed results are possible with paint-type graphics, especially if the graphics consist of line art, which can be resized into almost any proportion and size and still look good (without using the Ctrl key). Images with tight, regular patterns do not display well (they appear muddy). If you use the Ctrl key while resizing, which limits you to sizes that print best at your printer's resolution, you can still get excellent results. The limitation may force you to use a slightly larger-sized image than the reduced image size that you wanted, but you can use PageMaker's cropping tool to further reduce and edit the placed image. For details about how PageMaker works with graphics files from popular painting programs, see Appendix B.

Draw-Type Graphics
PageMaker places graphics files saved in the popular draw-type graphics

formats, including files created by Windows "Draw!" and "Graph!" (Micrografx), In*A*Vision and Designer (Micrografx), Corel Draw (Corel Systems), AutoCAD (AutoDesk), and programs that save files in the Windows Graphics Device Interface (GDI) metafile format, as well as the multiple-platform standard format known as Encapsulated PostScript (EPS or EPSF). Most professional Windows drawing programs, such as Corel Draw and Micrografx Designer, can save either a Windows metafile or EPSF file.

Other graphics programs are supported by filters that you can install. These include filters that support Computer Graphics Metafiles (CGM), Hewlett-Packard Graphics Language (HPGL), Lotus 1-2-3 and Symphony charts (PIC files), Videoshow (NAPLPS) graphics files, and Zenographics Mirage files.

Drawing programs give you precise tools for drawing geometric shapes. Usually, the drawing tools emulate drafting tools such as a compass, a T-square, a precise ruler, and a grid, and there are extra tools for quickly drawing perfect squares, circles, and geometric shapes. Amateur and professional graphic artists may find the drawing tools harder to learn than the painting tools, but these tools produce precise shapes and perfectly proportioned squares and circles. In addition, drawing programs save graphics in a format that is independent of the resolution of the display and drawing device, so that when you print the graphics, PageMaker uses the highest possible resolution of the printing device.

Draw-type graphics, which are described with a command language rather than expressed as a series of dots, can be resized freely (there are no limitations, unlike paint-type graphics). Draw-type graphics can even be stretched or compressed with very little or no distortion. You resize a draw-type graphic image in the same way that you resize a paint-type image, by dragging one of its corners. Hold down the Shift key to resize the image in equal proportions. There is no need to use the Ctrl key to resize draw-type graphics. If you want to create a graphic image to be a specific size on the final page, use a drawing program. This approach lets you resize the graphics to precisely the measurements that you want, not just to the measurements that PageMaker builds in for printing paint-type graphics.

In many cases, you can transfer text used in the graphics to PageMaker with excellent results. In other cases, you may have to delete the text from the graphics first, place the graphics on the page, and then replace the text using PageMaker to get the best results. For details about how PageMaker works with graphics files, see Appendix B.

Business Charts and Graphs

Programs that generate charts and graphs (bar and pie charts, x-y graphs, scatter plots, and combinations of these forms) usually save the result in a graphics file compatible with one of the draw-type graphics programs already mentioned. For example, Lotus 1-2-3 and Symphony create business graphics and store them in .PIC files. Micrografx Charisma is another excellent chart and graph program that can automatically create business graphics from spreadsheets, and then save them in graphics files that can be used with PageMaker.

Usually no graphics experience is required in order to use these products, because their function is to generate graphics automatically for business-minded people who are not skilled in graphics. Programs such as Charisma, Microsoft Chart, Lotus 1-2-3, Symphony, and Freelance Plus can save charts and graphs as draw-type graphics that can be scaled to any size without distortion. All of the rules that govern the use of draw-type graphics apply to business graphics that are saved in EPSF and other draw-type graphics formats.

Image and Text Scanning

Most publishing operations require the use of existing information, but how can you put existing text and graphics into the computer? Expensive text and image digitizers are currently used by large publishers and by the government, but inexpensive desktop models are also available to handle much of a desktop publisher's needs.

The technology of scanning text, called *optical character recognition* (OCR), has not yet caught up with the technology of typesetting. Today's desktop scanners only have high accuracy rates with typewritten text or text printed in the Courier font on a laser printer. The desktop scanners can store text in simple ASCII format, however, which can then be edited with a word processor.

Text scanning works best either with clean, crisp originals that were printed using a Selectric-style typing element or a daisy wheel with carbon-film ribbons, or with clean copies of the originals. If a character is broken, or a bad photocopy is used, the software can't automatically recognize the character. The text-scanning process is fastest when you use a clean original and place it flat on the glass platen so that the lines of text are parallel to the top of the platen. The OCR software reads slanted text (which results from the paper being placed askew on the platen), but the scanning speed is slower than usual.

Desktop scanners can also sense images that contain up to 256 different shades of gray, and some can scan in color. PageMaker accepts images stored in the Tag Image File Format (TIFF and compressed TIFF), which is supported by most desktop scanner manufacturers. (Compressed TIFF provides a method to compress the image data into a file of a manageable size.) TIFF describes an image that contains 256 shades of gray, and Color TIFF stores color images that can be displayed on PageMaker pages. PageMaker also accepts images stored in other formats, such as EPSF (Encapsulated PostScript).

Scanner manufacturers, such as Logitech, Xerox Imaging Systems, Microtek, and Hewlett-Packard, offer software to control the scanner. Image-editing programs, such as Micrografx/Astral Development's Picture Publisher), control the scanner so that you can improve a scanned image immediately after scanning it, without switching programs. A black-and-white scanned image (without shades of gray) is similar to a paint-type graphic image, but offers higher resolution when printed. Images with shades of gray are called *gray-scale images* and can be edited only with image-editing programs that support gray scales (such as Picture Publisher, or Aldus SnapShot for editing still video images). Images with color can be edited with programs that can display and change colors, such as Picture Publisher.

When Scanning Is Cost-Effective
A desktop scanner scans typewritten pages faster than the fastest typist

can type, and can continue at top speed all day long. If you want the most efficient method, however, there is no substitute for writing and editing by computer. No matter how quickly the technology of inexpensive text scanners develops, the scanners will probably not match the efficiency of creating the data electronically in the first place.

Scanners are most useful for scanning pages of text that will be processed or filed by computer, for scanning line art and sketches that will be improved with drawing software, and for scanning photos and slides. Although laser printers are not capable of reproducing a photo with the same quality as a photographic halftone, the higher-resolution PostScript imagesetters can produce magazine-quality halftones and color separations from desktop-scanned photos.

Many publications can use scanned images, including scanned line art that is then cleaned up by a drawing program such as Micrografx Designer or Corel Draw. Real estate listings can be updated frequently by scanning the photos of new houses and preparing the listings with PageMaker. Personnel reports can contain scanned photos of employees. Architectural studies can be typeset with scanned drawings of building plans and scanned photos of the landscape. Scanned images are finding their way into art and design magazines, as well as into newspapers, newsletters, and business reports. Subsequent chapters discuss the use of scanned images in publications, both as final artwork and as temporary placeholders for designing text and page elements around halftones that will be dropped in later.

Halftones

PageMaker can print scanned images at actual size, or at reduced or expanded sizes, with excellent results if you use the automatic resizing feature (by holding down the Ctrl key and the Shift key while resizing the image). PageMaker also has an image control feature that lets you change the lightness (brightness) and contrast of an image, and change the type of line screen and the screen frequency for creating a halftone.

A *halftone* is a continuous tone image converted to dots, or *halftone cells*, that simulate gray shades on a black-and-white printer. Photos and other continuous tone images must be converted, either by a digital device or a photographic device, into halftone cells. The photographic process for the production of halftones involves the use of a line screen at a particular density. The screen density determines how large the halftone cells in the image will be, which can make the difference between a muddy reproduction and a clear reproduction. *Density* is measured by the number of screen lines per inch, and the appropriate lines-per-inch measurement depends on the printing method. Newspapers typically need a 65- or 85-line screen. For advertisements, commercial work, and magazine pages, use screens with 120-, 133-, 150-, or more lines per inch.

You can mix conventional photographic methods with desktop publishing methods for cost-effective production. PageMaker lets you draw a black-filled box on the page, to represent a window for a negative. Camera services and print shops can produce halftones either as negatives to be stripped in by the printer, or as screened prints that you can paste onto artboards. A screened print is usually less expensive, but a negative provides better results because the image is photographed only once. Unless you are producing a special effect, do not produce a halftone of a halftone—when you overlay dots on dots, you can create a *moiré effect* (a wavy pattern caused by the repetition of a pattern on top of another pattern).

With the introduction of standard graphics file formats (such as TIFF), PostScript typesetters, and inexpensive hard disks for mass storage, the placement of scanned images on the page using PageMaker is an excellent opportunity to cut costs. At the very least, the scanned image can serve as a placeholder for a conventionally produced halftone. At most, it can serve as a substitute for the halftone, eliminating the need for the photographic halftone process.

To make the equivalent of a halftone cell with digital data, the printer combines several small dots into one halftone cell dot. Printers with a resolution of 300 dpi can produce the equivalent of a 60- to 65-line screen (newspaper-quality) halftone with gray scales. You can raise the resolution of the image, but the result is a denser image with less gray scales. The typical 300-dpi laser printer prints some halftones better than others, but commercial publications need higher-resolution devices.

The Linotype Linotronic 300 Imagesetter (with a resolution of 2540 dpi) can produce a commercial-quality halftone and color separation directly onto film, and it is a PostScript device. You can use a PostScript laser printer to print proof pages, and then send the output to a high-resolution Linotronic in order to get a high-quality halftone on the page.

PageMaker's Image control command gives you control over the density (frequency) and the angle of the line screen for creating halftones, and over the lightness and contrast values. The Image control command is introduced in Chapter 4.

Laser Printers, Typesetters, and Imagesetters

The motivating force behind desktop publishing is the advent of inexpensive laser printers and the ability to transfer pages to higher-resolution typesetters and imagesetters.

You may start your publishing efforts with scanning and word processing, but the quality of your results is directly related to your output device. Laser printers have grown in popularity because they offer better fonts plus image printing at medium resolutions, compared to the fonts and resolutions offered by conventional dot-matrix and letter-quality printers.

Most laser printers offer near-typeset quality with a resolution of 300 by 300 dpi, although some are 400 by 400 dpi, or 300 by 600 dpi. Laser printers are also capable of emulating daisy-wheel and dot-matrix printers at much better resolution and print quality, although some printers offer only partial-page graphics at 300-dpi resolution.

The most popular line of laser printers is the Hewlett-Packard LaserJet series (currently the LaserJet IIP and III). PageMaker works very well with these printers. However, desktop publishing tasks sometimes require that you prepare output on devices that are higher in resolution than 300 dpi.

The Apple LaserWriter has been the recognized leader in desktop publishing applications because it was the first to use the PostScript page description language, developed by Adobe Systems. Adobe PostScript is now available as an option for Hewlett-Packard LaserJets as well as laser printers from IBM, Texas Instruments, Digital Equipment Corporation, and many other manufacturers.

PostScript laser printers are compatible with each other and with higher-resolution laser typesetters and imagesetters from Linotype,

Varityper, and Compugraphic. For example, a PostScript-type laser printer such as the AST TurboLaser/PS (300 dpi) is entirely compatible with the Varityper plain-paper typesetter (600 dpi), and with the Linotype Linotronic class of PostScript-type imagesetters, including the Linotronic 100 (1270 dpi) and 300 (2540 dpi).

Typesetters and imagesetters are still out of most business's price range and not suitable for the fast-printing chores required in business computing applications. A typesetter or imagesetter produces output of such high quality that most businesses would only want to use it for the final typesetting step. The paper used with the typesetter has to be developed by a chemical-based processor, so a ventilated room (preferably a darkroom) for the processor is necessary.

Desktop publishers who need both the speed and the flexibility of laser printers, plus the high resolution of typesetters or imagesetters, can use the PostScript typesetters and imagesetters available as output devices in copy centers and typesetting services. You can prepare pages for these devices directly or use a PostScript laser printer to proof your pages inexpensively before using the devices. The combination of a PostScript laser printer and a Linotronic imagesetter was used to produce this book.

To use a printer with Microsoft Windows, you need to install *printer driver* software that communicates with and controls that specific type of printer. PageMaker uses Microsoft Windows printer drivers. Nearly all of the major laser printers available on the market support Windows, including page printers from IBM, Digital Equipment Corporation, Hewlett-Packard, AST Research, QMS, Qume, Cordata, Texas Instruments, and Epson. Windows can drive any PostScript printer, and any printer that can emulate an Epson FX-80 dot-matrix printer or an HP LaserJet.

Most laser printers print only on standard page sizes (8 1/2 by 11 inches or smaller). The Dataproducts LZR-2665 and some other laser printers can print tabloid-size pages (11 by 17 inches).

PageMaker can control collation, the use of input paper trays, page orientation, and different resolution factors with certain printers (such as HP LaserJets and Apple LaserWriters). PageMaker can also set its pages to use a certain font cartridge for HP LaserJet printers.

When you add a printer to your Windows system, be sure to add both the fonts supplied with the printer on disk, and the screen fonts that display representations of the printed fonts. Dot-matrix fonts display on the screen exactly as they print and may be useful for decorative purposes, but look more jagged at the edges than higher-resolution laser printer fonts. Add screen fonts to Windows by double-clicking the Control Panel's Font icon.

You can use a font manager such as Adobe Type Manager (ATM) from Adobe Systems, which is supplied with PageMaker 4, to display and print outline fonts (and forego the use of bitmap fonts altogether). ATM provides the essential scaling and display functions for outline fonts. It is far more convenient to have one outline for the font stored on disk rather than many bitmap versions representing different point sizes. The one outline can be scaled to any point size for display and printing. ATM provides the best quality with Adobe's Type 1 outline fonts.

Windows designates one printer as the *default* printer. You can change the default printer at any time. Your computer may be connected to several printers, or you may be composing publication files that will be used with a different computer and printer than the one you have now.

Before starting a publication, choose a printer that will serve as the final output device, using the Target printer command in the File menu. PageMaker composes the pages with settings for line lengths, page breaks, fonts, and built-in sizes for images depending on the target printer you've chosen. If you switch printers for a publication, PageMaker asks if you want to recompose the entire publication for the new printer.

The recompose operation ensures that the print will be the best in quality. However, line endings may change, so you will have to go back and check all of the pages for undesirable changes. The recompose operation does not take long with a short file, but it can take a few minutes with a 100-page publication. You can open a copy of a PageMaker publication file and perform the recomposing on a copy, preserving the original's target printer settings.

You can use PageMaker to create a print file of the pages, rather than actually print the pages, and then transmit that print file to another computer over a network, a modem, or by disk. The receiving computer does not have to run PageMaker in order to send the file to the printer, but the printer must be the same type (such as a PostScript printer, even if resolution differs). You can download the print file directly to the printer using a PostScript download utility. For more information, see the printing tips and techniques in Chapter 5.

Complete Systems

The rest of the hardware and software that you need depends on your application. Most writers and newsletter publishers need enough disk storage to accommodate a year's worth of text (an 80-megabyte hard disk is usually appropriate).

Because files can be copied from a floppy disk in a few seconds, you can effectively use whatever hard disk storage you have, but you must *always* copy files to floppy disks or to tape cartridges for backup in case your hard disk fails. Gray and color image files and some publication files may be too large to fit on a standard floppy disk. PageMaker can import images in compressed TIFF, which is usually smaller than other formats for images, so that you can use an image editing program that saves compressed TIFF files.

PageMaker requires a computer that uses the 80286, 80386, or 80486 processor, has at least two megabytes of RAM (random access memory), and runs Windows 3. It is recommended that you have more than two megabytes of RAM for faster performance. Windows 3 offers memory management modes for utilizing RAM, so no third-party memory managers are necessary.

A Super-VGA or standard IBM-compatible VGA display and color monitor is recommended, but any display and monitor that works with Windows 3 will also work with PageMaker, including MCGA (used in IBM PS/2 Model 30 computers), and EGA and compatible adaptors. For black-and-white display, you can use VGA, EGA, or the Hercules Monochrome graphics board (or a compatible board). You can connect a high-resolution monochrome (black-and-white) monitor to all of these adaptors except MCGA (which is not high resolution). Higher-resolution full-page monitors are also available for Windows from Micro Display Systems, Radius, Sigma Designs, and Moniterm.

Desktop Design

If you are not a designer by trade, prepare yourself by reading books about design and production. A few good books are listed in Appendix E. There is no substitute for a good designer, but it is possible for desktop publishers to learn good design techniques and to put them to use without paying top dollar for a professional designer. Your research will help you know which design elements you are judging when a top designer provides thumbnail sketches and finished artwork for your approval.

The purpose of this book is to show you how to use PageMaker to produce general types of publications. A subordinate mission of this book is to teach a few design skills. All of the desktop publishing software in the world can't save a badly designed publication. The best approach is to practice using PageMaker, read some good design books, and then seek advice from a professional designer. Finally, use this book to refresh your memory on how to use PageMaker.

2 | A Newsletter Tutorial

This chapter introduces PageMaker and provides a few layout and production techniques that can save you time and money. Although you may not be interested in producing a newsletter, the newsletter format provides a very straightforward way to demonstrate PageMaker's features. This book and the Aldus manuals were produced with PageMaker, which is perhaps the best way to show off the program's features for book design and production. Keep the *PageMaker Quick Reference Guide* (supplied as a tear-out card at the back of the *Aldus PageMaker Reference Manual*) at hand as you complete the examples in this book, in order to become familiar with PageMaker in the shortest possible time.

This book is not a crash course in design, but feel free to borrow from some of the designs used for the examples. In addition, many excellent books provide lessons in design skill and related design information. (See Appendix E for a sampling.) This book uses examples to describe many basic production techniques, typesetting and printing terms, and design considerations.

Start with a simple design effort in order to acquaint yourself with the limitations of PageMaker, as well as with the conventional constraints of typical printing presses. Before starting any publishing project, find out how the presses work. The number of copies that you want to print (the size of the press run), the page size (which partially depends on your choice of stock), the number of pages, and the use of color can all be factors in determining which printing presses and binding machines are appropriate for your job. Read *Pocket Pal* (see Appendix E) in order to learn printing and production procedures and terms, so that you can then provide a written description of your job to several printers, or to a print broker, who can help you determine the mechanical specifications for your publication and can offer price quotes for the paper, ink, printing, binding, and other services. The use of PageMaker could quickly reduce your production costs enough to pay for upgraded printing, such as the additional use of color or a better grade of paper, or other services.

Always start with an idea about how big the publication will be (the number of pages and the size of each page) before you design the pages. This chapter uses the example of a typical 8 1/2 by 11-inch, four-page newsletter (Figure 2-1). PageMaker's default settings are used for the image area.

Starting Up PageMaker

PageMaker 4 is supplied in compressed form on several disks. You must run the Aldus Setup Utility to decompress the files and install the program on your hard disk. You can install PageMaker 4 on any 286-, 386-, or 486-based PC that has at least two megabytes of RAM and at least 20 megabytes (preferably 80 or more) of hard disk space. You should have at least six megabytes of free disk space to install PageMaker, and at least eight megabytes to install PageMaker with all of the import/export filters, the tutorial files, the Table Editor program, and the templates. The rest of the disk is used for Windows, other programs, data files, and publication files.

PageMaker 4 runs under Microsoft Windows 3 (or later versions). If you have an older version of Windows, your PC dealer can supply the new version, or you can order it directly from Microsoft.

Installing ATM and PageMaker
You must install Windows 3 before using PageMaker 4. Follow Microsoft's instructions for installing Windows. Some computers are shipped with

July 1990 (vol. 3, no. 7)

Member: International Explorers Association
Stockholm, Sweden

Newsletter of the World Explorers Network

Founded: July, 1987
Editors: Tony Bove & Cheryl Rhodes

Learning From Marco Polo

There is no sea innavigable, no land uninhabitable.
— Robert Thorne, merchant and geographer (1527)

Too far East is West. — English proverb

We open this issue with an excerpt from the first printed travel guide of Western Society on how to travel to the Near and Far East. This guide was written 70 years after Marco Polo embarked on his historic visit to China. The following text is from a handbook written in 1340 by Francesco Balducci Pegolotti, agent for the Bardi banking family in Florence:

"In the first place, you must let your beard grow long and not shave. And at Tana you should furnish yourself with a dragoman. And you must not try to save money in the matter of dragomen by taking a bad one instead of a good one. For the additional wages of the good one will not cost you so much as you will save by having him. And besides the dragoman it will be well to take at least two good men servants who are acquainted with the Cumanian tongue. And if the merchant likes to take a woman with him from Tana, he can do so; if he does not like to take one there is no obligation, only if he does take one he will be kept much more comfortably than if he does not take one. Howbeit, if he do take one, it will be well if she be acquainted with the Cumanian tongue as well as the men...

"Whatever silver the merchants may carry with them as

The Mysterious Sea Crags!

When in Northern California, explore the caves and abalone hideouts of Sea Crags near Gualala. Page 5.

far as Cathay the lord of Cathay will take from them and put into his treasury. And to merchants who thus bring silver they give that paper money of theirs in exchange. This is of yellow paper, stamped with the seal of the lord aforesaid. And this money is called; and with this money you can readily buy silk and other merchandise that you have a desire to buy. And all the people of the country are bound to receive it. And yet you shall not pay a higher price for your goods because your money is of paper..."

Figure 2-1. Sample newsletter page.

Windows already installed on the hard disk, but you may need to install new printers, fonts, and other Windows programs besides PageMaker. Make a backup copy of the Aldus disks before using the Aldus Setup program (ALDSETUP.EXE) to copy the programs to your hard disk.

If you have more than two megabytes of RAM in your system, it is recommended that you use a font manager such as Adobe Type Manager (ATM) from Adobe Systems with PageMaker 4. ATM is supplied with the PageMaker 4 package, and you should install ATM before installing PageMaker.

To install ATM, be sure to have at least 750K of free disk space (ATM occupies about 250K of disk space, and each font occupies about 40K). Insert the ATM program disk into your floppy disk drive (drive A or B). Then run Windows 3 as usual. Select the Run command from the File menu, and type the following command line: **A:\INSTALL** (if Disk 1 is in drive A) or **B:\INSTALL** (if Disk 1 is in drive B). Press the Enter key. The ATM Installer window appears, and you can change the paths and directory names for the directories to hold the outline fonts and font metrics files, or accept the default paths and names. Click Install to begin the process.

ATM Installer asks if you want to install optional PCL bitmap fonts for HP LaserJet (or compatible) printers. The PCL bitmap fonts are not required but they improve printing performance for LaserJets. You can change the path and directory name for these fonts or accept the defaults.

When ATM Installer finishes, click OK to leave the Installer, then restart Windows. You must restart Windows after installing ATM. The Main window contains the ATM Control Panel for turning ATM on or off, for adding or removing fonts, for specifying the size of the font cache (system memory for temporary storage of font information), and for setting the option to use prebuilt or resident bitmap fonts in the printer (if they exist). Do not use this option if you intend to control the spacing between characters in PageMaker (using PageMaker's kerning features). For more information, see the instructions supplied with ATM.

To install PageMaker 4, first run Windows 3, and then insert Disk 1 of the Aldus disks into drive A or B. Select the Run command from the File menu, and type the following command line: **A:\ALDSETUP** (if Disk 1 is in drive A) or **B:\ALDSETUP** (if Disk 1 is in drive B). Press the Enter key.

The Aldus Setup program starts up, and if this is the first Aldus program you've installed, Setup displays a dialog box for specifying where to install the Aldus shared files on your hard disk. (You can store the shared files on one disk, and the actual PageMaker program on another—you specify the program's location later.) The default path for the shared files is C:\ALDUS. Click OK to accept this default, or change the path and/or directory name and then click OK.

The Aldus Setup program then displays its main window with options to install the PageMaker program, the templates (example files you can use to start designing a publication), and the tutorial files (for use with the tutorial section of the Aldus manuals). The PageMaker program, the tutorial files, and the filters (for importing and exporting information from other programs) are highlighted for installation, and you can select more options (such as PostScript and PCL templates) to install. A Help button is provided that explains the options.

The templates and tutorial files are optional, but you should install them if you have enough disk space. You need about eight megabytes of free space on your hard disk to install PageMaker 4 and all of its filters, tutorial files, and templates. Once installed, all of these files occupy about six megabytes of disk space (the Aldus Setup utility program needs extra space temporarily to decompress the files). You may want to skip installation of the templates and tutorial files if you have limited disk space.

Another window appears with an entry for the path to the directory in which to install the PageMaker files. You can change the entire path or any part of the path, and change name of the directory if you wish. The default pathname is C:\PM.

A window is displayed for "personalizing" your copy of PageMaker. Type your name, the name of your company, and the serial number of this copy of PageMaker. If you need help for this process, click the Help button. The serial number is reprinted on the original PageMaker disk, on the registration card, and on the bottom of the box. Type all the numbers and hyphens in the serial number, but exclude any letters you may find at the beginning of the number. Click the OK button when finished.

Setup then displays a window asking if you would like Setup to automatically modify the AUTOEXEC.BAT file in your system. This file controls how DOS is executed upon system startup. If you don't want

Setup to do this, you can click the No button, but you will have to manually change this file to accommodate PageMaker. You can click Yes to have Setup automatically make the required changes.

Setup automatically amends the PATH statement in AUTOEXEC.BAT to include the PageMaker directory (or a PATH statement is created if it does not exist), and the **SET TEMP=C:\TEMP** statement is also added. Setup can automatically perform these modifications, or you can perform them yourself from the Aldus Setup main window by choosing the files from the View menu.

The next step is to choose your filters. Filters are used to bring text and graphics from word processing files into PageMaker publications (*importing* files), and to save text from PageMaker publications in external files using other word processing file formats (*exporting* files). Import filters are provided for a variety of word processing file formats, and export filters are provided for certain key formats, such as Microsoft Word 3.0/4.0 and ASCII Text. You must install an import filter for any word processing program whose files you intend to use with PageMaker publications.

Many of you will want to install all filters in order to keep PageMaker as flexible as possible for dealing with files from other users. Choose one filter by clicking on its name; choose more than one by holding down the Control key while clicking their names. Choose all filters by clicking the Select All button.

The Select filters window shows how much disk space in required and how much you have available in the designated drive for the PageMaker program (C: by default). Deselecting filters reduces the requirement, but you can also switch from this window to the Program Manager and double-click the File Manager in order to delete files to create more room.

After selecting filters, you can then select templates in the same manner (if you chose to install templates earlier in Setup's main window). Again, the window shows how much disk space is required for the selected templates, and how much space you have left.

The Aldus Setup program then copies and decompresses the files from each disk automatically, prompting you from time to time for the next disk. Then a message appears asking for the next disk, remove the current disk from drive A (or drive B if you started the setup from drive B), and insert the next disk, then click the OK button.

When Setup finishes the installation, it displays the Setup main window again. This window offers several options, including the ability to run system diagnostics (Figure 2-2). We recommend that you at least try the two options in the View menu: viewing the README1.TXT and README2.TXT files. These text files contain last-minute information about the installation and use of PageMaker 4.

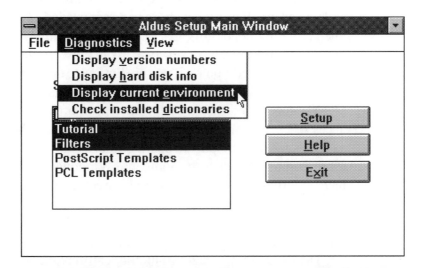

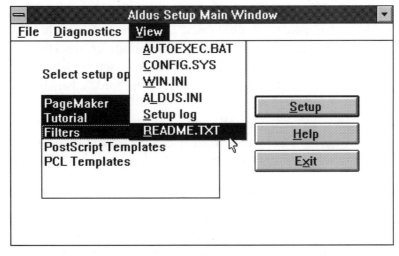

Figure 2-2. The Aldus Setup Main Window offers diagnostic options and the ability to view last-minute installation instructions and notes.

After finishing the installation process, close Windows and restart your computer (reboot DOS). Then start Windows again. You must do this so that modifications to AUTOEXEC.BAT actually take effect before you run Windows and PageMaker.

There are several restrictions on using PageMaker in only one megabyte of RAM—for example, performance is affected because the entire program can't fit in RAM (parts of it must be kept on the hard disk and loaded into RAM when those parts are needed). In addition, you can't open more than one Story Editor window or edit style definitions while in the Story Editor. The best way to avoid these limitations is to add more memory to your computer. If you are limited to one megabyte of RAM and you've added Windows enhancements such as Adobe Type Manager (ATM) for better display of fonts, or more screen fonts and desk accessories, you may not have enough RAM to run the program. In such cases, PageMaker displays a message that it can't run, and you have to add more memory or reduce the number of Windows enhancements (you may have to turn off ATM). Since RAM is not too expensive, it may be wiser to simply add more RAM. PageMaker works best when it has at least 1.5 megabytes of RAM at its disposal (such as when you have 2 megabytes, with 0.5 megabytes taken up by enhancements such as ATM).

The Aldus Setup program automatically creates the PageMaker 4 icon and the Aldus window in the Program Manager window, to make it easy for you to double-click the icon and launch PageMaker. The setup program also creates the Table Editor icon and the Aldus Setup icon in the Aldus window. These icons are used to launch these programs. The programs are actually stored on the hard disk in the directory you specified (or C:\PM by default).

You can install additional language dictionary files that are available as separate packs from Aldus. Refer to the installation manual supplied with the packs for step-by-step instructions for installing other languages.

Choosing a Target Printer

Before you produce a publication, you should know what kind of printer (laser, dot-matrix, typesetter, and so on) you will use for the final version of the publication. With this knowledge, you can change the size of graphic images and assign fonts to text knowing full well that those graphics and fonts will print properly. One of the benefits of using PageMaker is that you can change printers at any time, and use a different printer for printing drafts of the publication than the target printer for printing the final version.

When you change the printer, the publication is automatically recomposed (if necessary) to compensate for the fact that different printers use different fonts and options. A publication's line lengths, weights, and screen densities can be affected by a change in resolution from one output device to another. In addition, different printers use different fonts, and if the same size font is not available, PageMaker reformats the text to use the size closest to (but smaller than) the font you chose.

By selecting a target printer before starting a new publication, you ensure that PageMaker sets the line lengths, page breaks, available fonts, and graphics scaling percentages correctly for the target printer.

You install printers using Windows as described in the previous chapter. You can select any installed printer as the target printer. Every printer is controlled by a piece of software called a printer driver. You can install the driver even if you don't have the printer. The printer does not have to be connected to the computer in order to install the driver.

Windows is supplied with several drivers pre-installed or ready to install. They include drivers for PostScript-compatible printers (such as the Apple LaserWriter IINT and the Linotronic and Agfa PostScript imagesetters), PCL printers (such as Hewlett-Packard's LaserJet models), and dot matrix printers (such as the IBM Proprinter and Epson LQ models).

New printer drivers for Windows are provided with PageMaker 4 to take advantage of new features in PostScript and Hewlett-Packard LaserJet printers. The PostScript driver (version 3.4A) provides better support for Linotronic imagesetters. The HP LaserJet Series II (PCL 4) printer driver (version 3.4) is much faster than the earlier version provided with Windows 3.0.

To select the target printer, choose the Target printer command in the File menu. A list of the installed printer drivers is shown in a dialog box. Choose a printer driver, then click the Setup button in order to define the actual characteristics of that driver. For example (Figure 2-3), you might pick the PostScript driver for your target printer driver, then after clicking the Setup button, you might pick a specific type of PostScript printer such as a Linotronic 300 imagesetter. The target printer you select remains in effect until you change it.

If you intend to print the final version of a publication at a service bureau, you should consult the service bureau for the type of printer, and use that printer as your target printer regardless of the type of printer you have. By selecting the final-version printer as the target printer, you avoid having incompatibilities affect the appearance of the final version.

Whichever printer you select, be sure that you have installed the fonts available for that printer as described in Chapter 1. ATM fonts can be printed on all types of printers.

Starting a New Publication

After you install PageMaker, you are ready to begin creating publications. To start PageMaker, double-click the PageMaker program icon in the Aldus window of the Program Manager, or double-click a PageMaker publication or template file icon in a File Manager window.

To start a brand new publication, drag down on the File menu to choose the New command. The Page setup dialog box appears for specifying the size of the pages. Click the OK button (or press the Enter key) to accept the default Page setup settings (Figure 2-4).

You can bypass the design activities by choosing a template and loading it into PageMaker using the Open command in the File menu. A *template* is a predesigned publication file that is empty or contains dummy text and graphics used as placeholders, but is ready for use in page makeup. However, we assume in this chapter that you want to design a completely new publication so that you can learn how to use all of PageMaker's tools.

Designing a Layout

In the newsletter example, every page has two columns. Therefore, you can set the two-column format on the master pages so that all new pages start with a two-column format automatically. You are not locked into this

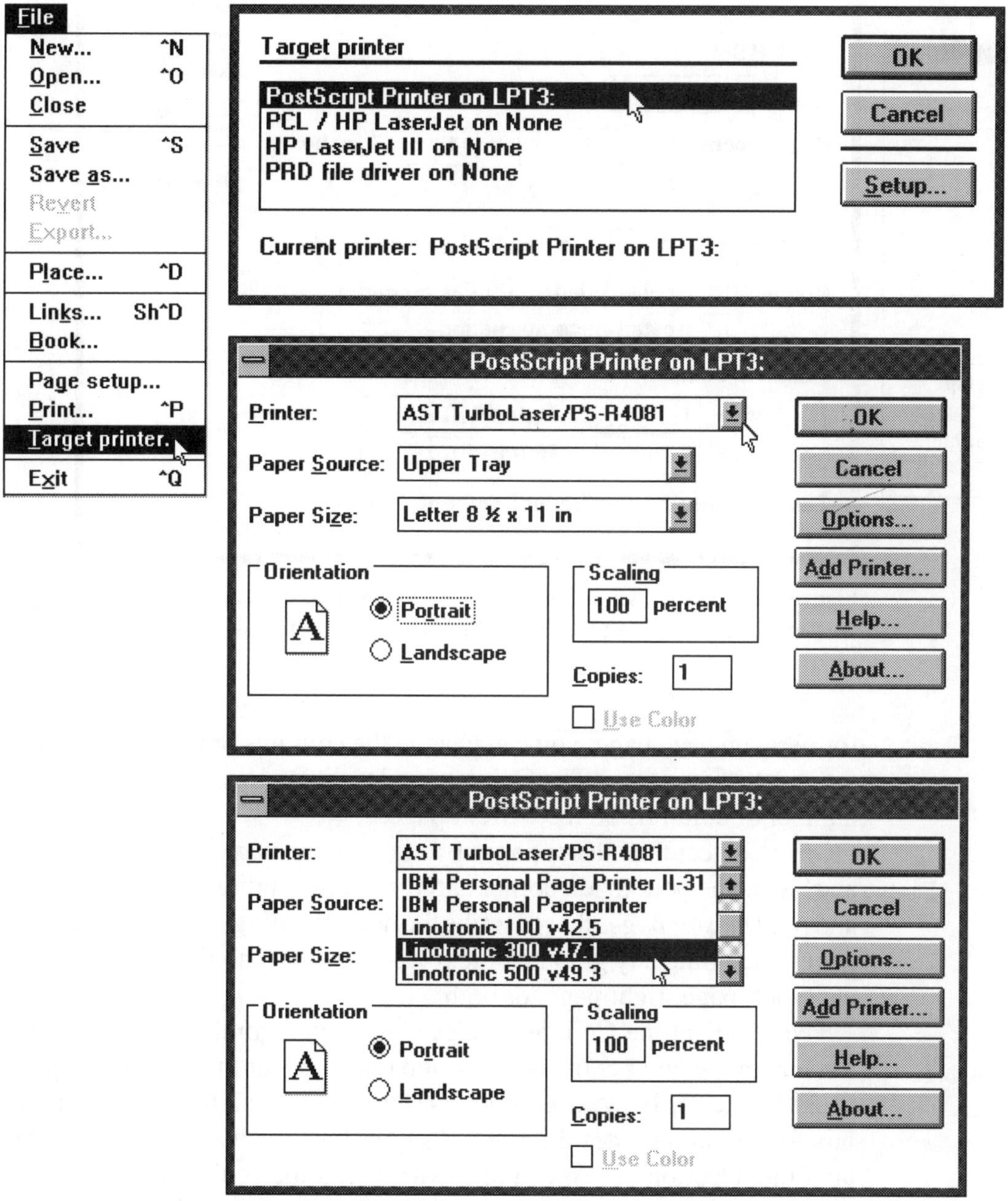

File

New...	^N
Open...	^O
Close	
Save	^S
Save as...	
Revert	
Export...	
Place...	^D
Links...	Sh^D
Book...	
Page setup...	
Print...	^P
Target printer.	
Exit	^Q

Target printer

PostScript Printer on LPT3:
PCL / HP LaserJet on None
HP LaserJet III on None
PRD file driver on None

OK

Cancel

Setup...

Current printer: PostScript Printer on LPT3:

PostScript Printer on LPT3:

Printer: AST TurboLaser/PS-R4081

Paper Source: Upper Tray

Paper Size: Letter 8 ½ x 11 in

Orientation
  A   ● Portrait
      ○ Landscape

Scaling
  100 percent

Copies: 1

☐ Use Color

OK
Cancel
Options...
Add Printer...
Help...
About...

PostScript Printer on LPT3:

Printer: AST TurboLaser/PS-R4081

Paper Source: IBM Personal Page Printer II-31
                IBM Personal Pageprinter
                Linotronic 100 v42.5
Paper Size: Linotronic 300 v47.1
                Linotronic 500 v49.3

Orientation
  A   ● Portrait
      ○ Landscape

Scaling
  100 percent

Copies: 1

☐ Use Color

OK
Cancel
Options...
Add Printer...
Help...
About...

Figure 2-3. To display the Target Printer dialog box, choose Target Printer from the File menu. Select a target printer in the dialog box before creating a publication so that PageMaker is aware of the printer's resolution.

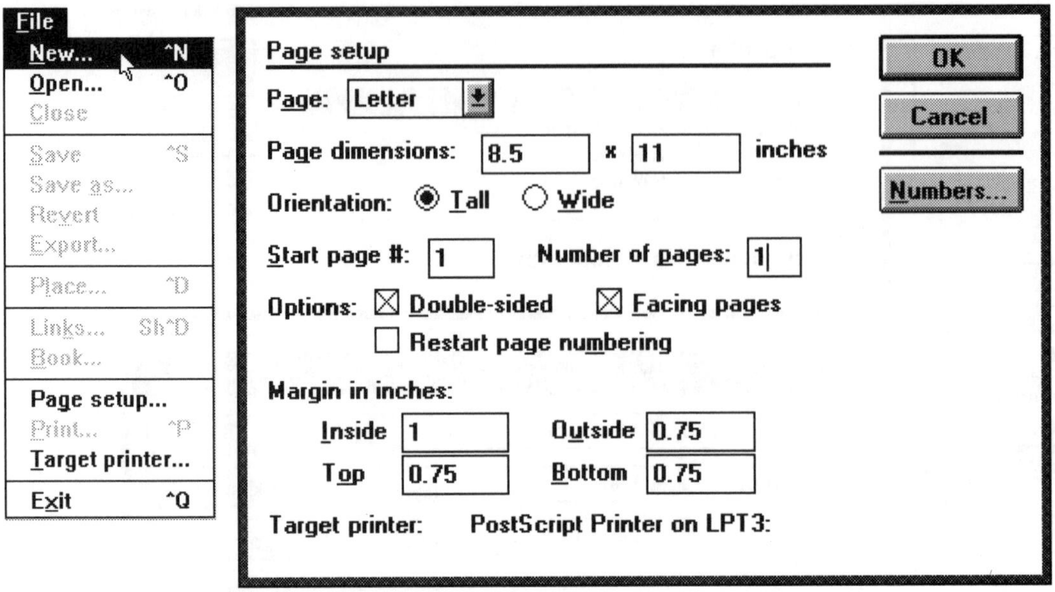

```
┌─────────────┐
│ File        │
├─────────────┤
│ New...    ^N│
│ Open...   ^O│
│ Close       │
│             │
│ Save      ^S│
│ Save as...  │
│ Revert      │
│ Export...   │
│             │
│ Place...  ^D│
│             │
│ Links... Sh^D│
│ Book...     │
│             │
│ Page setup..│
│ Print...  ^P│
│ Target printer..│
│ Exit      ^Q│
└─────────────┘
```

Page setup

Page: Letter

Page dimensions: 8.5 × 11 inches

Orientation: ● Tall ○ Wide

Start page #: 1   Number of pages: 1

Options: ☒ Double-sided   ☒ Facing pages
☐ Restart page numbering

Margin in inches:

Inside 1   Outside 0.75
Top 0.75   Bottom 0.75

Target printer: PostScript Printer on LPT3:

OK   Cancel   Numbers...

Figure 2-4. The Page setup dialog box, invoked by the New command, for defining the page margins, size, and orientation for a new publication.

format—on each page, you can change the columns or retain the format set in the master page. The Column guides dialog box always shows the number of columns on the current page.

First, select the master pages by clicking the page icons labeled "L" and "R" at the bottom left corner of the window. Figure 2-5 shows the left and right *master pages* that describe the default settings of all left and right pages, including any graphic or text elements that should be repeated on every left page, right page, or both.

Next, select the Column guides command from the Options menu. Type **2** for the number of columns, and type **0.25** for the amount of space to use for the gap between columns (1/4 inch). Figure 2-6 shows the dialog box for Column guides. Figure 2-7 shows how the master pages appear after the selection of two columns with a 0.25-inch column gap is made.

Back in the page setup menu (Figure 2-4), you could have selected a single-page orientation by clicking the marked box next to Double-sided in order to delete the "X" in the box and turn the Double-sided option off. The Double-sided option, which is usually on, sets up left and right master

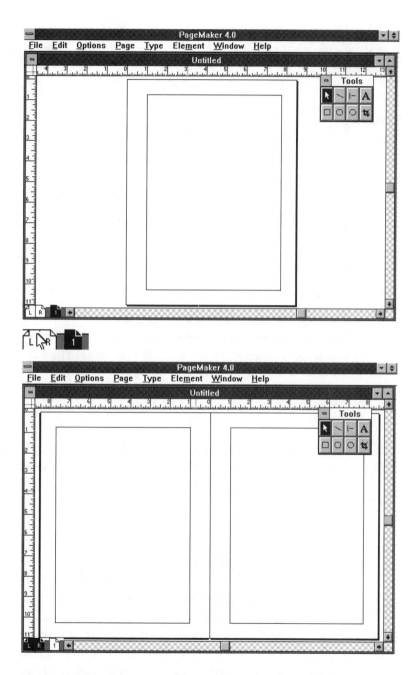

Figure 2-5. The first page of the publication as defined by the Page setup dialog box. Click the master page icon at the bottom left of the PageMaker window to display the master pages.

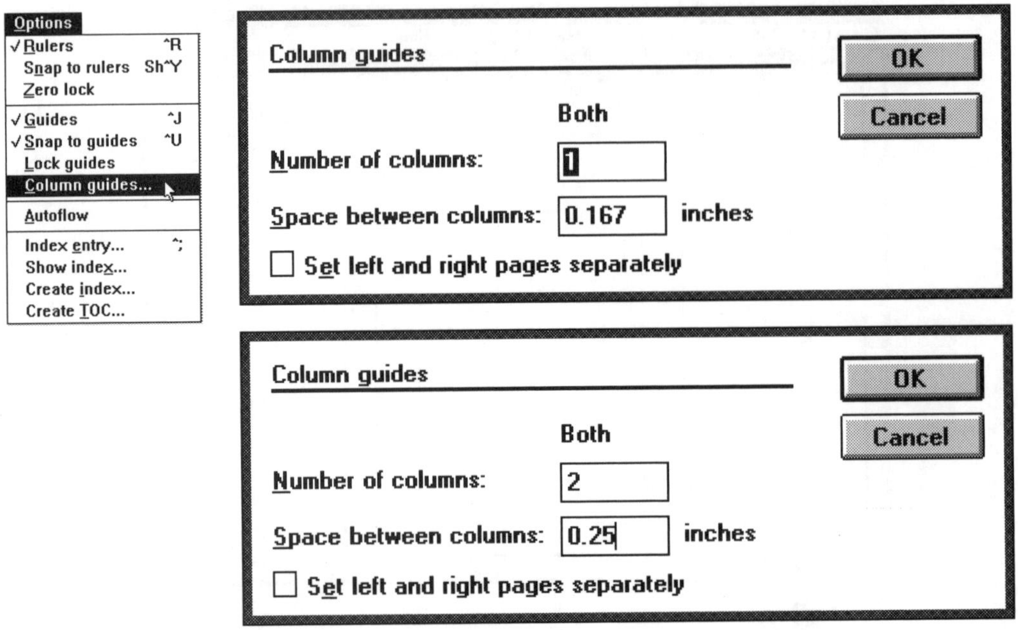

Figure 2-6. Change the master pages to a two-column format by using the Column guides command in the Options menu. Type the number of columns (2), and drag across the column width to select that value and type the new width (0.25 inches). Click OK to finish.

pages with margins properly offset from the spine where pages will be bound. Clicking this option off causes PageMaker to set up only one master page, and assumes that the publication does not have double-sided pages. Most publications use double-sided page styles, starting with a title page as a right-hand page, followed by two-page spreads.

Adding Footers with Page Numbers

The master pages are designed to include the text and graphics that you want repeated on every left or right page (or both pages) of the publication file. For example, you probably want to have page footers appear on each page with the proper page number. You set this up by creating page footers on the master pages in order to repeat the footers on each page. Each footer can hold a marker for the page number that should be printed on each page.

You can zoom into a more detailed view in order to type the footers.

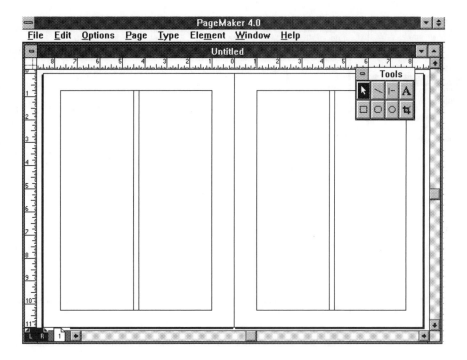

Figure 2-7. The master pages, after changing the number of columns to two.

Choose Actual size from the Page menu. Click once in the right scroll bar below the scroll box, and once to the left of the bottom scroll box, so that the bottom left corner of the left master page is in view.

Next, choose the text tool, click an insertion point at the left margin (Figure 2-8), and choose the Type specs option from the Type menu. Select Helvetica as the font by clicking in the font pop-up menu (Figure 2-9). Set the text to be 10 points in size by clicking in the point size pop-up menu. Finally, click the box next to Bold, then click the OK button (Figure 2-10). You can now type the text of the footer. (If you are not using the text tool, switch back to it before typing your text.)

Start with the automatic page number marker: Hold down the Control, Shift, and **3** keys. PageMaker displays the marker LM to mark the place of a page number in the left master page. Type a space and the text of the footer, as shown in Figure 2-11.

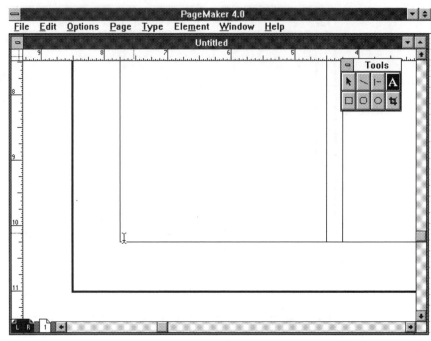

Figure 2-8. Change the Page View to Actual size, and scroll to the bottom of the left master page. Click an insertion point at the bottom left edge of the page.

After typing the footer, choose the pointer tool, and click anywhere in the middle of the footer's text. Two parallel lines appear above and below the footer (Figure 2-12). The lines have handles on them, indicating that the element is a text element.

Now choose Copy from the Edit menu in order to copy the footer to the Clipboard (a scratchpad area provided in Windows to hold elements temporarily). Click to the right of the bottom scroll box, or drag the bottom scroll box, to view the right master page (Figure 2-13). Choose Paste from the Edit menu, and a copy of the footer appears on the right master page (Figure 2-14).

To drag it into position, click and hold down the mouse button inside the text element until a cross with arrows replaces the pointer icon as the cursor, then drag to the bottom right corner of the right master page (Figure 2-15). It should be easy to drag the element into position because

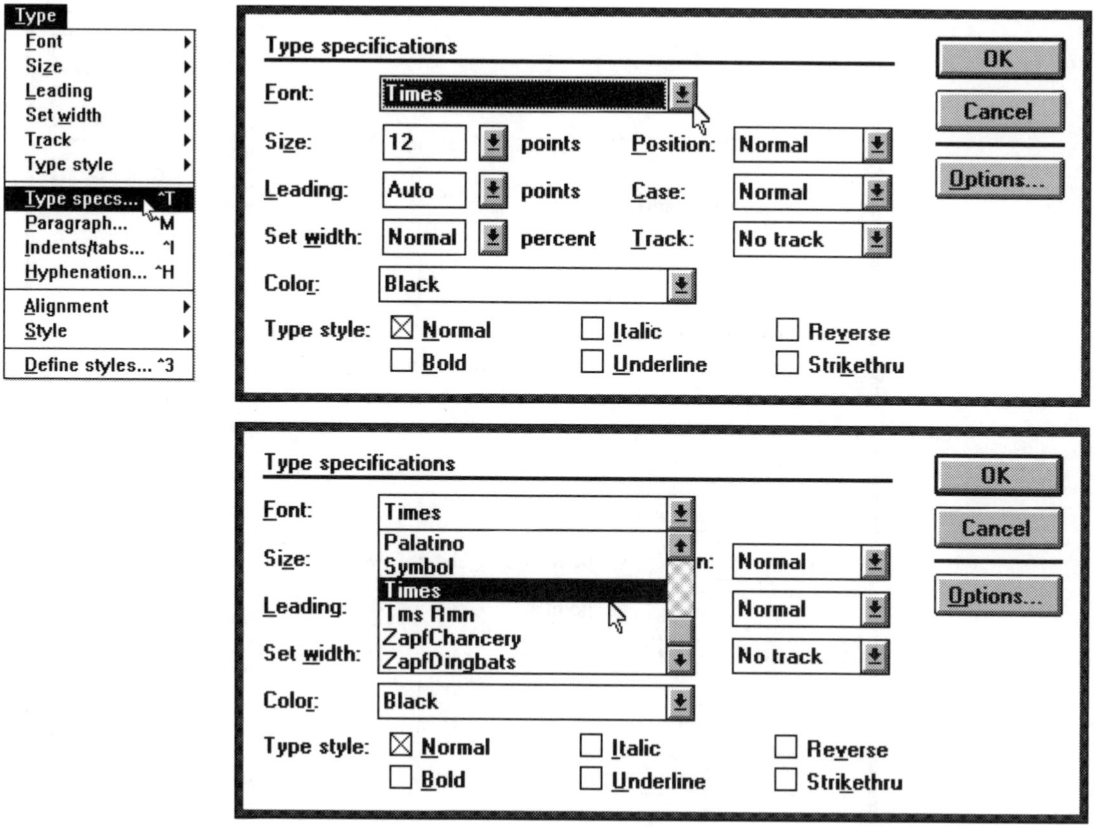

Figure 2-9. Using the Type specs dialog box from the Type menu, change the Type Specs to Helvetica by clicking in the font pop-up menu.

the column guides and the bottom guide act as magnets. This is because the option "Snap to guides" is turned on (it is usually on when you start PageMaker, but if it isn't, you can turn it on by choosing Snap to guides in the Options menu. A check mark indicates that it is on).

The copied footer is still left justified because it is a copy of the left master page footer. To change it, switch to the text tool, drag the text pointer across the footer text, and choose the Align right command from the Type menu (Figure 2-16).

To finish the job, click a text insertion point to the right of the page-

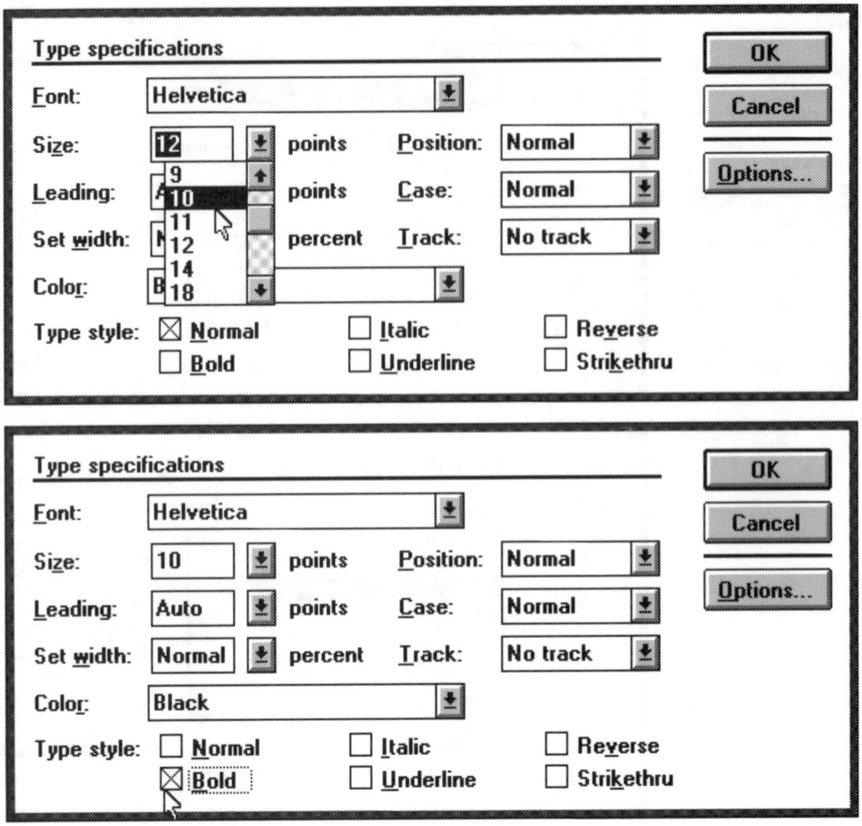

Figure 2-10. Using the Type specs dialog box from the Type menu, change the point size to 10 points in the point size pop-up menu, and to bold by clicking the Bold check box.

number marker (now shown as RM for the right master page) in the footer. Drag to select just the marker, and choose Cut from the Edit menu in order to cut the page marker (Figure 2-17). Click another insertion point at the end of the footer against the right margin, type a space, and choose Paste from the Edit menu (Figure 2-18). The footers are now complete, including automatic page numbers.

It is time to save your publication file (you should save it often). Since you started from scratch with the New command, choose the Save command from the File menu (Figure 2-19) so that you can use the same

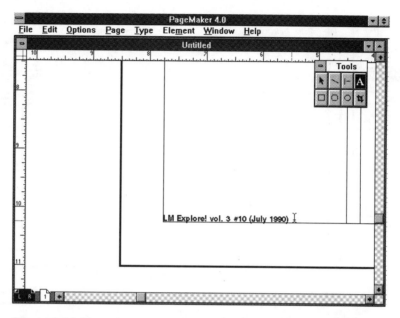

Figure 2-11. Type the page number marker and footer text for the left master page.

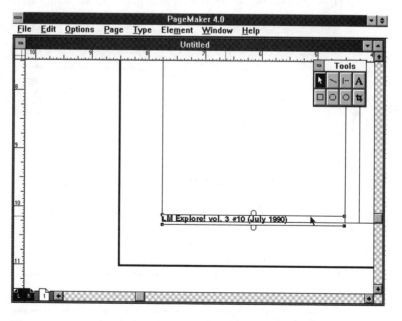

Figure 2-12. Select the footer text for copying.

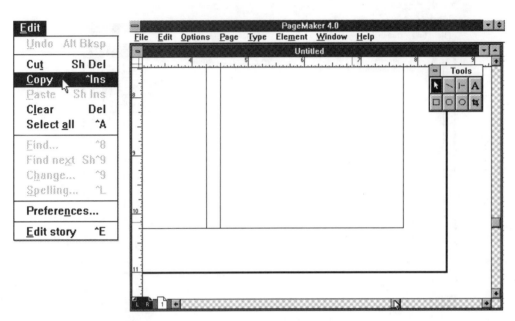

Figure 2-13. Copy the footer text, then scroll (using the bottom scroll bar) to the right (bottom) side of the right master page, before using Paste.

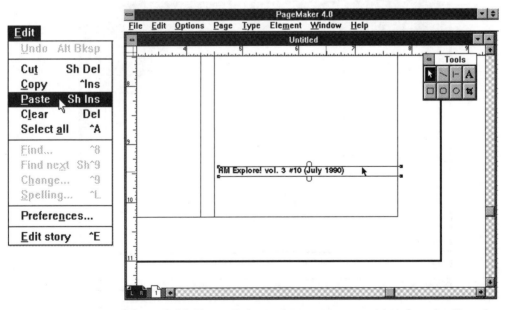

Figure 2-14. The copied text element appears on the page after Paste is used.

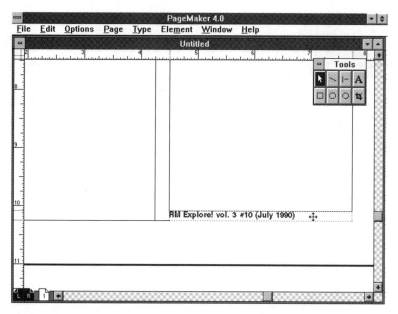

Figure 2-15. Move the copied text element into position to make a footer for the right master page.

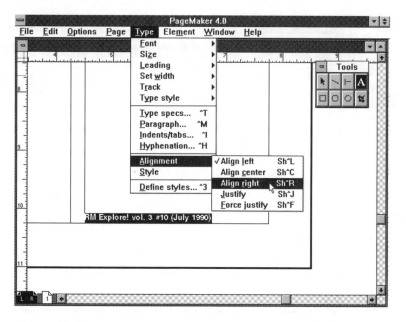

Figure 2-16. The Align right command changes the alignment of the selected text in the text element. (First, select the A tool and drag the text pointer over the text to select it.)

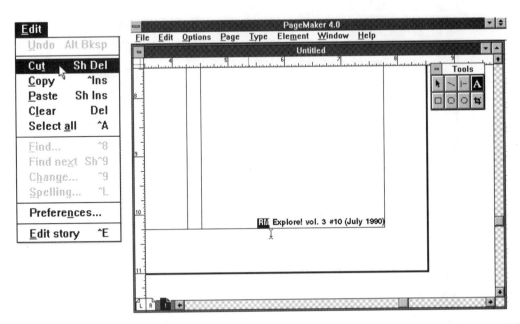

Figure 2-17. Cut the page marker from the left side of the text element (after first selecting it with the text tool).

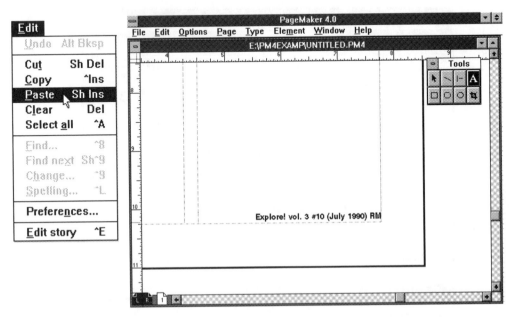

Figure 2-18. Move the text cursor to the right side of the text (at the end), type a space, and use Paste to paste the page-number marker back into the text element (so that the page number appears at the end of the text).

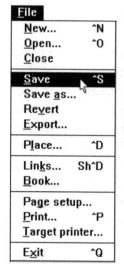

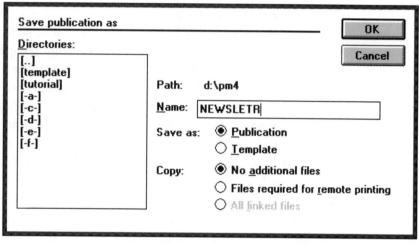

Figure 2-19. The Save (and Save As) dialog box lets you type a name for the newly created publication file. PageMaker automatically appends the ".PM4" file type to the eight-character name you supply.

design for new publications without having to redefine the master page. Name the file **NEWSLETR** and press Enter or click OK. PageMaker saves the publication file with the name NEWSLETR.PM4 (appending the "PM4" file type automatically).

You can now quit the program if you wish, and resume this example later by simply double-clicking this publication file in order to start PageMaker with this file exactly as it was when you last left it.

You can also start PageMaker directly by double-clicking the program, and open this file by selecting the Open command from the File menu, then clicking on the name of this publication file (NEWSLETR.PM4) to open the file.

Designing the Title Page

The style of a newsletter is characterized by its title page (page one), which can say more about your publication than a carefully worded statement. A simple design was chosen for this example in order to move quickly through PageMaker's features. To move to Page 1 of the newsletter, click the page 1 icon in the lower-left corner.

This page displays the footer designed previously in the right master page. However, the footer should not appear on page one of the newsletter, even though it should appear on every other page.

To turn off the footer (and any other master page elements) for page one, choose the Display master items option in the Page menu. If this option has a check mark next to it, the check mark disappears when you select it. The check mark means that master page items are displayed on the current page; with no check mark, it means that no master page items will be displayed for the current page. Therefore, you would turn this option off (no check mark) for a blank title page (Figure 2-20).

It may help your design task to display a ruler. PageMaker usually displays a horizontal and vertical ruler unless you turn off the ruler display by selecting Rulers from the Options menu. You turn the ruler back on by selecting Rulers again. PageMaker automatically uses inches, but you can change the unit of measurement to centimeters or to picas with points by selecting Preferences from the Edit menu. For the examples in this chapter, the ruler is measured in inches.

You may also want to use guides on the page because you can attach text and graphics blocks to them without the need to position a mouse exactly—the guide acts as a magnet so that when you move an element close to it, the element snaps to it. The Snap to guides command in the Options menu controls this feature, which is is on until you turn it off by selecting it. To turn it back on, select it again.

To create a ruler guide, click anywhere in the ruler and drag the ruler guide to the desired position on the page, using the dotted lines in both the horizontal and vertical rulers for measuring. Figure 2-21 shows a guide placed 2 inches below the top of the page, in Fit in window view and in 400% size page view (exactly on the 2-inch mark), to indicate the baseline of the newsletter title text.

Use the 400% size page view (the most accurate view for lining up items on a page) and ruler guides to be sure that elements are aligned properly. To switch to 400% size view, choose 400% size in the Page menu, or hold down the Control key (CTRL key on some keyboards) and type **4**.

The Control-**4** keyboard shortcut is just one of many shortcuts you can use to bypass the program's menus for quick action.

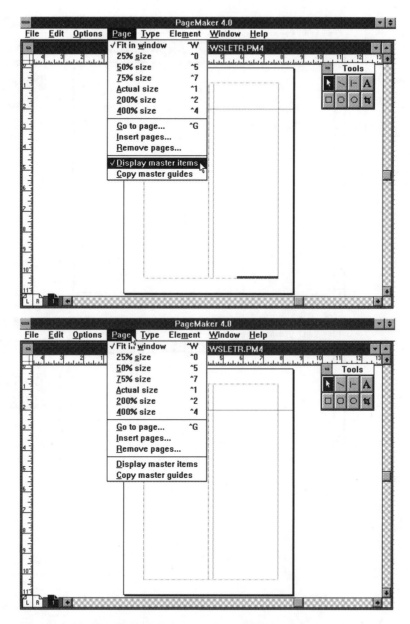

Figure 2-20. The blank title page, before and after the master page items were turned off (the footers are defined as master page items for all pages, but should not be used on the title page).

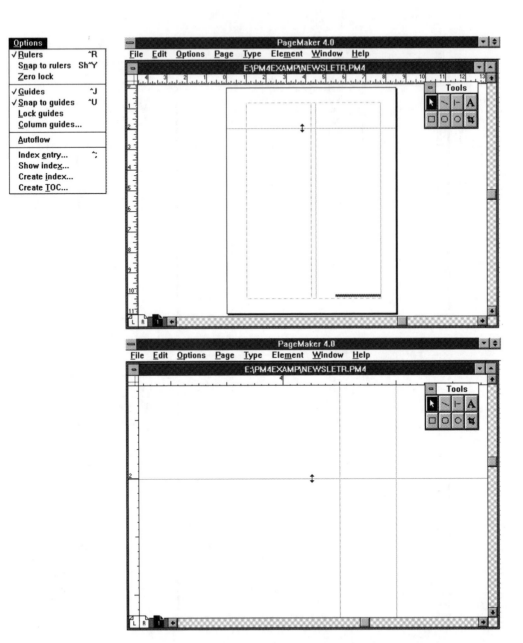

Figure 2-21. Add a ruler guide at the 2-inch mark to help place text and graphic elements accurately. This example shows the fit-in-window view and 400% view.

Use the pull-down menus until you learn the keyboard shortcuts, which are displayed in the menus. As you learn PageMaker, you will remember the shortcuts for the commands that you use most often, and you will not need to use their menus. To switch back to Actual size view, type Control-**1**; to switch to Fit in window view, type Control-**W**.

Ruler guides can be positioned anywhere on the page, horizontally or vertically, and can be locked into position, or unlocked, moved, and deleted. When the Snap to guides option is on (in the Options menu), the placement of elements is easier and their alignment is guaranteed. Ruler guides should be used whenever you want to align anything, or use them to create a page grid, and elements can then be aligned to the grid. You can have up to 40 separate ruler guides in the page display.

Changing Fonts, Sizes, and Leading

To add a title, switch to Actual size view (most accurate for viewing line endings), click the text tool, click an insertion point on the page on top of the ruler guide, and type the title, as shown in Figure 2-22 (the title is "Explore!").

The title is way too small, so you must change its type specifications—the font name, its size, its style, and the amount of leading. To do this, first select the text with the text tool by dragging across it (the entire text should be highlighted after doing this).

With the text selected, you can change the font, type style, size, and leading with the Type specs command in the Type menu as shown previously, or by dragging to the right of the Font, Size, Leading, and Type style options in the Type menu to use the pop-up menus (Figure 2-23). When using the pop-up menus, changes are shown immediately. The Helvetica font (a Type 1 font) was chosen for the title, with 100 points for its size, automatic leading, and both the bold and italic styles. When changing a Type 1 font's size, you can specify any size in one-tenth point size increments (such as 10.1 points).

Note: our font examples may look better than yours, because we are using Adobe Type Manager (ATM) with Windows to display Type 1 outline fonts. Without ATM, a 100-point Helvetica character looks more jagged because a 100-point screen version is not available. When using

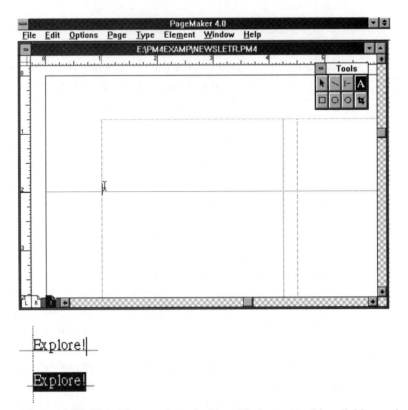

Figure 2-22. Type the newsletter's title with the text tool by clicking an insertion point on the ruler guide, followed by typing the title. Then select the text to change its type specifications.

Windows with TrueType fonts (to be available in 1991), 100-point fonts display with the same quality as Type 1 fonts with ATM. We suggest that you use either ATM with Type 1 fonts, or TrueType fonts (to be available in 1991), for design work.

The *leading* amount measures the space between lines, either from the tops of uppercase letters from one line to the next, or from the baselines of the two lines.

The *baseline* is an imaginary line that aligns the bottoms of each character's body, not including descenders. For example, the baseline of the title runs along the bottom of the letters of "Explore!", but "p" has a descender that descends below the baseline, and "o" and "e" are rounded at the baseline and extend a little bit below it. These embellishments help

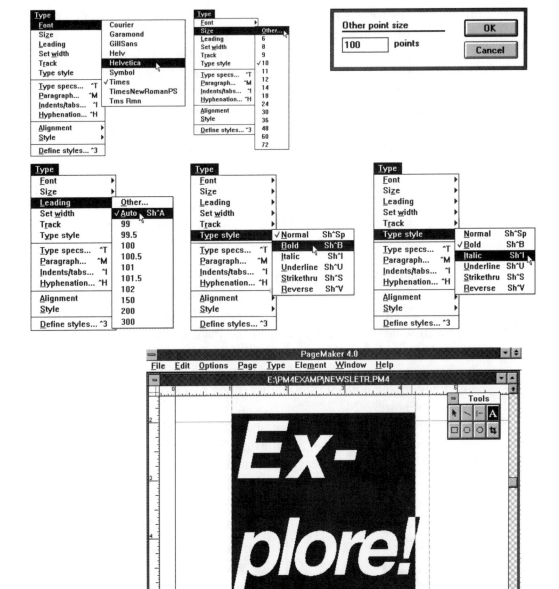

Figure 2-23. Change the font, size, leading, and style of the title from the pull-down menus. As shown, other sizes can be specified, even if they are not on the menu, by selecting the Other option and typing the size. You can set text to be bold *and* italic to combine those styles.

make type in fonts easier to read than other forms of type (such as typewriter or dot-matrix type). In this example, you are using the ruler guide at the 2-inch mark as the baseline for the title text. Ruler guides don't print, so you can leave them on the page and use them as baselines for text.

Automatic leading was chosen for the title. With automatic leading, PageMaker increases the size of the leading to accommodate the size of the font, including the size of any individual characters that are set to a larger size than the rest of the text. It is a useful setting if you are experimenting with the font's size to get the right fit in a section of the page. You can always switch to a specific leading amount (which you can specify in tenths of a point, from 0 to 1300 points). To keep lines from overlapping, use automatic leading or specify a leading amount that is at least 20% greater than the font size.

Text Element Width and Alignment

The title text now wraps around within the column width. However, you want the newsletter title to span both columns. To see the title better, select the Fit in window display option in the Page menu, or hold down the Control key and type **W.**

You can change the text block's width by switching to the pointer tool and dragging the bottom right corner of the block of text to be wider, as shown in Figure 2-24.

To move the title into position (using the pointer tool), press and hold down the mouse button over the title until the four-arrows symbol appears (Figure 2-25). Without releasing the mouse button, drag the title into the

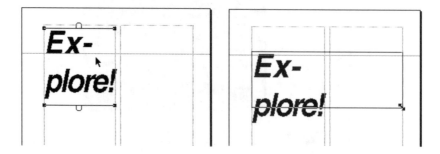

Figure 2-24. Change the column width of the newsletter's title by dragging the bottom-right corner with the pointer tool.

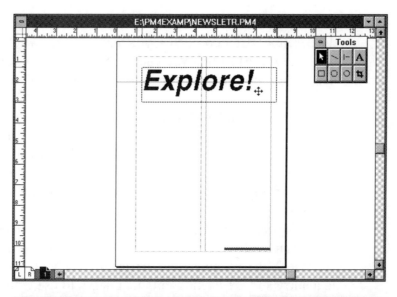

Figure 2-25. Move the text element into position by holding down the mouse button until the pointer turns into four arrows, and then drag the element up so that the ruler guide becomes the baseline for the title. Switch to another page view (such as 75% shown here) to align the text element precisely.

proper position so that the title uses the ruler guide at the 2-inch mark as the baseline. After doing this, you may want to switch to a 75% view (in the Page menu) so that you can see the entire top of the page in closer detail, then use this technique again to move the element into precise position.

The title should be changed to be aligned along the right margin of the page. To change the alignment, select the text of the title with the text tool, and use the Alignment pop-up menu (in the Type menu) to select the Align right option (Figure 2-26). The title is aligned, or *justified*, to the right margin of the text element box (the box is indicated by the lines with handles).

Some designers start with the finished newsletter logo and title, while others start with imaginary text blocks and a blank space for a graphic logo and title. You can choose any starting method with PageMaker. If you are in a hurry and are lacking graphic images to use with this example, just draw a box with the box tool or an oval with the oval tool to act as a place holder for the graphics. You can adjust the title and add graphics later.

Placing Graphics

When you are designing the title page and plan to use graphics in the title, place the graphics (or rough versions, if the images are not finished) onto the page so that you can see the entire layout with the graphics. If the graphics are not yet available, use PageMaker's toolbox to create a simple representation of the graphic's outline for now.

For example, the logo for this newsletter includes a graphic image of the Earth (courtesy of the Comstock *Desktop Photography* catalog) for the left side of page one. If you have nothing suitable, you can draw a circle to represent the globe graphic image.

To draw a circle, select the oval-drawing tool from the toolbox, and move the crosshairs cursor to the top-left corner of the page. Hold down the Shift key and drag downward and to the right in order to create a perfect circle, as shown in Figure 2-27. (If you don't hold down the Shift key, the shape will be an oval.)

PageMaker can import a variety of graphics files (described in Chapter 1). If the graphics can be copied to the Clipboard, use the Paste command to place the graphics on the page. However, for the best results,

Figure 2-26. Select the title text and use the Align right option in the Alignment pop-up menu, which is in the Type menu.

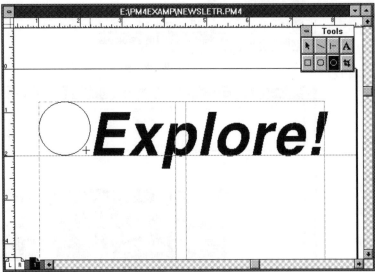

Figure 2-27. Draw a perfect circle with the circle drawing tool by holding down the Shift key while drawing.

use PageMaker's Place command to place the graphics directly from the file onto the page.

Choose the Place command from the File menu, and the Place dialog box appears (Figure 2-28) containing a list of files and directories. Directories and drives have brackets around their names. To look inside a directory or drive, double-click the directory or drive name. As you open a subdirectory that is contained within another directory, you are moving down through an organized set of directories (as if you were going up a tree from the root) until you reach the file that you want. If the list of names is longer than the dialog box window, scroll bars appear for scrolling up and down the list. To operate the scroll bar and see more names in the list, click below the white box in the gray area, click the up or down arrow, or drag the white box up or down.

The graphic image for this example is a TIFF image file from the *Comstock Desktop Photography* CD-ROM disc (which contains a catalog of TIFF image files for publications). TIFF image files usually have ".TIF" as the file type.

Select the graphics file and click the Place button (or double-click the filename). Because the graphics file contains a TIFF image, the pointer

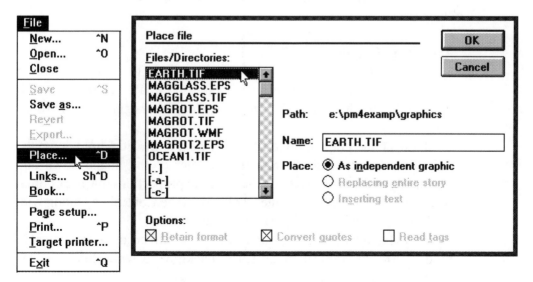

Figure 2-28. The Place command's dialog box.

turns into the image icon. Move the icon to the upper-left corner of the title area of the page, and click to place the image (Figure 2-29).

Use the same method to place a draw document (an object-oriented graphic image, represented by a pencil icon), a paint document (a paintbrush icon), or a graphic image saved in EPS (Encapsulated PostScript) format (a PS icon). PageMaker's pointer icons tell you what type of graphics file you are placing.

Scanned photographs and other TIFF images that contain color or gray areas occupy a great deal more disk space than Windows Bitmap graphics. They also take considerably more time to redraw on the screen. Therefore, PageMaker normally places a low-resolution version of the image for display purposes. You can change the display of images from the normal setting to a high-quality setting (for higher resolution), or to a gray box (for faster display), in the Preferences dialog box (Preferences is an option in the Edit menu).

When you print the publication, the high-resolution version is usually substituted for the display version so that you get the best possible print quality. Displaying images at high resolution is described in Chapters 4 and 5.

Do not be alarmed if the graphic image seems a bit jagged—print the page to see what the result will look like. Printing is described later in this chapter.

Arranging Graphics and Text

During a design effort, one new idea may cause you to change something else. The image of the Earth is nice, but it is too small. The first step is to enlarge the graphic image in size by *scaling* it (resizing it proportionately).

To scale the graphic up to fit snugly next to the title, hold down the Shift key and drag the bottom-right corner of the image down and diagonally to the right. To scale the image in proportions that are optimal for the resolution of your printer, hold down the Control key along with the Shift key while dragging (Figure 2-30).

Now that the Earth is next to the title, it would be an improvement to the design to have these items on a black background, with white text. This is simple to do.

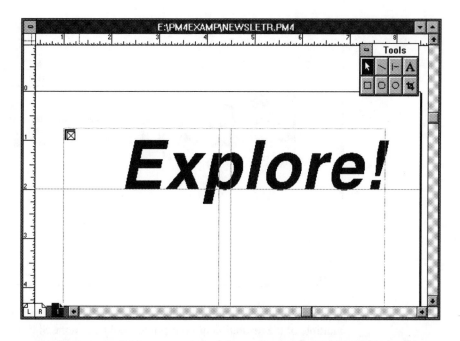

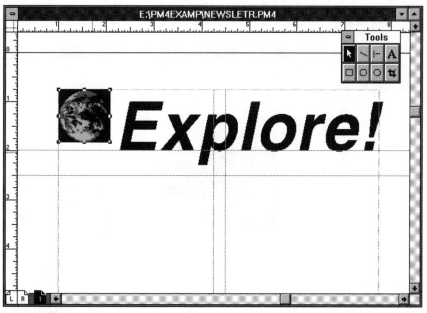

Figure 2-29. Place the TIFF graphics file in the upper left corner of the title area.

Figure 2-30. To scale the image in equal proportions, and to a dot size that is a multiple of the resolution of your printer, hold down the Shift and Control keys while dragging a handle on any corner.

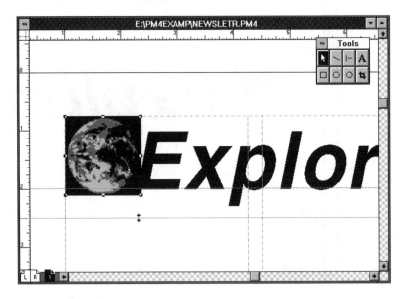

Figure 2-31. Drag a ruler guide to the 2.5-inch marker to represent the bottom of a black background for the title.

First, drag a ruler guide to the 2.5-inch marker to represent the bottom of the black background (Figure 2-31). Next, draw a rectangle with the rectangle tool that extends from the margins to the new ruler guide, covering the title elements (Figure 2-32). The edges of the rectangle should snap to the column and ruler guides as long as the Snap to guides option (in the Options menu) has a check mark.

After drawing the rectangle, it should have remained selected, with tiny handles on each corner for scaling. If it is not selected, select the rectangle now, using the pointer tool (Figure 2-33). Change it to a black rectangle by selecting the Solid option in the Fill submenu of the Element menu. Solid is a pattern fill that solidly fills the rectangle with the current color—in this case, black.

To place the black rectangle behind the other title elements, select the Send to back command in the Element menu (Figure 2-34).

The Earth image now appears in front of the black rectangle. The text is also in front, but it is still black characters on a black background. To change the text to white, switch to the text tool, and drag across the area where the text was placed (Figure 2-35). Then choose the Reverse option in the Type style pop-up menu in the Type menu, to change the letters to be reversed from black to white (Figure 2-36).

A few more adjustments are required. The title's exclamation point extends beyond the black rectangle, but you adjust the column width of the text element to bring the exclamation point back inside the rectangle. First, select the title with the pointer tool, then adjust the width of the text element by dragging the right-bottom corner of the element inside the black rectangle (Figure 2-37).

Now the title is fine, but the Earth image is too big. Select it with the pointer tool, then while holding down the Shift and Control keys, drag its lower-right corner up and toward the left, so that the image snaps into a size that is smaller (Figure 2-38).

We have another graphic image to include in the newsletter title: an Encapsulated PostScript (EPS) file modified using Aldus FreeHand, a PostScript drawing program. This EPS image comes from the *T/Maker ClickArt EPS Professional Art Series* of PostScript clip art, which you can use in your publications as many times as you wish without paying any royalties. This series and other collections of electronic clip art can be

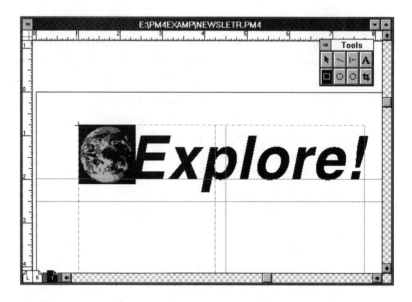

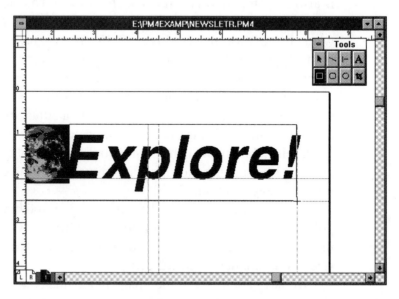

Figure 2-32. Draw a rectangle with the rectangle tool over the title elements.

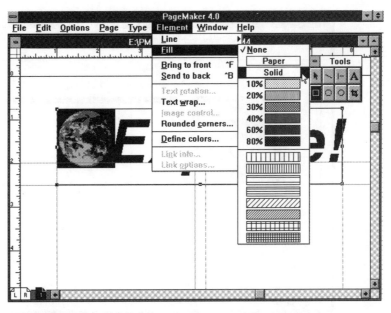

Figure 2-33. After selecting the rectangle with the pointer tool, change the Fill to Solid (black) in the Element menu.

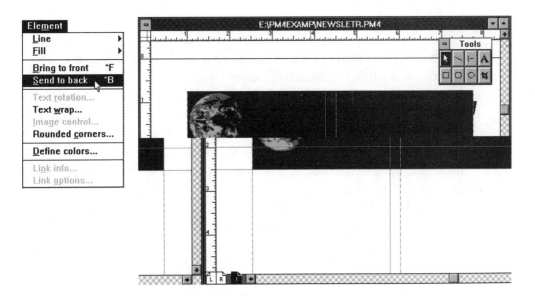

Figure 2-34. Select the Send to back command in the Element menu to place the black rectangle behind the other title elements. (The title text is not visible because it is also black.)

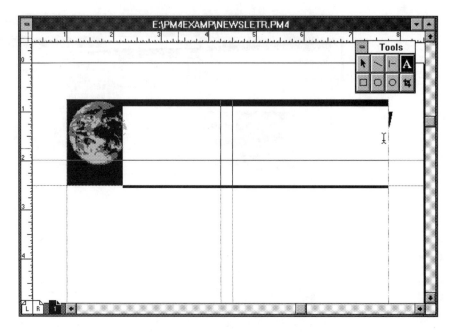

Figure 2-35. Drag across the title text with the text tool; the text appears reversed where it is selected.

purchased from your computer dealer or directly from T/Maker.

You place this graphic image in the same manner as before: using the Place command (Figure 2-39) to select the graphics file, and move the graphics placement icon to a position on the page. Click the graphics placement icon to place the graphics (Figure 2-40). After placement, the image is selected and can be moved to any position on the page—click inside the image until the cursor changes to a cross with arrows, then drag the image (Figure 2-41).

Don't be alarmed if the white areas inside the EPS image seem to disappear, showing the black underneath. EPS graphic images often do not display in Windows applications exactly as they will print. The printed page will show the white and gray portions of the EPS image overlaying the black.

To add the subtitles underneath the title, drag a few ruler guides with the pointer tool from the top ruler to the 2.75-, 3-, 3.25-, and 3.5-inch markers (Figure 2-42). Type the text for the subtitles the same way as before: switch to the text tool, click on one of the ruler guides, and type

Figure 2-36. Change the selected title to Reversed type.

Figure 2-37. Adjust the text element for the title so that the exclamation point is within the black rectangle.

Figure 2-38. Adjusting the graphic image by scaling it with the Shift and Control keys depressed, to scale it proportionately and to a dot size that is a multiple of the printer's resolution.

the text. Select the text after typing it (Figure 2-43), and choose the font, size, leading, and style pop-up menus, as described earlier, to change the font to Helvetica, the size to 10 points, the leading to automatic, and the style to bold and italic. Type the second-level subtitles to extend for two lines by pressing Enter to break the lines into two lines. You should have text appearing below the title as shown in Figure 2-44.

The final touch is a horizontal *rule* (a line) that should be drawn along the 3.25-inch ruler guide. Switch to the perpendicular-line tool from the toolbox, and draw the rule by dragging from the left to the right margin (Figure 2-45). Then select the Line pop-up menu in the Element menu, and select a double-line style for the rule.

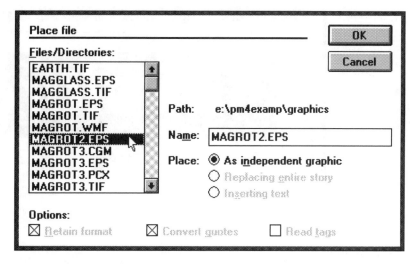

Figure 2-39. Place another graphic image (an EPS file) for the title page.

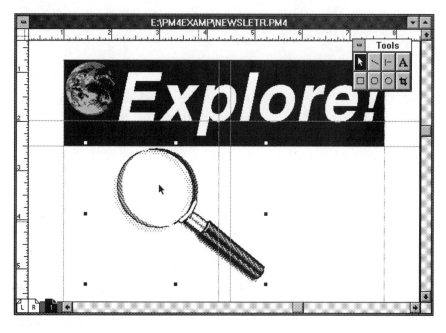

Figure 2-40. The placed EPS graphics file from the T/Maker ClickArt Professional
EPS Images Series.

Figure 2-41. Drag the selected EPS image into position.

Figure 2-46 shows the newsletter title in its final form (displayed, not printed). At this point, it is wise to save the file by choosing the Save command from the File menu.

Saving a Template File

Since the publication contains a completed title and nothing else, you may want to save it as a template. This approach lets you both preserve the original file and have a custom version. First, you design a publication's master pages and title, then save it as a template file for starting future versions of the publication. Later you open the template file as a new, untitled publication that you can supply a new name for, and thereby preserve the original template.

To create a template, use the Save as command, and click the Template option to save the publication as a template (Figure 2-47). Close the publication by selecting the Close command in the File menu, or by clicking the close box in the upper-left corner of the publication window.

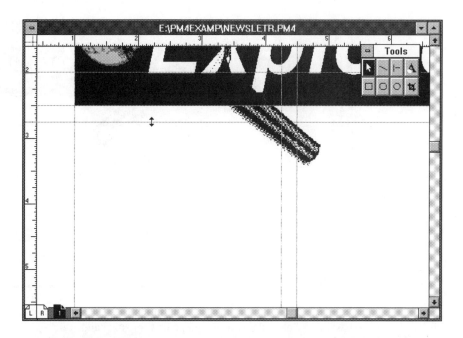

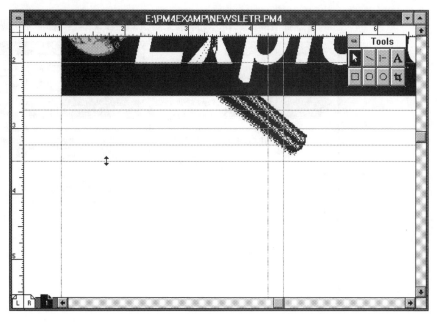

Figure 2-42. Drag more ruler guides to align the text beneath the title.

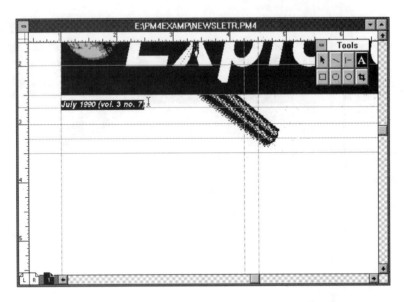

Figure 2-43. Type the text of the subtitles with the text tool, using the ruler guides as baselines. Select the text to change its font, size, and style.

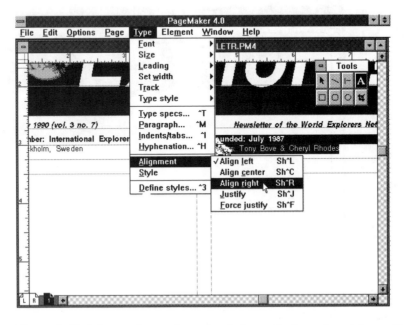

Figure 2-44. Select each text element and change its font, size, style, and leading. For the right-hand text elements, change the alignment to Align right.

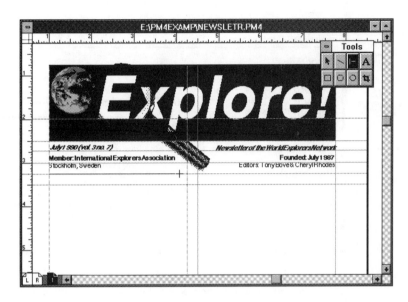

Figure 2-45. Drag a straight rule with the perpendicular-line tool from the left to the right margin, on top of the 3.25-inch ruler guide.

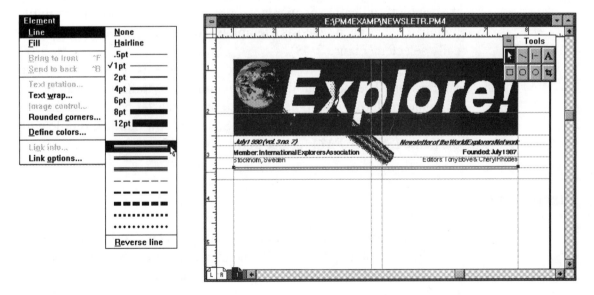

Figure 2-46. The title section, with the horizontal rule defining its bottom.

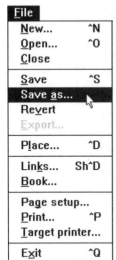

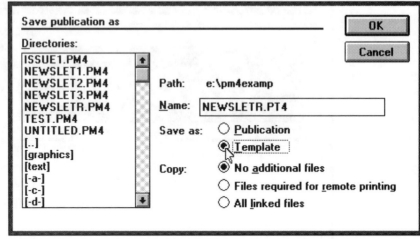

Figure 2-47. Save the publication file as a template, so that when you open it again, you open a new untitled version and preserve the original template.

Later when you reopen the publication, you have a choice of opening the original publication or opening a copy of the publication. The example publication has been saved as a template, so the Copy option is automatically selected (Figure 2-48).

Open the template as a copy, so that it opens as a new untitled publication. The new publication contains everything that was in the template, including the footers defined on the master pages, and the text and graphics placed on the title page. Save this new publication file with the name **ISSUE1.PM4** for use in the rest of this chapter's examples.

Placing Stories

The best page designs have a certain order—elements are balanced so that the page does not appear overly designed. A good page design should catch the reader's attention and direct the eye movement across and down the page.

We deliberately left out of the template many design decisions about how to place stories in the newsletter, because a story's content—

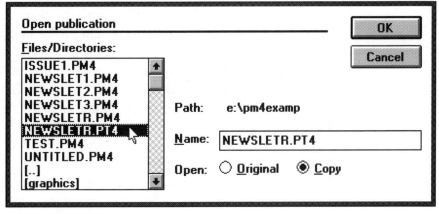

Figure 2-48. Opening the template file as a copy, so that you can create a new publication with the identical title and preserve the original template.

especially its title and any accompanying graphics or images—may not fit into a predesigned notion of how a generic story should be layed out. However, we did leave in one ruler guide—the guide at the 3.5-inch mark—to act as a starting point for the page-one stories of the newsletter. We also defined all pages to have the two-column format by default. We can always change this arrangement, but the default settings make it easier to place stories quickly.

We'll place one entire story, with a graphic image, on page one, and we'll place another graphic image on page one to advertise another story inside the newsletter. The first story's headline, or title, should be in a size that is not too large to be confused with the newsletter title, but not too small to be insignificant next to the text. The headline must also be close enough to any graphic image or photo that accompanies the article so that the reader's attention moves from the graphic or photo to the headline.

Another decision to make is where to put a graphic image or photo that accompanies the first story, and where to put the other image used to draw attention to an inside story. With conventional layout methods, you need to leave space on the page for the images, but you have the classic problem of not knowing how long the text will be when it is in typeset form. With PageMaker, you can solve this problem by placing electronic versions of the text and graphics. You can then adjust the elements as you wish to fit the space on the page, without spending a lot of time measuring and making copies of images and text galleys.

If you have a large, eye-catching image to use on the front page, you may want to start your publication effort by placing that image first, so that you get an idea of how the image stands out and how to balance it with other elements.

Placing and Cropping an Image

PageMaker supports a variety of graphics file formats. In particular, TIFF (Tag Image File Format), EPS (Encapsulated PostScript), PCX (PC Paintbrush), Targa (Truevision), and Windows Bitmap formats are used to store digitized images from scanners and video digitizers (also called *frame grabbers*).

Perhaps the easiest way to obtain a royalty-free image, if you have a camcorder, is to use a video digitizer or frame grabber to freeze a frame of video and store it as a TIFF, EPS, or Targa file. Video images are not as high in resolution (number of dots) as photographic images from a 300-dpi desktop scanner, but at small sizes, many people don't notice the difference. Video images are certainly cheaper to make and take less time than photographic images, depending on the type of equipment you use.

For this example, you can scan any photograph if you have a scanner, or you can digitize any image if you have a video digitizer or frame grabber. If you have none of these, you can draw a simple box to represent the image at a size that matches the final size we use for the video image. Figure 2-49 shows a box, drawn with the box tool, that acts as a place-holder for an image. The black box can serve two purposes: it can be a temporary placeholder that can be replaced later with a scanned or digitized image, or it can be printed or typeset with the page and used as a mask in the prepress stripping process, where a conventional photo-graphic negative is dropped into the black space (which turns into a white space when the page negative is made, so that the negative can be placed in the space easily by the stripper).

However, by scanning or digitizing an image and placing it directly on the page, you can sidestep the costly stripping of negatives, and you can make design changes and perform digital image retouching with graphics

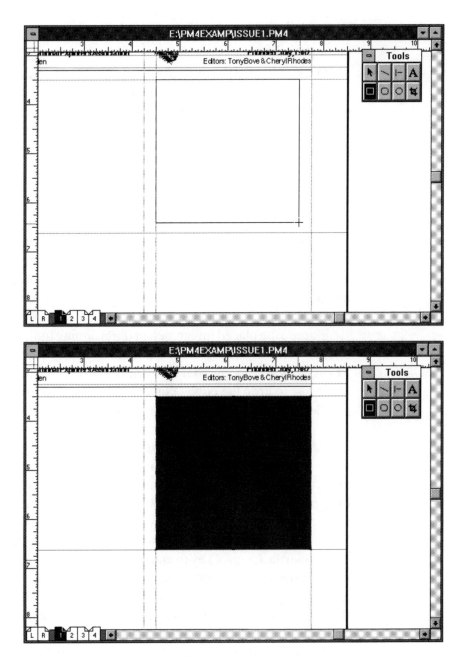

Figure 2-49. Draw a box to act as a placeholder for a graphic or photo.

programs in a cost-effective way, unlike costly conventional photographic techniques.

Once you have the image in an electronic file on disk, you can place the image onto the page, as shown earlier with the Earth image in the newsletter title. Use the Place command to select the file, and when the graphics placement icon appears indicating the type of image, you can place the image into the position on the page where you want it to appear (Figure 2-50).

The image may appear too large for the page, but you can scale it down. Before scaling, however, you may want to take advantage of the large image size to *crop* the image first.

Cropping an image is a process of clipping off the edges of an image that you don't want to show. The cropping tool in PageMaker is useful for cropping the edges of a rectangular image—it does not change the original image, but hides the edges so that they don't appear on the screen and don't print.

To crop the placed image, select the cropping tool, and click inside the image to display handles on the corners and sides of the image (Figure 2-51). Align the cropping tool over one of the handles, and drag inward into the image to crop the edge. You can crop one edge by dragging a center handle, or crop two edges at once by dragging a corner handle (Figure 2-52).

After cropping, scale the image to the appropriate size to fit on the page. If the graphic is a line drawing, such as an EPS file or Windows metafile (WMF) created by a drawing program, you can scale it by dragging a handle until the graphic is the correct size for your layout. If it is a paint-type graphic image with a pattern or fine detail, a TIFF, EPS, PCX, Targa, or other type of scanned image, or a digitized video image, hold down the Control key to automatically snap the image into one of the optimal sizes that best matches the dot resolution of your printer (Figure 2-53). In addition, hold down the Shift key while scaling in order to keep the same proportions; otherwise, you can distort the image by stretching or compressing from any of its sides.

By holding down the Shift key, you constrain the scaling of the image to retain the same ratio. By holding down the Control key, you scale the image only to sizes that work well with the selected printer, and you avoid

Figure 2-50. Place a digitized video image (or any image, if you have one) in the right-hand column just under the 3.5-inch ruler marker.

Figure 2-51. Select the image with the cropping tool to crop the image.

Figure 2-52. Crop by aligning the cropping tool over a selection handle and dragging inward into the image. You can crop one edge by dragging a center handle, or crop two edges at once by dragging a corner handle.

Figure 2-53. Scale the image with the pointer tool by holding down the Shift and Command keys while dragging the lower-right corner handle up and into the image.

having unwanted patterns (such as moirés) in the image. Without holding down the Shift key, you can stretch or compress an image or graphic, as well as change its size. Without holding down the Control key, you can scale the image to any size, even to sizes that are not optimal for your printer. Remember to release the mouse button before you release the Shift and/or Control keys to achieve the desired result.

No matter how you stretch or compress an image, you can snap it back to a size equally proportional to the original by holding down the Shift key while scaling the image. If you hold down the Control key, the image snaps into the sizes that work well with the selected printer.

The image occupies the top of the right column, leaving space below for more text. You are now ready to place the text of the first story.

Placing Unformatted Text
A newsletter operation may include several reporters, editors, and writers. There is no reason why these people can't use different word processors

to prepare their stories, and submit them to the PageMaker user who puts them together into a newsletter. PageMaker can import every popular PC word processing program's file format, and can even import text from not-so-popular programs.

Although your text file may be properly formatted by the word processing program for printing, you will probably want to change the type specifications when placing the text in the newsletter. For example, you may have picked 12-point type with automatic line spacing in the word processor, but you really want 10-point text with 12 points of leading (more precise control than line spacing) in the newsletter.

This example assumes that you did not format the text in advance or you wish to override the format that was set by the word processor. Thus, you could have used any word processing or text editing program to prepare the text.

The first step is to define the default type specifications for text placed with the Place command. This step is not necessary—you can always change the type specifications after placing text—but it saves time to set them in advance.

With the pointer tool selected, use the Type specs command in the Type menu. Select the Times font at 10 points, with 12 points of leading, in the Type specs dialog box (Figure 2-54), and click OK.

You will be pouring text slowly, one column at a time, so check that the Autoflow option in the Options menu is turned off (no check mark). Be sure also that the Snap to guides option is turned on (with a check mark), so that you can attach elements easily to guides on the page.

Choose the Place command from the File menu to place the text. Select a text file and turn off the Retain format option by clicking the box so that the "X" disappears. With this option the Place command does not retain the formatting settings from the word processor—PageMaker's Type specs settings are used instead. Click the Convert quotes option on (Figure 2-55), and click the Read tags option off. Finally, click Place (or press the Enter key).

If the text file is not recognized as a word processing file, PageMaker will display the Smart ASCII Filter dialog box before placing the text (if the file is recognized, PageMaker skips this dialog box). When this appears, you have several choices for importing text files, such as

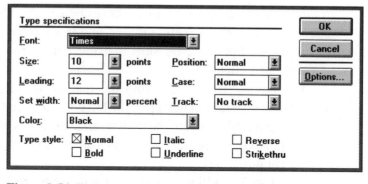

Type

Type	
Font	▶
Size	▶
Leading	▶
Set width	▶
Track	▶
Type style	▶
Type specs...	^T
Paragraph...	^M
Indents/tabs...	^I
Hyphenation...	^H
Alignment	▶
Style	▶
Define styles...	^3

Type specifications

Font: Times

Size: 10 points   Position: Normal

Leading: 12 points   Case: Normal

Set width: Normal percent   Track: No track

Color: Black

Type style: ☒ Normal   ☐ Italic   ☐ Reverse
☐ Bold   ☐ Underline   ☐ Strikethru

OK   Cancel   Options...

Figure 2-54. The type specifications for the text body were set before placing the text file so that they control the format of the text (and override any format selected in the word processor).

File

File	
New...	^N
Open...	^O
Close	
Save	^S
Save as...	
Revert	
Export...	
Place...	^D
Links...	Sh^D
Book...	
Page setup...	
Print...	^P
Target printer...	
Exit	^Q

Place file

Files/Directories:

CAPTION1.TXT
CAPTION2.TXT
POLOTRAV.TXT
PRODUCTS.TBL
QUESTIO2.WRI
QUESTION.DOC
TRAVEL.DOC
[..]
[-a-]
[-c-]
[-d-]

Path: e:\pm4examp\text

Name: POLOTRAV.TXT

Place: ⊙ As new story
○ Replacing entire story
○ Inserting text

Options:
☐ Retain format   ☒ Convert quotes   ☐ Read tags

OK   Cancel

Smart ASCII import filter, v1.2

Remove extra carriage returns:
☐ At end of every line
☐ Between paragraphs
☐ But keep tables, lists and indents as is

☐ Replace 3 or more spaces with a tab
☐ Monospace, import as Courier
☒ No conversion, import as is

OK   Cancel

Figure 2-55. Use the Place command to place the text of the lead article, with the Retain format and Read tags options off and the Convert quotes option on. Use the no conversion option with the Smart ASCII Filter.

removing extra carriage returns. These choices are described in Chapter 3 in the section on importing tables, and in Chapter 5 in the section on placing text. For now, be sure that the option for No conversion is checked, and click OK.

The pointer should turn into the manual text-flow icon, and you should place the icon at the top of the left column below the 3.5-inch ruler guide (Figure 2-56). Click the mouse, and text flows all the way down to the bottom of the page and two handles on the text block (top and bottom) appear (Figure 2-57).

The story's headline must be changed. Switch to 75% view or actual-size view to see the text, and choose the text tool. Select the headline text by dragging over the text to highlight it (Figure 2-58).

Choose the Size, Leading, and Style pop-up menus in the Type menu (Figure 2-59) to change the the headline to bold italic, 18 points in size, with 20 points of leading.

Now that the title is the correct size, the left column is too long—the bottom of the column is too close to the bottom of the page. It helps to

Figure 2-56. Using the manual text-flow icon to place text on the page.

Figure 2-57. Text flows down the left column and stops when Autoflow is off. In the Fit in window display, the text is "greeked" for the display because the characters are too small to be discernible (and drawing them would take up too much time).

place a guide at the bottom of the page that runs across the text measure, so that the right column's text can be aligned with the left column's text. Switch to the pointer tool, and drag a ruler guide down from the horizontal ruler at the top of the page. Release the mouse button when the guide is located at the $9^5/8$-inch ruler mark (Figure 2-60).

Use the pointer tool to select the text element again. The bottom handle of the left column displays a + symbol, signifying that the text file has more text to place. To shorten the column, click the + symbol and drag the bottom handle up as if you were pushing up a window shade; the text block is shortened as you move it. Align the text with the guide, then release the mouse button (Figure 2-61).

To continue the text to the next column under the image block, point to the bottom handle of the first text block and click it (Figure 2-62). The program changes your pointer to the manual text-flow icon. To place the next block of text under the image block, move the manual text-flow icon to the mark at $7^3/4$ inches. Click the mouse button to place the rest of the

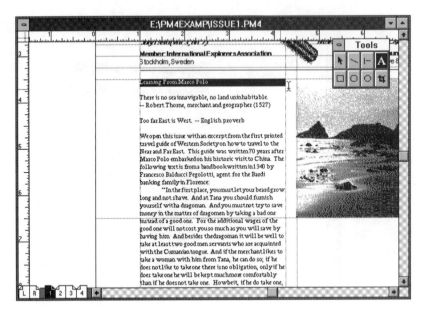

Figure 2-58. Select the story's headline with the text tool.

story in the second column. The top handle of the right column contains a + symbol, indicating that the text continues from that location back to another location (in this case, it continues to the bottom of the left column). The bottom handle contains nothing, which signifies the end of the text file.

The text has ended, but not at the end of the column. Even though we've left room for a caption for the video image, there is still plenty of room to add a graphic image somewhere in the story, perhaps with the headline to balance the video image.

Flowing Text Around Graphics

PageMaker offers the capability to automatically flow text around a graphic image. You can see how this works by adding a graphic image to the story you've just placed.

Scroll up to the headline for the story, and use the Place command as before to place the graphic image. Use the PRACTICE.TIF file in the BASICS subdirectory of the TUTORIAL directory supplied with PageMaker 4. When you place the graphic image (Figure 2-63), it

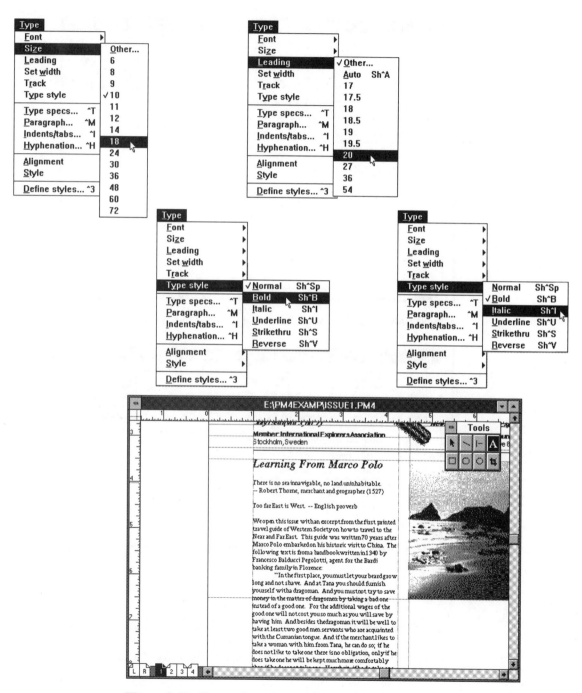

Figure 2-59. Change the headline text to 18 points with 20 points of leading, and bold italic.

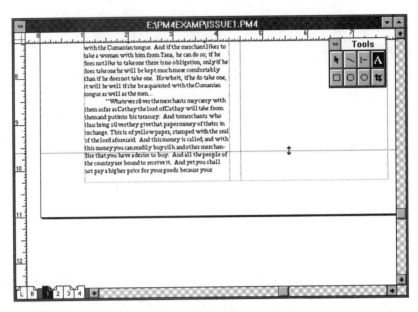

Figure 2-60. Set a guide at the bottom of the page to help align text blocks.

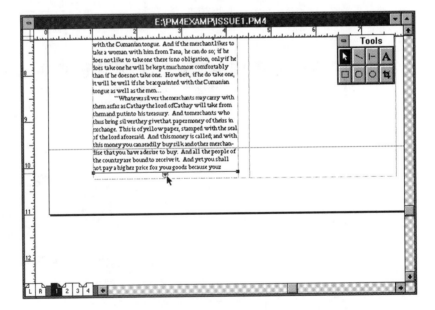

Figure 2-61. Shorten the text block in the left column by dragging up on the text element handle.

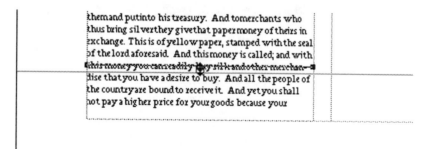

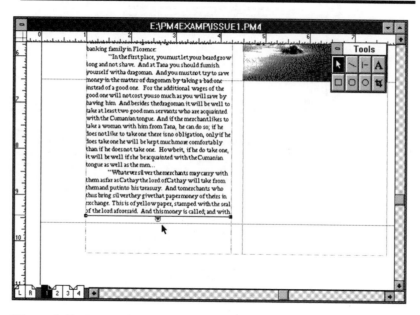

Figure 2-61. Continued.

obscures part of the top of the text block. (The image is actually supposed to represent Aldus Manutius, the famous Renaissance printer. We can borrow it to represent Marco Polo, at least for this example.)

After placing the image, it should still be selected. Choose the Text wrap option in the Element menu to define the way text wraps around the selected graphic image. A dialog box appears (Figure 2-64) with icons representing three options: no wrap, a rectangular wrap (the middle icon,

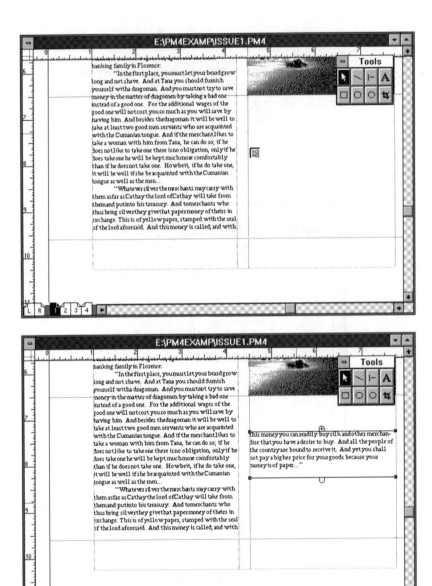

Figure 2-62. After clicking the + symbol in the left-column text block, place the rest of the story in the right column.

Figure 2-63. Place a graphic image at the top of the left column over the top of the text element.

selected in the example), and an irregularly shaped wrap. PageMaker lets you define either type of wrap, and also lets you adjust the wrap by dragging points in the dotted outline surrounding the graphic image. We describe irregularly shaped text wraps in Chapter 4.

The text wrap boundary remains in effect even after resizing the graphic image—the boundary is resized with the image (Figure 2-65). In the headline, the second line should be broken for the name "Marco Polo" by typing a Enter before the name. Switch to the text tool and click an insertion point at the beginning of the name, then press Enter. The text continues to wrap around the boundary even after editing the text.

Selecting and Editing Text

A few changes should be made to the text at the beginning of the story to make it more attractive. For example, the quotations at the beginning of the story should be changed to italics. To do this, drag with the text tool

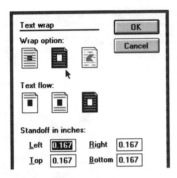

Figure 2-64. Use the text wrap feature to define how text wraps around the image. The straightforward rectangular wrap is defined because the image is rectangular.

across each section of text to be changed, and select Italic from the Type style pop-up menu in the Type menu (Figure 2-66).

When making minor editing changes to text on the page, you can click directly with the text tool an insertion point for typing or deleting text. You can also use the keyboard cursor movement keys and the editing keys to move an insertion point to another location in the text element. Depending on your keyboard, the cursor movement keys and the editing keys may be the numeric keypad keys, or they may be separate keys. If you use the

Figure 2-65. Resize the image to allow more room for text, and the wrap boundary stays in effect. Break a line in the headline, to keep the name intact, by clicking an insertion point with the text tool before the name, and pressing Enter to break the line.

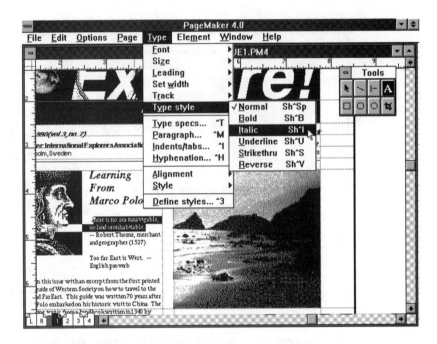

Figure 2-66. Change the selected quotation to italic.

numeric keypad, the 4 key acts as a left arrow key, the 6 key acts as a right arrow key, the 8 key moves up, and the 2 key moves down.

The left/right arrow cursor movement keys move the insertion point by a single character or space, and the up/down keys move the point by a single line. Holding down the Control key when pressing a left or right arrow key (or the numeric keypad equivalents) moves the insertion point to the beginning of the next word or the previous word. If an up or down key (or the numeric keypad equivalents) is pressed along with the Control key, the point moves to the beginning of the next paragraph or the previous paragraph. Press the 7 key to move the insertion point to the beginning, or the 1 key to move to the end, of the current line (or of the next line, if the point is already at one of those positions). When the Control key is pressed, the 7 key moves the point to the beginning of the next sentence, and the 1 key moves the point to the previous sentence. You can also move up or down in the text block quickly with the 9 or 3 keys. With the Control key pressed, the 9 or 3 keys move the insertion point to the beginning or to the end of the text that has been placed.

There are several different ways to select text. Select a single word by double-clicking the word; then drag in any direction to select a group of words. To select a single paragraph, triple-click anywhere in the middle of that paragraph. To extend a selection from an existing selection, hold down the Shift key and click a new ending point (Shift-click). (You may also use the cursor movement keys, rather than the mouse.)

Another way to select a large area of text is to click a starting point at one end, then Shift-click the ending point at the other end. The easiest way to select all of the text is to click anywhere in the text once, and then choose the Select all command from the Edit menu (or press the Control and A keys).

While the text is still highlighted (selected), change the tab spaces at the beginning of each paragraph with the Indents/tabs option in the Type menu. You can change the tab settings so that the space at the beginning of each paragraph is much smaller. You may want to switch to Actual size or even to 200% size (in the Page menu) to increase the detail in the ruler. Select the Indents/tabs option from the Type menu, and move the first tab marker on the ruler in the Indents/tabs dialog box (Figure 2-67) to approximately 1/8 inch. In the dialog box, a fractional number changes as you move the tab marker—when that number is 0.125, release the mouse button. Click OK and the paragraph tabs change in the selected text.

Adjusting Columns of Text

The story needs its columns adjusted so that they line up at the bottom. The easiest adjustment is to drag the right-hand column of text down.

Start by pulling down a ruler guide so that you can line up the text baselines for the two columns. Drag down on the top handle of the right column as shown in Figure 2-68, then drag down on the bottom handle to pull out the rest of the story.

You may want to change the display to Actual size (in the Page menu). A quick way to do so is to use the pointer tool and point to the area that you want to see in actual size, hold down the Alt and Control keys, and click the mouse. Try this combination again and the program changes the display to reduced size so that the entire page is displayed. You can switch back and forth from actual size to reduced size with this key-click combination. To quickly go to the 200% view from any other view, press Control 2; for 400%, press Control 4.

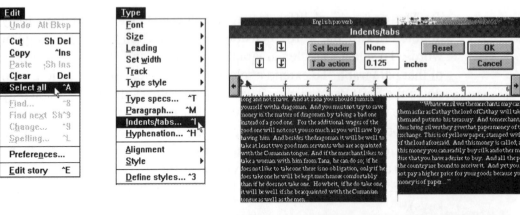

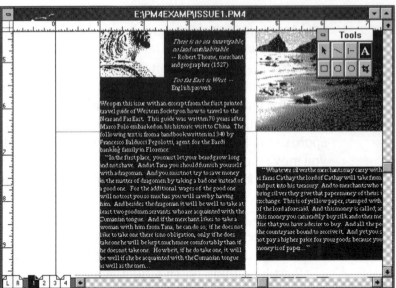

Figure 2-67. The Indents/tabs dialog box for changing paragraph indents and tab settings.

Switch to Actual size to make most text adjustments. For the most accurate view of the page as it will look when printed, check the alignment by going to 400% size (Control 4), and then make any final adjustments in that view. You probably don't want to be slowed down by working at the 200% or 400% size all the time because it requires more scrolling. The

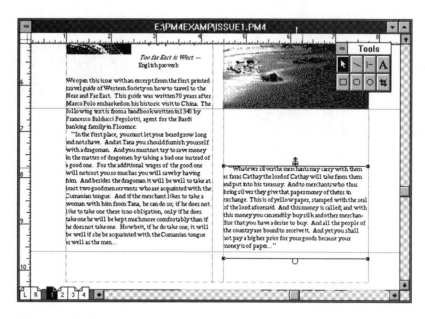

Figure 2-68. Line up text in two columns, using a guide to line up the baselines.

fastest way to move the window is with the grabber hand (press the Alt key and then drag). The grabber hand can also be constrained by the Shift key to move vertically (press the Alt and Shift keys and drag up or down), or horizontally (press the Alt and Shift keys and drag left or right). When you move the window with the grabber hand or by using the scroll bars, you have to wait for the screen to redisplay. If you use a full-page display screen, you will find it is easier to work in the 200% size, because you can increase the size of your window to see more of the page at once.

You can now draw a two-column rule at the bottom of the page to provide an even look. Switch to the perpendicular-line drawing tool and align the crosshairs cursor (+) to the left margin of the left column at the 10-inch ruler mark. Drag across the column to the right margin of the right column. The program draws a straight horizontal rule (Figure 2-69).

The final touch for page one is to add a caption for the image, which advertises the story that is inside the publication. Separating the caption from the other story is another column rule. You should already know how to switch to the text tool, type some text, and then use the Font, Size, and

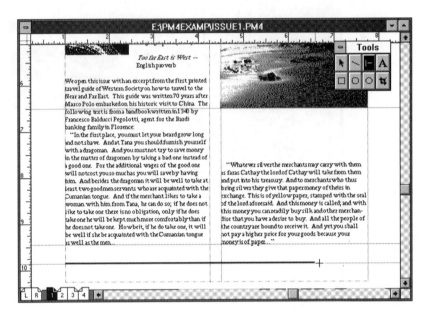

Figure 2-69. Draw a rule (line) across both columns at the bottom of the page, using the perpendicular-line drawing tool.

Type style pop-up menus to change the type specifications for the text. Figure 2-70 shows how the caption and rule should be placed on the page.

Now is a good time to save the publication, if you have not done so already. Choose the Save command from the File menu.

Inserting New Pages

You can add pages to this publication file by choosing the Insert pages command from the Page menu. The Insert pages dialog box (Figure 2-71) automatically adds two pages after the displayed page if you click OK, or you can change that number to add more or fewer pages. You can also decide to insert the pages before the current page. If you displaying a two-page spread, you have the option to insert new pages between the displayed pages.

PageMaker automatically uses the column settings, plus any graphic or text elements stored on the master pages, as long as both the Display master items option and the Copy master guides option in the Page menu are on (checked). Normally, these two options are on (have check marks).

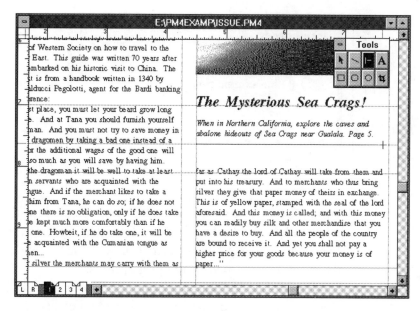

Figure 2-70. After adding the caption text with the text tool, changing its type specifications as described before, draw a one-column rule to separate the caption from the story.

When the Display master items option is not checked, the text and graphic items defined on the master pages are hidden so that they do not print or display. When the Copy master guides option is not checked, the column and ruler guides are hidden in the master pages. Keep these options turned on, unless you need to remove master items or guides from a page.

Placing Formatted Text

Rather than placing an unformatted file, this time you can try placing a file that has been prepared and preformatted in a word processing program. As described in Chapter 1, word processors can be used to preformat text for PageMaker, depending on how many formatting options are available in the word processor.

This example assumes that you used a word processor such as Microsoft Word or WordPerfect, both of which have options for italic and bold type styles, as well as font selection. For this example, a Times 10-

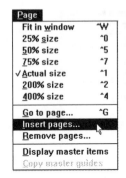

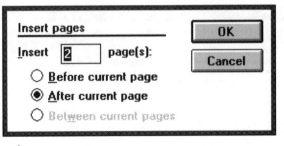

Figure 2-71. Use the Insert Pages dialog box to add two pages.

point font with 12 points of leading was selected for the body of the text, with subheadings set to bold at 12 points, and the title bold at 14 points. PageMaker can read this information with the text and place the text using these already-defined formatting options.

To start the second story on page two, click the icon for page two (lower-left corner of the screen). PageMaker displays two facing pages (two and three) in the Fit in window view. To center the display window at Actual size on Page two, point to the left-hand page and click the mouse while holding down the Control and Alt keys.

Because the story to be placed is already formatted, and you want to use, or *retain*, the word processor formatting when you place the text, use the Place command with the Retain format option turned on (Figure 2-72). Point and click at the spot on the page where the second story should begin—leaving enough space for the story's headline.

Next, select the title and subtitle of the story with the text tool, and use the Cut command to cut it to the clipboard (Figure 2-73). Click the text pointer to a place above the article and use the Paste command to paste the title and subtitle text there. PageMaker creates a new text element that is separate from the body of the story.

Select the separate title and use the Size, Leading, and Type style pop-up menus (Figure 2-74) to change the title to 36 points with 38-point leading, and the subtitle to 24 points with 26-point leading, set to italic as well as bold (the title is already bold). Drag the bottom-left corner of the title and subtitle text block out toward the right margin to stretch the block so that the entire title fits on one line (Figure 2-75).

Continue the story into the next column by clicking the bottom handle of the text block (the pointer becomes a manual text-flow icon if Autoflow

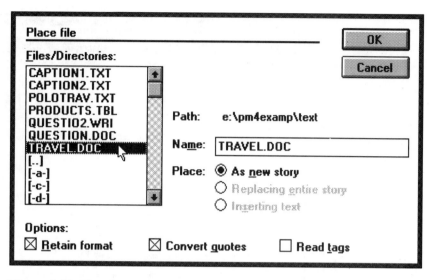

Figure 2-72. The Place dialog box, with the Retain format and Convert quotes options turned on.

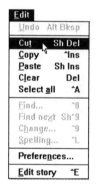

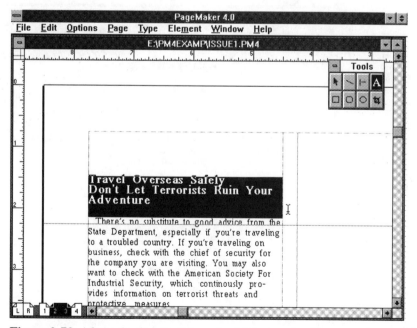

Figure 2-73. After selecting the title and subtitle text, use Cut to cut it out of the text element and place it temporarily in the clipboard for the next use of the Paste command.

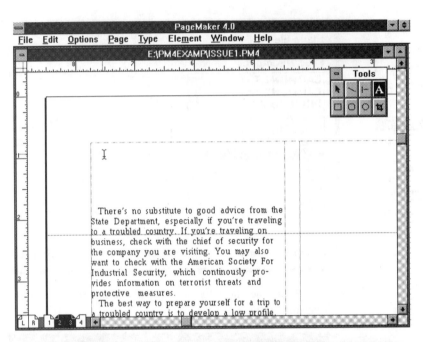

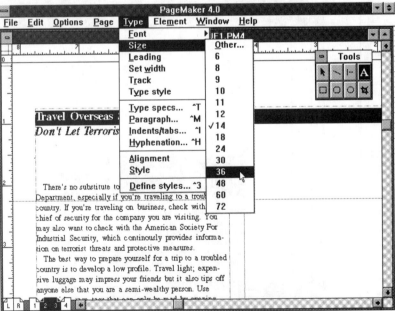

Figure 2-74. Click an insertion point and paste the title text. Then change the type size and leading. Also change the subtitle to italic as well as bold.

Figure 2-75. Stretch the title (which is now a separate text element) so that the title and subtitle each fit on one line.

is off) and clicking at the top of the next column. The text flows down to the bottom of the page. Extend the article to the next page by clicking the bottom handle of the text block to get the text-flow icon, and then clicking at the top of the column on Page three. With a long text file, you can continue to place text in columns on pages by clicking the bottom handle to get the text-flow icon, and then switching pages by clicking the page-marker icon. (You can switch pages or select options from some menus while using the text-flow icon, but you can't switch tools.) If you have not yet begun to place a file and you change your mind after choosing Place from the File menu (and the text-flow icon has appeared), select another tool from the toolbox to cancel the text placement.

Drag a ruler guide down to the mark at 9 3/4 inches, then move up (use the scroll bar to move quickly) and drag another ruler guide down to the mark at 2 1/4 inches. Pull up the top handle of the text block to close up the space between the text block and the title, lining up the text with the ruler guide, as shown in Figure 2-76. Adjust the bottom of the text block by using a ruler guide, as described earlier.

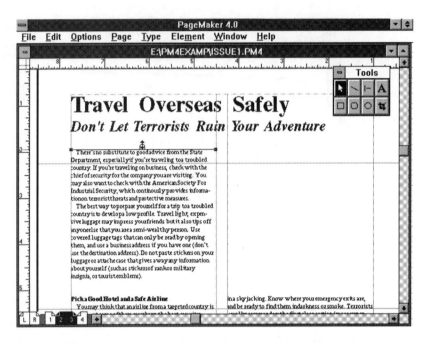

Figure 2-76. Adjust the top of the text block with the pointer tool, using a ruler guide for guidance.

Enhancing the Layout

PageMaker is versatile—you can try one layout and then change to another very quickly, without losing the first attempt. If you have enough space on disk, use the Save as command in the File menu to save the publication file under another name as a second version before changing the layout, so that you can later go back to the first version.

You may want to enhance the layout of the second and third pages. Assume that the second story does not fill up the entire two pages, and that you want to include a special section (a "sidebar" to the story). You can move the text block in the left column of Page two (Figure 2-77) and in the right column of Page three out of the way so that you can use the space for the sidebar.

The sidebar consists of two lists, each with seven numbered items. The lists could be lined up side by side at the tops of the two columns as separate items, with each list surrounded by a 1-point box.

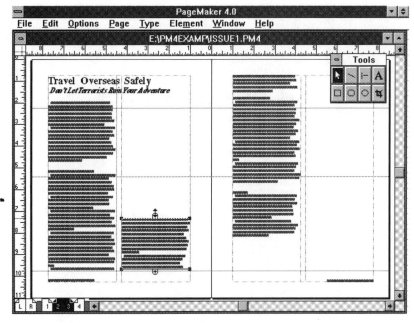

Figure 2-77. Move the text block in the right column out of the way to fit the special sidebar text.

Drag-Placing Text

Another way of placing text from a file into a space on the page, without having the text fill up a column, is to drag when placing the text. An outline of the text element appears as you drag, so you can set the size of the text element before the text appears.

Use the Place command in the File menu to select the sidebar text file. Move the manual text-flow icon to the top of the right column to place the sidebar text. However, don't just click the icon—this time drag the icon across and down the column (Figure 2-78).

Next, use the pointer tool to click the bottom of the text block at the seventh item (Figure 2-79), and continue drag-placing the rest of the block in the left column of Page three (Figure 2-80).

In order to put a box around a text block in a column, make the text block thinner than the column, and draw the box so that it aligns with the column margins. To make the text block thinner, select it with the pointer tool. Drag the bottom-left corner inward and the top-right corner inward

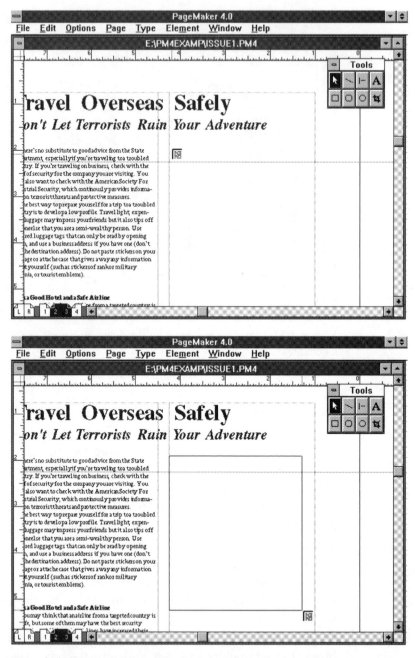

Figure 2-78. Use the Place command and drag-place the sidebar text into a space in the right column.

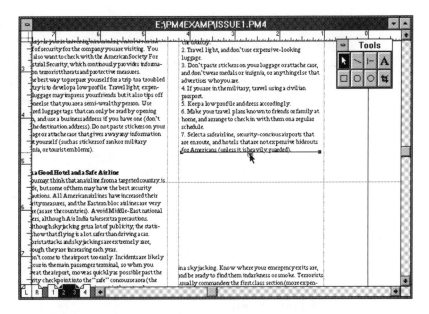

Figure 2-79. Click the bottom of the text block that holds the first seven items of the list.

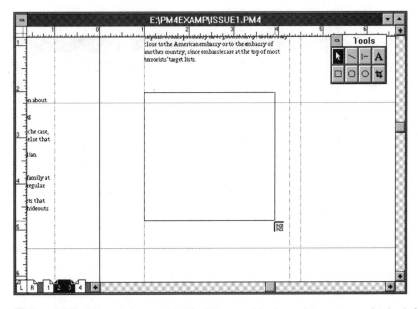

Figure 2-80. Place the second half of the text block on the next page in the left column.

in order to reduce the width of the text block equally on both the left and right sides (Figure 2-81). You will be able to move the text block more easily if you turn off the Snap to guides option in the Options menu. When the block is not attached to guides, it can be moved freely to a location very close to the guides without becoming attached to them.

Position the text block so that it is centered in the column and select the box tool. Draw a box around the text by clicking a starting point above the top-right corner of the text and dragging across the text to a point below the bottom-left corner. Line up the outer edges of the box with the column margins and, at the top and bottom, leave the same amount of space separating the box from the inside text. When you release the mouse, the program completes the box, as shown in Figure 2-82.

If you don't like the results, simply press the Delete key (or Backspace key) because the box is already selected (it has handles) to delete the box. You can also resize a selected box by dragging one of its handles with the arrow-pointer tool.

At this point, if the Fill pattern had been set to Paper or Solid, the box obscures the text. While the box is still selected (i.e., displaying its

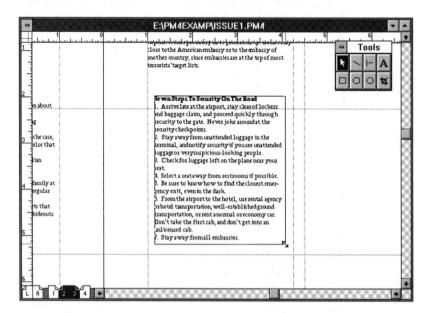

Figure 2-81. Change the text block's width to accommodate a box around the text.

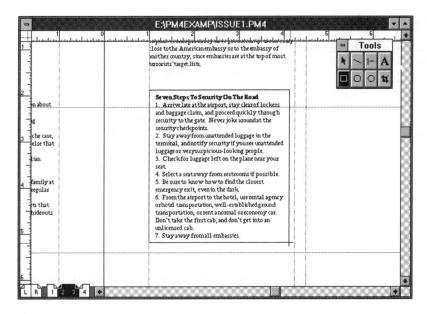

Figure 2-82. Draw a box around the text.

handles), choose None in the Fill pop-up menu (Figure 2-83) in the Element menu so that the box becomes transparent. (If you've already used the Fill pop-up menu, it may already be set to None.) Next, pick a line width from the Lines pop-up menu (such as a 1-point line) in the Element menu.

At this point you could also choose a color for the box, such as a light yellow or blue tint. (Color is discussed in Chapter 4).

Continue flowing the story around the sidebar box by clicking with the pointer tool in the bottom handle of the text block above the sidebar, and placing the text below the sidebar (Figure 2-84). Adjust the lower text block by dragging up on its top handle.

Apply the same treatment to the other section of the sidebar: Make the section of text thinner than the column, center it in the column, draw a box around it, and set the box line width to be 1 point and the fill pattern to be none.

Drag the top handles of the story up to fill the space below the sidebar. Use a ruler guide to line up the text with the first column and with the other columns. Drag the bottom handles down to the bottom ruler guide.

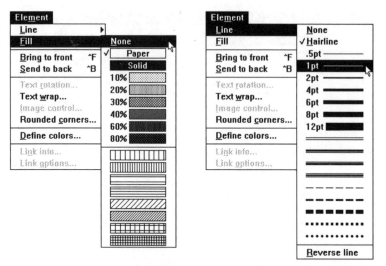

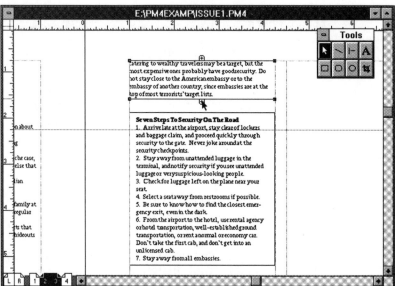

Figure 2-83. For the box, set the line width to 1 point, and the fill to None. Then click the bottom handle of the other story to continue flowing it below the boxed sidebar.

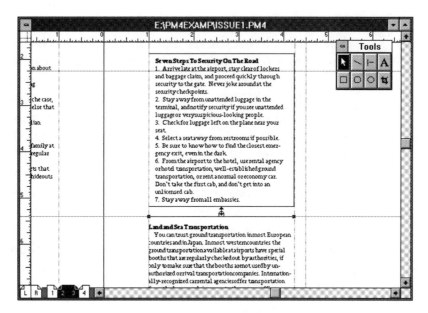

Figure 2-84. Continue the other story below the sidebar, and adjust the text block by dragging up on the top handle to fill in the space between the boxed sidebar and the story.

Final Touches

You now have full first and second pages, and a partially full third page. You can add more pages and place more text to fill out the pages. You would follow the same techniques already described in this chapter for placing text and adjusting text elements.

One editing change you may want to make to the story on Page one is to add quotation marks to the excerpted section from the first printed travel guide for the Far East. You can add quotation marks by clicking an insertion point on the page with the text tool and typing the quotation marks, but there is another way that may be faster for making a slew of editing changes at once. PageMaker provides the Story Editor, which is a fully functional word processor, to edit text that is already placed (or about to be placed) on the page.

Move to Page one, switch to the text tool, and click an insertion point anywhere in the story about Marco Polo. Then choose Edit story from the Edit menu (or type Control-E). A new window appears, with the text from the story shown in a large readable font (Figure 2-85). The benefit of the Story Editor is that you can make several editing changes quickly without having to wait for the text to be composed after each change.

Click the text tool at the point where you want to insert an open quotation mark. Type Control-Shift-[(left square bracket) for the open quotation mark (Figure 2-86). Repeat this procedure with the first line of the subsequent paragraph. Then go to the end of the story, click another insertion point with the text tool, and type Control-Shift-] (right square bracket) for the closing quote mark. To close the Story Editor window, click the close box in the upper-left corner, or choose the Edit layout command in the Edit menu (Control-E again).

For more embellishments, you can add more graphic elements to the pages, such as vertical lines (called *column rules*) between the columns on each page. You would draw a vertical column rule in the same way that you drew other rules, using the perpendicular-line drawing tool. It helps

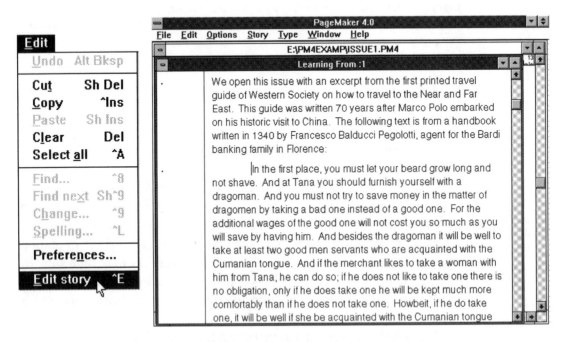

Figure 2-85. Use the Story Editor (click with the text tool somewhere in the text, and choose the Edit story command) to make several editing changes quickly without having to wait for the text to be composed after each change.

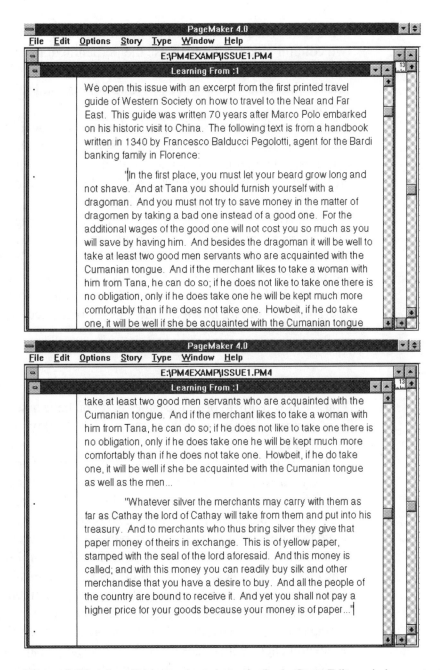

Figure 2-86. After clicking an insertion point in the Story Editor window, enter the open quotation mark by typing Control-Shift-[(left square bracket). Do the same with the first line of the subsequent paragraph. Then go to the end of the story and type Control-Shift-] (right square bracket) for the closing quote mark.

to move a vertical ruler guide into position directly in the middle between two column guides, and then use the perpendicular-line drawing tool to draw the line along the guide. You drag a vertical ruler guide from the side ruler in the same manner that you drag a horizontal ruler guide from the top ruler.

Allow extra time to print pages that have vertical lines or hairlines. Many designers prefer to see white space, rather than rules between columns. The goal is to balance all of the elements on the page without crowding them. White space is considered to be as important an element as text, line art, rules, color, and halftones.

Save your file when you finish making changes. PageMaker performs a mini-save whenever you turn the page, so that even if the system crashes, you will not lose much of your work. You can revert back to the state of the publication file at the last full-save operation by using the Revert command in the File menu. You can also revert back to the last mini-save operation by holding down the Shift key when selecting Revert.

Printing

You are now ready to print the pages that you have assembled. Select the Print command from the File menu, which displays the Print window shown in Figure 2-87.

Depending on your printer, you can select several print options, or else click OK to accept the default settings or the last settings that you chose for printing (one complete copy at 100% scaling factor, printed in the usual order of pages for your printer). You can select any number of copies and/or specify a specific range of pages to be printed. Other options include *thumbnails* (mini-pages useful in design and production planning), collated copies, reverse order, paper source (if your printer has different paper trays), and scaling the pages by a percentage to be larger or smaller than the original page size. You can even print with tiling settings for oversize pages. (*Tiling* is the process of printing a large image on several pages with edges that can be overlapped and pasted together.)

You specified page margins in the Page setup dialog box when you first created the publication file. The default settings are usually fine for

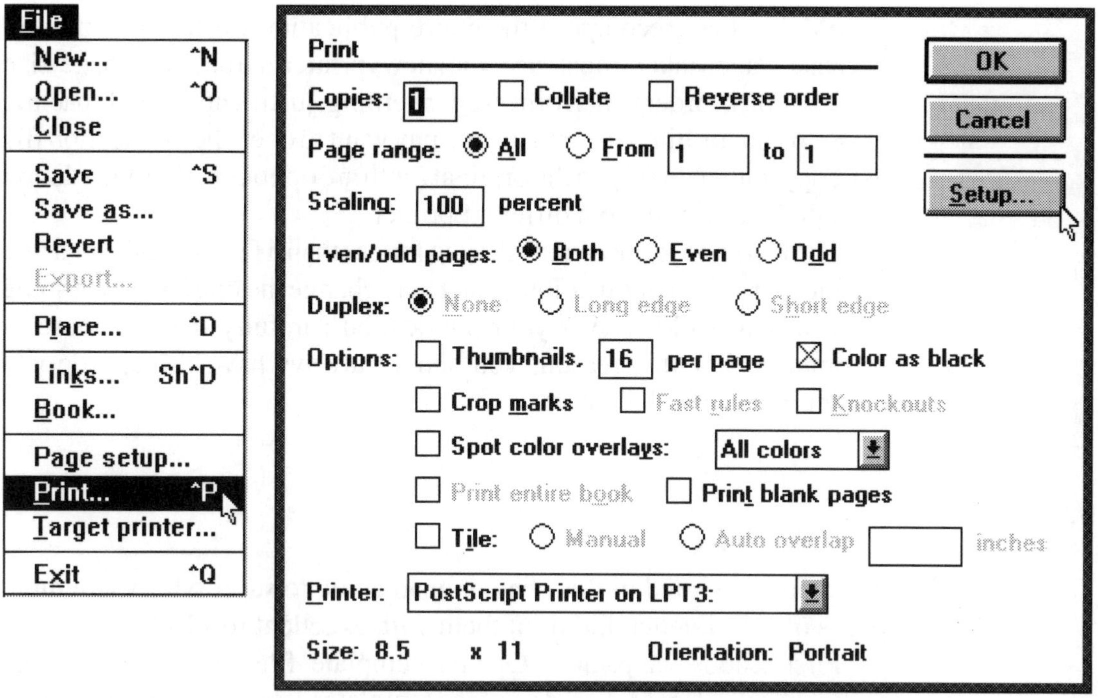

File

New...	^N
Open...	^O
Close	
Save	^S
Save **a**s...	
Re**v**ert	
Export...	
P**l**ace...	^D
Lin**k**s...	Sh^D
Book...	
Pa**g**e setup...	
Print...	^P
Target printer...	
E**x**it	^Q

Print

Co**p**ies: ☐ **1**   ☐ Co**ll**ate   ☐ Re**v**erse order

Page range: ◉ **A**ll   ◯ **F**rom ☐ 1   to ☐ 1

Scaling: ☐ 100   percent

Even/odd pages: ◉ **B**oth   ◯ **E**ven   ◯ O**d**d

Duplex: ◉ None   ◯ Long edge   ◯ Short edge

Options: ☐ Th**u**mbnails, ☐ 16   per page   ☒ **C**olor as black

☐ Crop **m**arks   ☐ Fast rules   ☐ Knockouts

☐ Spot color overla**y**s: All colors ▣

☐ Print entire book   ☐ Prin**t** blank pages

☐ T**i**le: ◯ Manual   ◯ Auto overlap   ☐   inches

P**r**inter: PostScript Printer on LPT3:   ▣

Size: 8.5   x 11   **O**rientation: Portrait

OK
Cancel
Setup...

Figure 2-87. To choose the type of printer for the publication, first set up the printer type in the Setup dialog box inside the Print window. Use the Print command in the File menu, then click the Setup button in the Print window. Choose a printer from the pop-up menu, and click OK.

all printers. If you change those settings, refer to your printer manual to be sure that your design does not extend beyond the maximum print area of your printer. You can choose Page setup from the File menu to change the margin settings, but that method will affect your layout and cause other changes that you may not want. To print the complete pages without changing the layout, scale the publication to less than 100% in the Print dialog box (if your printer supports scaling).

If you select a different printer than the printer you assigned earlier, and the new printer's printed page size is too small for your design, PageMaker displays a confirmation message warning you that the publication was composed for a different printer. You can cancel the new printer assignment, or continue with it by clicking OK. If you continue,

PageMaker may recompose the entire publication for the new printer, because PageMaker must use the new printer's font and page-size information in order to perform proper kerning, justification, and spacing. To keep your original file intact, you may want to open the publication file as a copy, rather than open the original (both are options in the Open dialog box), before printing to a different printer.

The recompose operation takes no longer than a few minutes (or a few seconds for a short publication), but it may change the line lengths of some lines of text, so look over your publication carefully if you choose to recompose. For this reason, you should always have the appropriate printer in mind at the outset.

Summary

The steps presented in this chapter enable you to successfully assemble pages of a newsletter and print them with excellent results.

First, choose a printer. Open a template file (use the templates included with PageMaker, download templates from the Aldus forum on CompuServe, or use templates from the *Aldus Portfolio: Designs for Newsletters*), or else choose New from the File menu. Use or modify the default page setup (which specifies double-sided, facing 8 1/2 by 11-inch pages, with a 1-inch inside margin and 3/4-inch outside, top, and bottom margins).

Choose Column guides from the Options menu to specify the number of columns (for setting up a layout grid, that can be changed later). Use the toolbox to create left- and right-hand footers, to place automatic page numbering markers, and to position all other elements that you want repeated on all left- or right-hand pages, on the left- and right-master pages.

Choose Save from the File menu, and give your new publication file a name. If you want to preserve the original file as a template file, choose Save as from the File menu, and click the template option. When you open that file again, it opens as an untitled copy, and you can give this copy a new name while preserving the template. As you work in the new file, continue to save the file as often as necessary to prevent lost work.

The Options menu offers Rulers, with a selectable unit of measurement. (Default rulers measure inches; select Preferences from the Edit menu to display centimeters or picas). The Options menu also offers Snap to guides (which are on by default), used to create an attraction between the elements you place and any column guides you have set. Elements automatically attach to the column guides they are closest to, creating automatic precision alignment of elements to columns.

Select Type specs from the Type menu and choose a font, style, size, and leading, and then click the text tool. Move the I-beam text editing pointer into position, click the mouse button to establish an insertion point (if Snap to guides are on, the insertion point will snap to the nearest guide), and start typing.

Text automatically wraps (and hyphenates, if hyphenation is set to automatic) to the next line if the text extends past the right-margin setting.

To change the width of a text block, select the pointer tool (the I-beam icon changes back into an arrow pointer) from the toolbox and drag the bottom-right corner of the text block to the desired width.

To move the title into position on the page, position the pointer tool over the title and press down, but don't release, the mouse button; the cross with arrows symbol appears. This symbol tells you that you can move the selected text or graphics element to a new position on the page. Release the mouse button to fix the element at the new position (if Snap to guides are on, they affect the placement).

To draw a circle, select the oval-drawing tool and move the crossbar icon into position on the page. Hold down the Shift key, while dragging to the right and down, to size the circle. (If you don't hold down the Shift key, you will draw an oval.)

To draw a line (*rule*), select the perpendicular-line tool. Move the crossbar pointer to the starting position, click the mouse to start drawing your line, and drag the line until you reach the end position.

To place graphics, select Place from the File menu. Select from a list of suitable graphics files (paintings, drawings, scanned images, charts, or graphs formats that PageMaker recognizes) and click the place button, or double-click the filename. Move the icon into position on the page and click to place the file. After placement, you can scale graphics by dragging a corner handle of the selected image. (You can also select an image at any time and scale it.)

Scale graphics in proportion without distortion by holding down the Shift key while dragging a corner handle of the image. For paint-type graphics, and scanned and digitized images, use built-in sizes for your target printer by holding down the Control (CNTL) key while dragging. Use both the Control and Shift keys to scale graphics in proportion to get the best results on the target printer.

You can also place graphics by using the Copy (or Cut) command from the Edit menu to copy the graphic from another publication or document in another application window, together with Paste to place the image on the PageMaker page.

Use the Place command to place either formatted or unformatted text. After selecting the Place command and a text file, you have the choice of placing formatted text (preformatted by a word processing program) with the Retain format option on, or placing text without formatting if this option is off (ignoring any formatting from your word processor). If you are not retaining the format, first change any of PageMaker's default type specs (as necessary) before you place the file.

Autoflow (in the Options menu) must be turned off if you want to manually flow text from column to column. Move the text-flow icon to the desired position on the page, clicking once to place the first column. (If Snap to guides are on, the column flows within the preset columns.) After selecting the article's title with the text tool, change the type specifications using the pop-up menus for Font, Size, Leading, and Type style (in the Type menu). Push up or drag down on the bottom handle of the text block to position the end of the column, and then click on the bottom handle to continue placing text in the next column.

After placing text, you can select text and change the tab settings for the entire story with the Indents/Tabs option. You can also edit text on the page and change the page-size view, or edit text in the Story Editor window for faster editing. You may insert pages, change settings that affect the page (such as Display master items and Copy master guides), turn the page, and place more text. Change the type specs and position of titles and subtitles by selecting them with the text tool and using the pop-up menus in the Type menu.

When drawing boxes around text elements (as in sidebars), adjust column widths of the text elements to be narrower to fit within a box. Draw vertical rules as column separators if desired, but if you have a dot-matrix printer (such as an Epson), the rules may take an extremely long time to print or may print heavier than hairline width, so you may want to avoid using them.

To print the publication, select the Print command from the File menu and specify print options (if your printer supports them) such as thumbnails, all pages or a specified range, the number of copies of each page, collated or not, in reverse order or not, or scaled in size to print smaller or larger than the original (or leave at 100% original size). If you select a different printer than the printer you had assigned previously, and the printed page size of the new printer is smaller, PageMaker displays a confirmation message to let you either cancel the new printer assignment or continue with the assignment. If you continue, PageMaker may recompose the publication for the new printer. You may want to open a file as a copy, rather than open the original file (in the Open dialog box) before printing to a different printer, so that the original file remains intact.

This chapter provided a step-by-step tutorial on nearly every feature in PageMaker. You can use this experience to design and produce any kind of publication—not just newsletters. A newsletter was selected because they are usually detailed and require some thought about design to make them attractive to read. Chapter 3 describes how to put together lengthier documents, such as business reports, manuals, and books, using some of PageMaker's automatic features for fast turnaround.

3 | Reports, Manuals, and Books

This chapter describes how to design and produce mid- to large-sized publications, such as an annual business report or a full-size instruction manual. One characteristic that these publications have in common is that they should be designed with a consistent format, both to present a unified image of the company and to make them more readable.

Use a simple design, with consistent treatment of titles, headings, charts, figures, and so on in order to present the information clearly. Your company logo, integrated with a unified design, can be effective for communicating the company image on business cards, letterhead and envelopes, product packaging, documentation, annual reports, and advertising. Your goal is to present a consistent image that will be remembered.

You can enforce a uniform style for a publication by creating master pages and saving the publication as a blank template publication file. Graphics from one publication can be easily copied into another, using the Copy and Paste commands in the Edit menu. You can also start with a template for one type of publication, modify it for another type, and use the Save as command to save the modified publication as a new template without changing the first template.

PageMaker is a good choice for producing an annual report, instructional manual, reference manual, catalog, or book, because it offers both word processing and table editing features, as well as the capability to build an index and a table of contents.

The program also accepts charts, graphs, and illustrations from different programs or even different types of computers. The report or manual can be printed on a laser printer for final proofing, updated very quickly, and then transferred to an imagesetter or typesetter for a very professional look.

PageMaker handles any type of document up to 999 pages in size. Most books, instruction manuals, and reference manuals are broken up into sections or chapters that are smaller than 999 pages. Even though you can combine all chapters or sections into one publication file (up to 999 pages), such a file might be too large to use. It is just as easy, and preferable in most cases, to create a separate publication file for each section or chapter. PageMaker's multiple-publication features let you link these sections or chapters for automatic page numbering (up to page 9999), automatic printing of all publication files in order, and automatic generation of an index and table of contents.

Designing a Business Report

Reports usually include charts, spreadsheets, and specialized graphics. (Chapter 1 describes all of the programs that can generate such elements for PageMaker pages—nearly every popular program for the Macintosh is supported by PageMaker.)

A report should also contain the company logo (sometimes placed on every page in the footer), a title page, and perhaps graphics or photos.

You can follow along with the example in this section by typing enough text to fill a few pages, or by borrowing text from a file you already have. You can also create a company logo that is similar to the logo in the following example by altering one of the supplied graphic files in the PageMaker tutorial, using a graphics program such as Paintbrush in the Accessories group supplied with Windows 3, or a professional illustration program such as Micrografx Designer or Corel Draw.

Charts and graphs can be produced by various programs, including Micrografx Charisma, Corel Draw, Micrografx Draw Plus, and Microsoft Excel. You can even use a charting or graphics program on the Macintosh and convert the charts and graphs to a PC format for use with the PC version of PageMaker. For these examples, we used Aldus Persuasion on the Macintosh to enhance an Excel graph, then converted the graph to a PC format before placing it onto a PageMaker page.

Setting Up the Master Pages

An annual report should look sophisticated and important. You should lay out the text with enough white space surrounding it to make the text look very significant. The design chosen for this example—one wide ragged-right margin, with headings and pull quotes in a thinner marginal column—helps preserve white space.

This example presents the *pica* and *point* measurement system that is more precise than inches for lining up elements on a page. There are 72 points (6 picas) to an inch, with 12 points in every pica. This system displays rulers in small increments of picas and points. When you change the measurement system, it automatically changes both the horizontal and vertical rulers, but you can change the measurement system for the vertical ruler separately.

To change the ruler measurement system, select the Preferences option from the Edit menu (Figure 3-1). A scrolling menu is available for the measurement system (for both rulers), and for the vertical ruler if you want to change it also.

Set both rulers to picas for the examples in this chapter, and click OK. You can change the measurement system or the vertical ruler at any time in the Preferences dialog box.

Start the business report example by designing a new publication file's master pages. Select the New command in the File menu to bring up the Page setup dialog box, which now displays the page's measurements in picas and points. Choose the Tall orientation (Figure 3-2) if it is not already chosen, and check the Double-sided and Facing pages options to turn them on, so that PageMaker creates two master pages: one for the right page and the other for the left page.

Define the Page setup of the publication to be at least nine pages (you

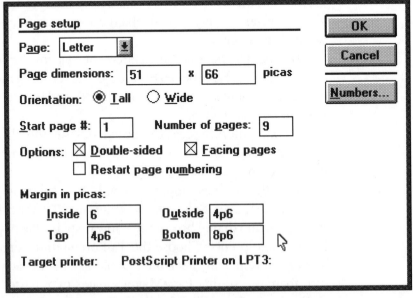

Edit	Options	Pa
Undo	Alt Bksp	
Cut	Sh Del	
Copy	^Ins	
Paste	Sh Ins	
Clear	Del	
Select all	^A	
Find...	^8	
Find next	Sh^9	
Change...	^9	
Spelling...	^L	
Preferences...		
Edit story	^E	

Preferences

Layout view:

Measurement system: Picas

Vertical ruler: Inches — points

- Inches
- Inches decimal
- Millimeters
- Picas
- Ciceros
- Custom

Greek text below:

Guides:
- ● Front
- ○ Back

○ Normal
○ High resolution

Show layout problems:
- ☐ Loose/tight lines
- ☐ "Keeps" violations

Story view:

Size: 12 points   Font: Times

Save option: ● Faster   ○ Smaller

OK   Cancel   Other...

Figure 3-1. Use the Preferences dialog box to set different ruler measurements. Here, both rulers are changed from inches to picas.

Page setup

Page: Letter

Page dimensions: 51 x 66 picas

Orientation: ● Tall   ○ Wide

Start page #: 1   Number of pages: 9

Options: ☒ Double-sided   ☒ Facing pages
☐ Restart page numbering

Margin in picas:
Inside 6   Outside 4p6
Top 4p6   Bottom 8p6

Target printer: PostScript Printer on LPT3:

OK   Cancel   Numbers...

Figure 3-2. The page setup menu appears immediately after selecting a New publication from the File menu. Change the Bottom margin to 8 picas, 6 points (8p6).

can always add more pages or delete extra pages). Change the default page margins so that the bottom margin is redefined to be 8 picas and 6 points (**8p6**), rather than 4p6, leaving enough space at the bottom of each page for a footer and white space. (Always design pages with some thought to leaving enough white space to create a more pleasing, less crowded appearance.)

Next, define the default column formatting for all pages of the report (which, of course, can be overridden on individual pages if you want). Switch to the left-right master pages. Then select Column guides, and change the number of columns to **2** (Figure 3-3) and change the space between columns to **1p6** (1 pica, 6 points).

The next step is to unlock the guides if they are locked. A check mark next to the Lock guides option (in the Options menu) indicates that the guides are locked; unlock them by selecting the option again so that no check mark appears.

With the guides unlocked, you can drag them as needed to change the column widths. Drag the right-hand column guide on the left master page (Figure 3-4) over to the left side of the page and line it up with the marker at 33p6. Scroll the screen over to the right master page and line up its right-hand column guide on the 19-pica mark. Both pages should now have the same column layout.

Now add page-number footers to the master pages (as shown in Chapter 2). Set the footer text to be in Helvetica 10-point type with automatic leading in the Type specs dialog box. Figure 3-5 is an up close view of the left-master page footer, which includes an automatic page number inserted by pressing the Control, Shift, and **3** keys (as in the newsletter example in Chapter 2). The footer also includes space for a logo, created by typing three em spaces (type the Control, Shift, and **M** keys to create each space) next to the page marker. (*Em spaces* are fixed spaces that are the width of a capital "M" in the chosen font. Unlike regular spaces between words, em spaces are not adjusted by PageMaker.) Also type one em space after the page marker to separate the page marker from the text of the footer.

The master pages automatically set all of the publication file's pages to start with these column settings and to include footers. On each page, you can override these settings and, for example, remove the footers or change the column layout.

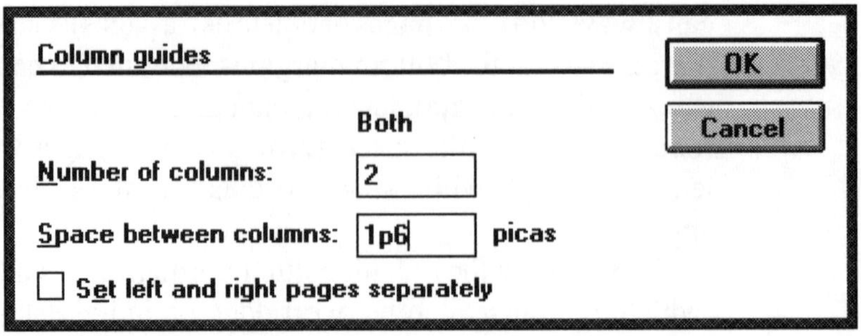

Column guides

OK

Cancel

Both

Number of columns: 2

Space between columns: 1p6   picas

☐ S**e**t left and right pages separately

Figure 3-3. Change the number of columns to two, and the space between columns to 1 pica and 6 points.

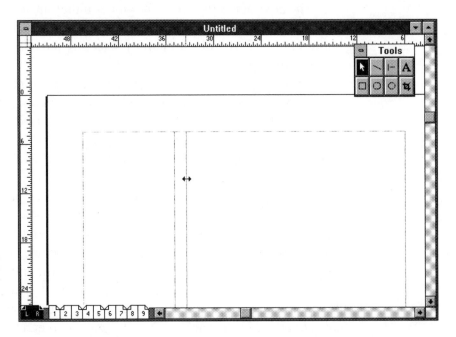

Figure 3-4. Move the unlocked column guide on the left master page to a custom position for all of the left-hand pages in the publication.

Adding a Company Logo

You can place a company logo on the master pages so that it appears in the report on every page at the same location. To create the logo, start with

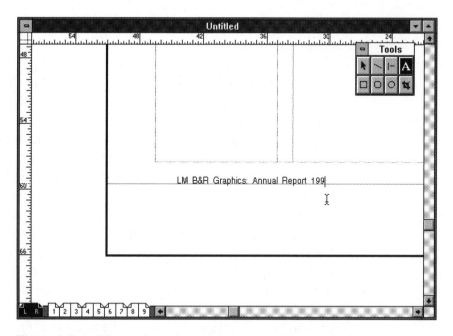

Figure 3-5. A different footer is used for left and right pages, with space to drop in a logo.

a sketch or a previously designed logo on paper, and digitize it with a desktop scanner. The scanner creates a file that contains a bit map of the logo. You can edit and retouch the pixels on the screen by using a paint program (described in Chapter 1), and then use the cleaned-up paint image as a template for tracing in a drawing program, such as Micrografx Designer or Corel Draw. PC graphics can also be converted or read directly (after being copied to the Macintosh over a network) and used by the Macintosh version of PageMaker, and Macintosh graphics can be placed in the PC version of PageMaker.

This example uses for a logo a modified version of the cropping-tool image used in PageMaker's toolbox, which you can create in a graphics program or by capturing the image on your screen with a utility such as Tiffany Plus (Anderson Consulting and Software, N. Bonneville, WA), which creates a graphics file containing the image of the screen. We added a few embellishments to the image such as text and a fine dot pattern. You can substitute any graphic image as a logo for this example, including any of the sample graphics files supplied in the PageMaker tutorial and template folders.

No matter which method you use to create a logo, you can manipulate the logo in PageMaker as long as you use a graphics file format compatible with PageMaker. (Chapter 1 describes graphics file formats and graphics programs.)

To add the logo to the master pages, switch to actual-size display, and then place the logo's graphics file using the Place command from the File menu. Select the left master page and click the mouse to place the image (Figure 3-6).

You can resize the graphic image by dragging one of the handles that appear when the image is selected. You can drag any corner handle to change the size of the image to one that is right for your layout. If the image is a paint-type graphic image, a scanned image, or a line drawing with patterns, you can obtain the best results by holding down the Control key to automatically select the optimal sizes for your target printer. In addition, hold down the Shift key while resizing in order to keep the same proportions in the resized image. Without using the Shift key, you may

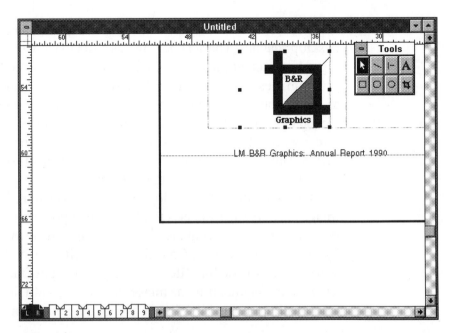

Figure 3-6. Place a logo on the left master page.

distort the image by stretching or compressing from any of its sides. In Figure 3-7, the logo is resized by holding down the Shift and Control keys while dragging the lower-right corner inward, scaling the logo down in size and by equal proportions.

After you scale the image to a size that fits in the space to the left in the footer, release the mouse button (and then release the Control and Shift keys). While the image is still selected, choose Copy from the Edit menu to copy the logo into the Clipboard. Switch to the master right page and choose Paste from the Edit menu. Move the newly pasted image into position next to the footer on the master right page (Figure 3-8). The logos and footers will be repeated on every left and right page, except those pages in which you turn off the Display of master items option (Page menu).

Saving a Template

At this point, it makes sense to save a version of this publication as a blank template for others in your company to use. It already has a convenient footer with a logo on each page. To use this set of master pages for any

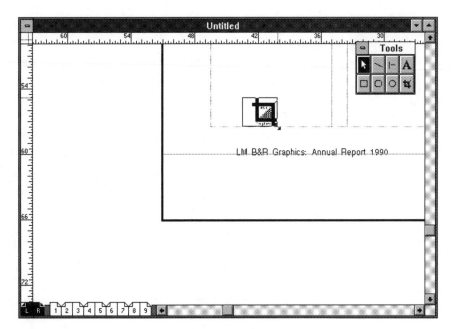

Figure 3-7. Scale the logo down in an equal ratio to the text.

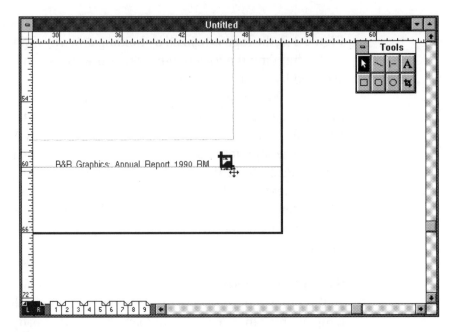

Figure 3-8. The logo placed on the master right page.

other type of corporate report, all you would have to do is change the text of the footer.

To save the publication as a template, choose the Save as command (or Save command, as this is an untitled publication), and check the box marked Template. Then type the name of the template file, such as **REPORTEM** (you have up to eight characters, but the first one must be a letter). PageMaker automatically appends a period and the three-character extension ".PT4" to make the file name REPORTEM.PT4.

When you open a file saved with the Template option, PageMaker automatically opens an untitled copy of the file, thus preserving the original template file.

You can then save the copy under another name, such as **REPORT1** (PageMaker automatically appends a period and the three-character extension ".PM4" to make the file name REPORT1.PM4).

For this example, use the Save as command to save the untitled copy as a regular publication file under the name **ANNUAL90** (which becomes

ANNUAL90.PM4). Click the box next to the Publication option in the Save as dialog box, and press OK.

Using the Story Editor

A new feature of PageMaker 4 is the Story Editor, which provides a text editing window for editing the text on the page. The Story Editor lets you write and edit text without recomposing the text for the page. You can alternatively edit text directly on the page, but PageMaker recomposes the text as you type it, making editing slower. If you plan to change only a few words, edit directly on the page, but if you plan to make a lot of changes, edit in the Story Editor window.

PageMaker offers extensive word processing features in the Story Editor window. You could use the program as a word processor, or you could use your favorite word processor for most of the writing effort, then use PageMaker's Story Editor for the editing phase. The choice depends on whether you are already using a word processor or not. If you are already using a word processor, there is probably no reason to change tools. You can use PageMaker to finish your pages.

For those who are not yet using a word processor, PageMaker can be an economical choice for several reasons. You need only buy one program to do both word processing and page makeup, and you can prepare a text file in almost any word processor format by exporting the text from PageMaker. Besides, you can check the spelling of all the text in the publication by opening a Story Editor window.

A *story* in PageMaker is a collection of text elements that can span many pages.

A single story can be typed and edited in the Story Editor, imported into the Story Editor, or placed directly on the page in layout view with the Place command and then edited with the Story Editor. A single story can be exported as a single file. The story's page elements are automatically linked so that text flows from the beginning of the story to the end, no matter where the elements are placed on the pages. You can even have a story flowing from one page to a previous page, though it is not a recommended style for readability!

The need to make last-minute changes is prevalent in the production of business reports of any kind, because the information can change at a moment's notice. PageMaker accommodates the need to make last-minute changes by providing several innovative features, such as the ability to search for and replace text, and the ability to automatically replace sections of the publication with new versions of the placed files. The report's text can be edited directly in the Story Editor, or you can replace the text with the contents of another file. A spreadsheet can be linked to the publication file so that when the spreadsheet is changed, the changes are copied to the publication file. The same is true of graphics files.

To use the Story Editor to start a new story, choose Edit Story command from the Edit menu (or type Control-E). To edit an existing story, click anywhere in the story with the text tool, or click a text block of the story with the pointer tool, and choose Edit Story (or type Control-E). The Story Editor displays a new window with the text displayed in a special font and size for editing.

You can open multiple Story Editor windows to edit more than one story at a time. This feature is particularly useful if you need to copy or cut text from one story and paste the text into another story (using Copy or Cut and Paste).

Creating and Importing Text

You can create text from scratch in the Story Editor window, or bring text from a word processing file into the Story Editor window for further editing. To bring text in, you can use the Import command in the Story menu (the Story menu appears when you open a Story Editor window), and choose the word processing file to import. Another way is to use the Copy command while in the word processing program to copy the text to the Windows Clipboard, and then switch to PageMaker's Story Editor window and use the Paste command.

To create the text for the report example, click anywhere with the text tool on Page one of the publication file, and select Edit Story from the Edit menu (Figure 3-9). You can then type text directly into the story (Figure 3-10).

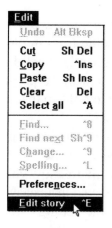

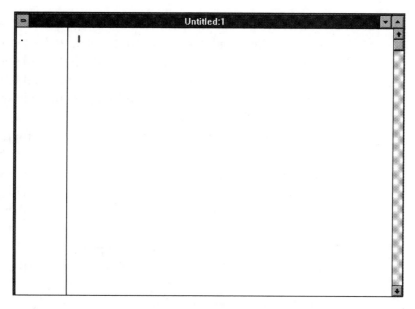

Figure 3-9. Use the Edit Story command to open the Story Editor window.

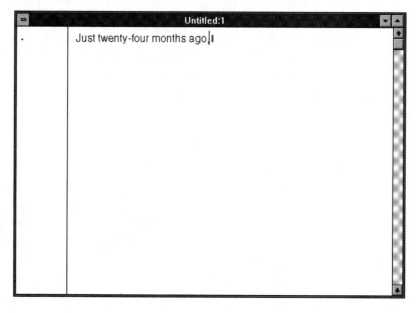

Figure 3-10. Type text in the Story Editor window, which acts like a word processor.

After typing the text, you can select any part of the text in the Story Editor window, and assign any font, size, and style to the text. In our example, we chose the entire text with the Select all command in the Edit menu (Control-A), and set it to be 12-point Helvetica with 16-point leading. The leading phrase of the first paragraph is set to bold so that it stands out.

The Story Editor does not display changes in font, size, and leading, and it does not display formatted columns. This is because the Story Editor is optimized for editing text as fast as possible. No matter how you style the text in the Story Editor window, the text is displayed in an easy-to-read font, size, and style. The program remembers the settings you chose and uses them when it recomposes the text for the page (when you close the Story Editor window). The program displays text in the Story Editor window in 12-point display font, rather than the settings you chose, because the text is easier to read and faster to edit. (You can change the Story Editor's display font and size in the Preferences dialog box to suit your preference.)

When you import text from a word processing file, the text may already have font, size, and style attributes. The Import dialog box provides the same options—Retain format, Convert quotes, and Read tags—as the Place dialog box for placing text. The Import dialog box lets you import the text as a new story, or as replacement text for the story's text. It also lets you insert the contents of the word processor file at the insertion point in the story, merging the imported text with the existing text of the story. For example, we imported a Microsoft Word text file into the Story Editor as a new story. The text was already formatted in Word (Figure 3-11).

Another reason why PageMaker's Story Editor is useful for word processing is its ability to assign *style definitions* for sections of text (also called *style sheets*). A style definition is a set of text formatting instructions that can be applied to a single paragraph or to multiple paragraphs in one step. (It is not the same as the *type style*, which can be normal, italic, bold, and so on.) A style sheet is first defined by the Define styles command in the Type menu, or it can be defined by a word processor that supports the use of style definitions, such as Microsoft Word. Once a style

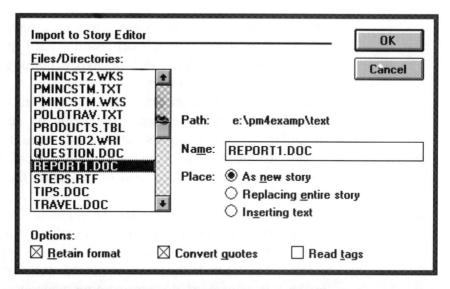

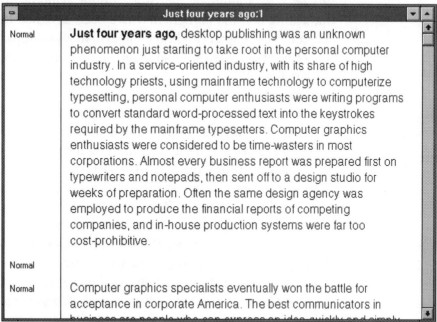

Figure 3-11. Text can be imported from a word processor file into the Story Editor window, with or without formatting characteristics. Note the use of the "Normal" style definition, imported from a Microsoft Word document.

sheet is defined, it can be assigned to a paragraph in the Story Editor window by means of the Style command in the Type menu (or by using the Style palette, which can be displayed by choosing it from the Window menu or by typing Control-Y).

Style sheets are an important innovation because you can change the text formatting of your entire publication by changing a few style definitions. The use of style sheets is another reason why a template file is valuable—it can contain predefined style sheets that can be assigned to incoming text without any need to remember the specifications of a design.

Style sheet definitions can also be imported along with a document. For example, we used the "Normal" style definition in the imported Word document, which was automatically brought into PageMaker along with the text. As a result, in the previous example the word "Normal" appears in the left column of the Story Editor window for each paragraph, indicating that the paragraphs have been assigned this style definition. Later in this chapter (in the technical manual example), we describe how to define or change a style sheet, and how to assign style sheet definitions to paragraphs.

Placing Stories

There are two ways to stop editing in the Story Editor window and return to the layout view to place the story on the page.

One way is to select the Close command from the Story Editor window's Control menu (Figure 3-12). Another is to choose Close story from the Story menu (or Control-Shift-E).

If the story has not yet been placed on the page, an alert box appears asking if you want to place the story or discard the story. Click the Place button, and a loaded text placement icon appears in the layout view so that you can place the story. Click the text placement option on the first page in the wide column at the 20.5-pica mark. Continue placing the text over pages (in the wide column only) until all of the text is placed.

If you want to return to layout view for a moment, but then continue editing in the Story Editor window, you can switch to layout view without closing the Story Editor window by clicking an exposed portion of the publication file outside the Story Editor window. If there are no exposed

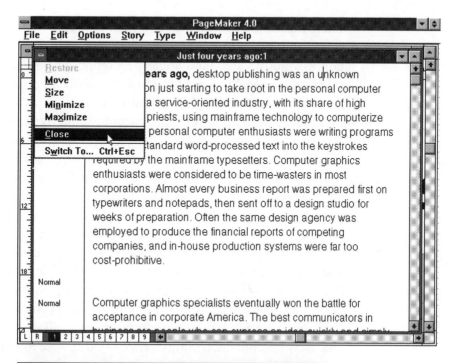

Figure 3-12. Close the story and place it on the page by choosing the Close story command in the Story menu, or the Close command in the Control menu for the Story window. The Place dialog box appears if the story has not yet been placed.

portions, choose the publication's name from the Window menu to switch to layout view. The Story Editor windows that are still open are also listed in the Window menu, so that you can switch back and forth. You can also return to the Story Editor window by clicking inside the window.

If you choose the Edit layout command (Control-E) in the Edit menu when a Story Editor window is active, PageMaker returns to layout view and to the same place on the page where the recently edited text appears. When you return to layout view, any stories you changed in the Story Editor windows are automatically recomposed for the page.

For closing a Story Editor window and placing text, PageMaker also provides the Place/Replace command in the File menu. The Place command closes the Story Editor window and bypasses the alert box to give you the loaded text placement icon for placing the story.

If the story has already been placed, PageMaker displays the Replace command rather than the Place command in the File menu. Replace replaces the placed story with the newly edited story.

You would use Place to close and place a new story and bypass the alert box that would appear if you just used Close story. You would use Replace to close the Story Editor window and replace the story on the page with the text in the Story Editor window (also bypassing the alert box). Replace is useful for changing the already-placed stories in a template file or another publication file—in a few operations you can select an existing story, open the Story Editor, import (replacing all the text) the new story, make any last-minute editing changes, and choose Replace to replace the old story.

It is a good idea to place all of the text in a publication first so that you can readily see how many pages of text you have. It is then easy to experiment and change the layout repeatedly. If you plan to use graphic elements, such as lines, you might prefer to select their position and place them before placing all of the text.

Using Find and Change

The Find, Find next, and Change commands let you find one or more instances of a particular set of characters, or a particular word or group of words, and change it to something else. The commands are available in the Edit menu when a Story Editor window is active.

The Find command can be used to find any word, phrase, or set of characters (including spaces, tabs, and paragraph endings). For example, you might want to search for every instance of a product name. You use the Match case option to find exactly the same letters—if you specify uppercase letters, it finds only uppercase letters. (In our example, the words "Crop City" will be found, but not "crop city" because we used uppercase letters in the Find entry.)

As an option you can also specify attributes for the words or characters, so that the program finds only those instances which have the same attributes. For example, your product name may be used many times in the text, but you only want to find the bold versions. Click the Attribute button (Figure 3-13) to display the attributes window, which has pop-up menus for the paragraph style sheet, font, size, and style (such as italic, bold, and so on). Select the "Any" style so that the Find command finds all instances of "Crop City" no matter how they are styled.

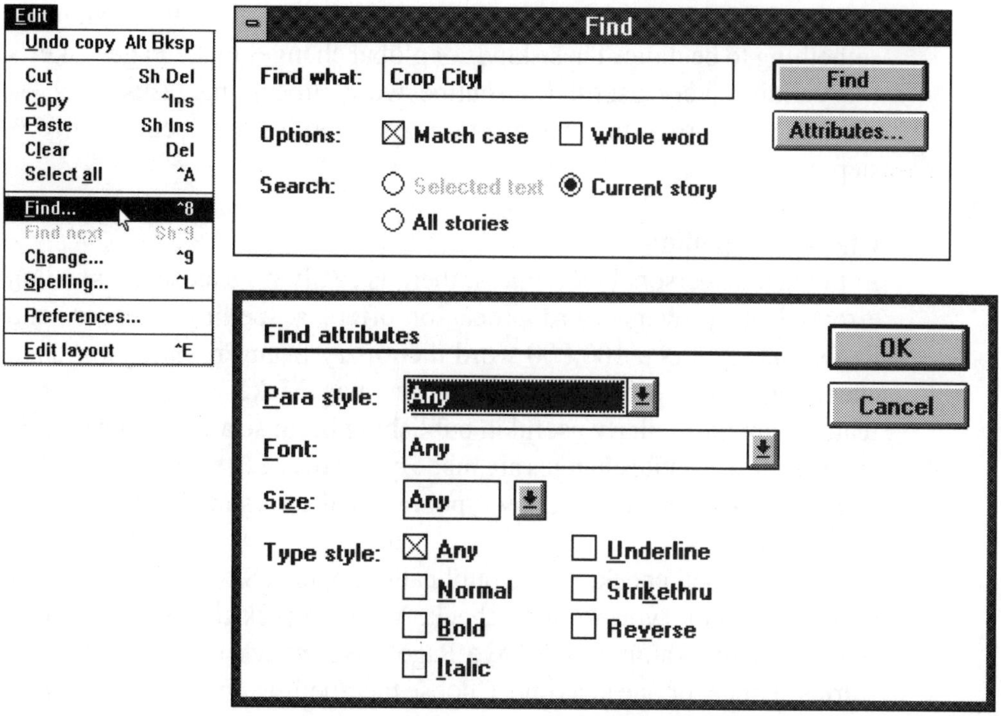

Figure 3-13. Use Find to locate one or more words or characters, such as the words "Crop City," in the current story opened by the Story Editor. Click the Match case option to match upper- and lowercase letters, and click the Attributes button to specify the attributes of the words, phrases, or characters to be found.

The Find command is useful for finding something and then returning to the Story Editor window and editing the text at that location. The Find next command can be used to find the next instance. You can use Find next continually to find each instance. The keyboard shortcut for Find is Control-8, and the shortcut for Find next is Shift-Control-9.

The Change command can find words and characters and also replace them with something else. You can specify the same options and attributes as with the Find command (Figure 3-14). You can, for example, change the words "Crop City" to "Crop City®" (type ^r in the change text entry area for the registered trademark symbol). You can specify that only the bold versions of "Crop City" should be changed, or that any version of "Crop City" should be changed. In addition, you can specify the attributes of the replacement, so you can change all bold versions of something to be italic. These kinds of global changes make PageMaker's Story Editor very useful for routine word processing tasks, such as changing the formatting of all the titles and subtitles of a document in one step.

Checking Spelling

In the age of personal computers, there is really no excuse for spelling errors. Nearly every word processor offers a spelling checker, and PageMaker offers a 100,000 word dictionary from Proximity for spell checking in the Story Editor window. PageMaker's spelling check features are particularly useful in publishing because after all the editing and final last-minute changes are made, you can check spelling as the last operation in order to catch any typographical errors made with the last minute changes.

To start spell checking in a publication, open a Story Editor window on the first story you want to check. You can pick the first story in a sequence, for example, and have PageMaker check the spelling in all stories at once, or one at a time. Choose the Spelling option from the Edit menu (Figure 3-15). The Spelling window appears and the program is ready to start checking. Click the Start button to start the operation.

When PageMaker finds a word that it can't find in the dictionary (which could be a proper noun, a technical word, a typo, an idiomatic expression, a slang word, a misspelled word, or a word rarely used), you

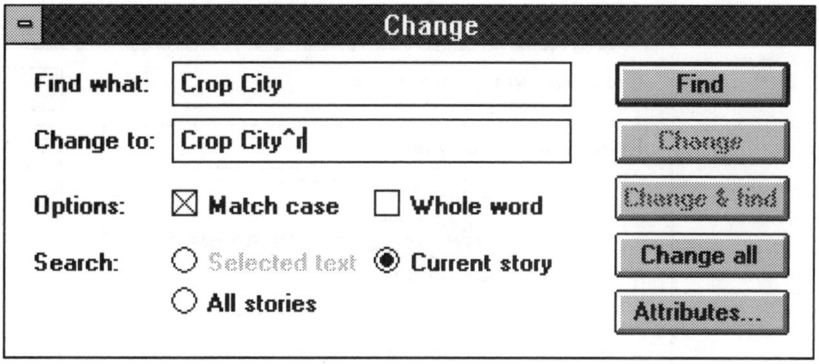

Change

Find what:	Crop City	**Find**
Change to:	Crop City^r	Change
Options:	☒ Match case ☐ Whole word	Change & find
Search:	○ Selected text ◉ Current story	Change all
	○ All stories	Attributes...

Figure 3-14. Use Change to replace one or more words or characters, such as "Crop City," with another set of words or characters, such as "Crop City®" (type ^r in the change entry to represent the registered trademark symbol).

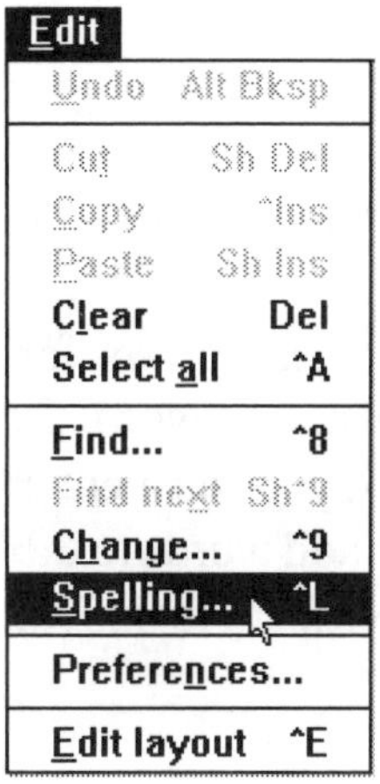

Edit

Undo	Alt Bksp
Cut	Sh Del
Copy	^Ins
Paste	Sh Ins
Clear	**Del**
Select all	**^A**
Find...	**^8**
Find next	Sh^9
Change...	**^9**
Spelling...	**^L**
Preferences...	
Edit layout	**^E**

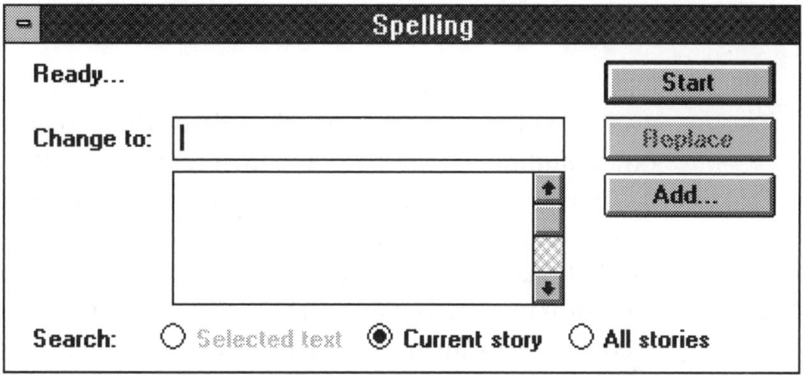

Spelling

Ready...   **Start**

Change to: | Replace

                                      Add...

Search: ○ Selected text ◉ Current story ○ All stories

Figure 3-15. Use Spelling to check the spelling of one or more stories. Spelling is available when a Story Editor window is active.

have the choice of ignoring that word, replacing that word, or adding that word to the dictionary. PageMaker displays a list of words it found in its dictionary that closely resemble the word in the text (Figure 3-16). Click the word in this list that is the correct spelling to replace the misspelled word, or click the options to ignore the word or add it to the dictionary. You also can type the correct spelling yourself, without clicking one of the words in the list.

If you click to ignore the word (the Ignore button), PageMaker never asks to change that particular word again in that publication file. How-

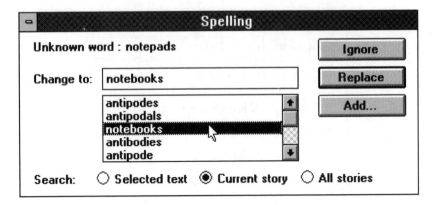

Figure 3-16. PageMaker displays the closest words, and you have the choice of clicking one of these words for replacement, or typing your own replacement. If the word should not be changed, you have the choice of adding the word to the dictionary or ignoring the word.

ever, it will pop up again as misspelled when you use PageMaker again (after quitting the program and then returning to it).

If you click the Add button, PageMaker displays a dialog box for adding and deleting words in the dictionary. You can also edit words in the dictionary. When adding or editing dictionary words, you must enter the words exactly as they will be typed. The capability to add words to the dictionary is useful if you intend to write a report that uses a lot of technical words and you want to be sure to spell them correctly.

Enhancing the Report

It is not enough to place the text on pages and expect the report to communicate effectively. For example, an annual report may contain sections that discuss market analysis, product information and life cycle, financial summaries, media campaigns, and anything else relevant to describing the business. Each section should follow a consistent heading format, so that the reader is not confused by the presentation.

Other touches, such as using a large initial uppercase letter dropped into the text, are designed to make the report look like it was produced by

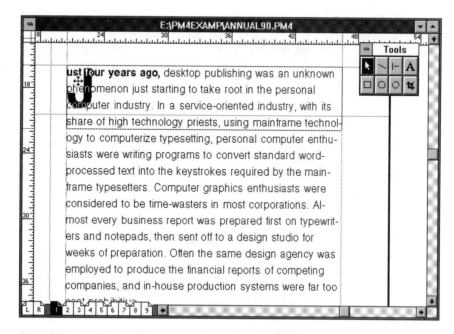

Figure 3-17. Move the large first character into position.

confident people. Subtle design touches, such as wrapping text around graphics, give the impression that the report has been well thought out in advance. These design qualities are intangible and depend a great deal on how well they are executed. Thus, your ability to use PageMaker is very important for the success of the report.

The first enhancement is to set the first letter to a large point size. The uppercase letter should descend into the article, not stand out by itself, so the rest of the opening sentence must wrap around the initial uppercase letter. This is called a *drop cap*. To do this, you must place one text block next to another in the same column.

Creating a Drop Cap

Move back to the first page to create a drop cap (the first letter of a paragraph, enlarged in size and extended below the baseline of the first line—sometimes called a *dropped initial cap*). Select the first letter by choosing the text tool and dragging across the letter. Use Cut to cut the

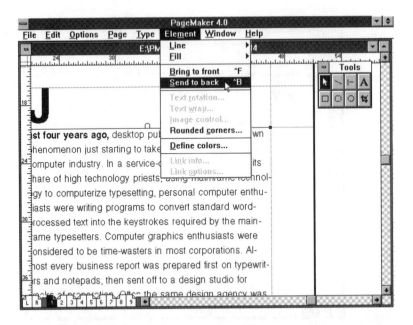

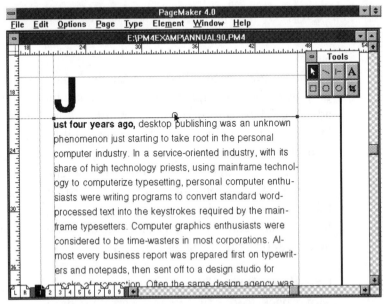

Figure 3-18. After using Send to Back in the Element menu to send the large first character to the background, push down on the body text from the top, then click the handle to get the text-flow icon.

letter from the text, and then use Paste to paste it back onto the pasteboard area next to the page, or onto the page above the body text. Click an insertion point immediately after the large letter and press the Return key. Choose the Type specs menu, and change the font size to 60 points with 70 points of leading.

Move the large letter back into the top part of the text, flush to the left margin of the wide column (Figure 3-17). Choose the Send to back command from the Edit menu, so that you can select the body text without selecting the large letter (Figure 3-18). Push the top handle of the body-text block down below the large letter, and click the mouse on the top handle to activate the text-flow icon. Drag the text-flow icon across the area of the column to be filled with text (Figure 3-19). When you release the mouse button, the first three lines should be in place next to the capital "J." You may now have to adjust the new text element in order to correct the spacing (Figure 3-20). (Hint: Drag a guide down from the ruler to make the alignment of the two blocks easier.)

Although the resolution of the screen is limited, PageMaker accurately displays the width of a letter in the Actual size page view. Use the 200% or the 400% view to align objects to ruler tick marks. You can always print the page and then adjust the column width next to the letter if necessary.

Adding a Title and Logo

To add a title to the report's first page, choose the text tool and click an insertion point at the left margin of the page and near the top of the page. Type the title with one space between each letter and two spaces between each word. Highlight the title and change the font to Helvetica, bold italic, 36 points with automatic (auto) leading. Stretch the title block by dragging a corner handle out to the right margin (Figure 3-21).

Switch to the perpendicular-line tool, choose an 8-point line from the Line pop-up menu in the Element menu, and drag a line at the 12-pica mark across the page under the title (Figure 3-22).

Complete the first page by moving the logo into place. To do so, copy the logo from the master page and Paste it on Page one. Resize the logo (Figure 3-23) by clicking the bottom-right handle while holding down the Shift key. (You can also hold down the Control key to get PageMaker's built-in sizes for the printer you selected.) Be sure that the footer is turned

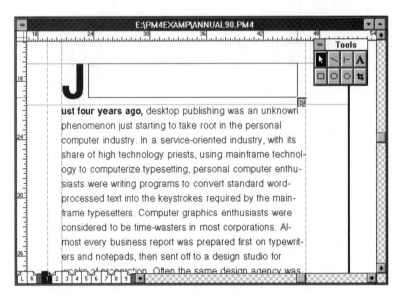

Figure 3-19. Drag the text-flow icon across the column to define the new text element for the first three lines of text.

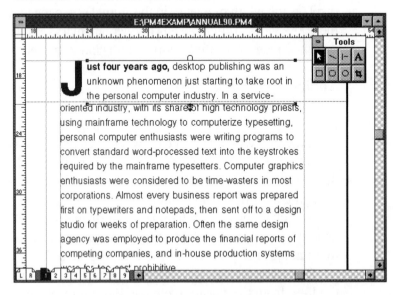

Figure 3-20. Pull down on the new text element's handle to correct the line spacing.

off on Page one by looking at the Display master items option in the Page menu: a check mark indicates that the option is on; no check mark shows that the option is off. The option is like a toggle switch: select the option to turn it on or off.

Enhancing Story Headings

A business report should be designed so that it is easy for a reader to browse through and read only those sections that are of interest. The narrow left-hand column is ideal for placing the headings of the report, so that they stand out from the rest of the text.

To move a heading from the body-text column to the narrow column, choose the text tool. Click and drag across the entire heading (Figure 3-24), and use Cut from the Edit menu. Click an insertion point at the left edge of the narrow column, and select Paste from the Edit menu.

If the heading is not formatted, drag across the heading again (while still using the text tool), choose the Type specs menu, and change the font size to 14 points with 18 points of leading. Finally, draw a 2-point line under the heading (Figure 3-25).

Repeat these steps for each heading in the report. For long headlines that should occupy two lines, select the text tool, click an insertion point where the heading should be broken (headings should not be hyphenated), and press the Return key to insert a carriage return. Subheadings should remain in the text block, but need to be changed to 14-point bold type.

Controlling Widows and Orphans

A problem that occurs with paragraphs in a layout is that one or more ending lines of the paragraph appear at the beginning of a column or page, separated from the rest of the paragraph that appears at the end of the previous column or page. This is called a *widow*. A similar problem occurs when one or more initial lines of a paragraph fall at the bottom of a column or page, separated from the rest of the paragraph that appears in the next column or page. This is called an *orphan*. You don't want a widow or orphan to detract from the presentation of your report. PageMaker lets you specify paragraph controls that automatically avoid these problems.

The Paragraph dialog box, displayed when you select Paragraph from the Type menu, changes the specifications that control the overall look of

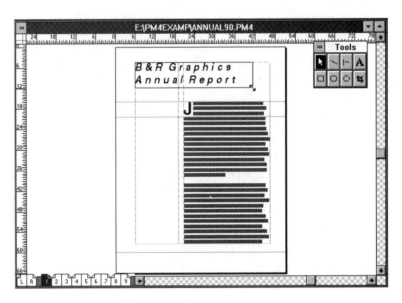

Figure 3-21. Stretch the title element to fit across the page.

Figure 3-22. Draw an 8-point line below the title.

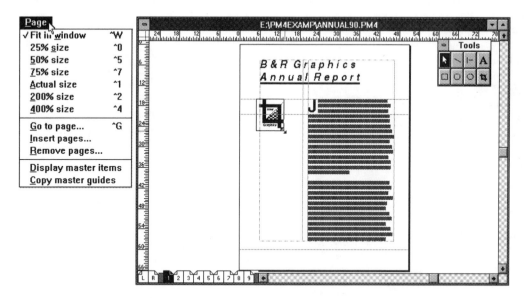

Figure 3-23. To turn off the footers for Page one, turn off the Display master items option in the Page menu by selecting it until the check mark disappears. Then resize the logo to fit in a prominent space on Page one.

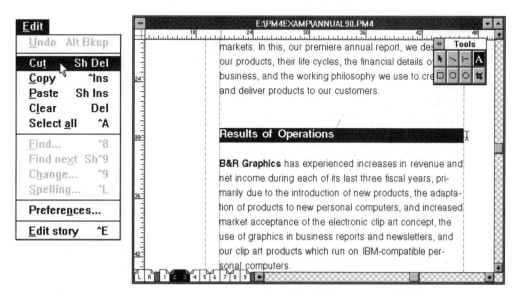

Figure 3-24. Select a section heading using the text tool and use the Cut command.

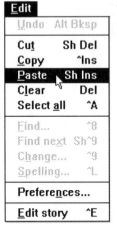
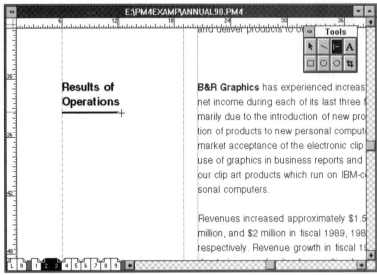

Figure 3-25. Use the Paste command to paste the section heading in the left column, and draw a 2-point line below the heading.

one or more paragraphs. The paragraph or paragraphs must already be selected if you are going to change the Paragraph settings for those paragraphs. (If no text is selected, the new Paragraph settings affect only the new text that you type after changing the settings.) One way to select all the paragraphs in a story is to use the text tool to click an insertion point somewhere in the story, and then use Select all in the Edit menu (or Control-A).

After selecting paragraphs or the entire story, choose Paragraph from the Type menu (or Control-M). The Paragraph dialog box is displayed (Figure 3-26), providing choices for indents, text alignment, line space before and after each paragraph, the current dictionary for hyphenation and spelling, paragraph rules, spacing attributes, and options for controlling lines, including widow and orphan control. In this dialog box you can specify which dictionary to use for spell checking and hyphenation for one or more selected paragraphs.

In the example, the widow and orphan controls are turned on, with one line set as the maximum number of lines for a widow and for an orphan

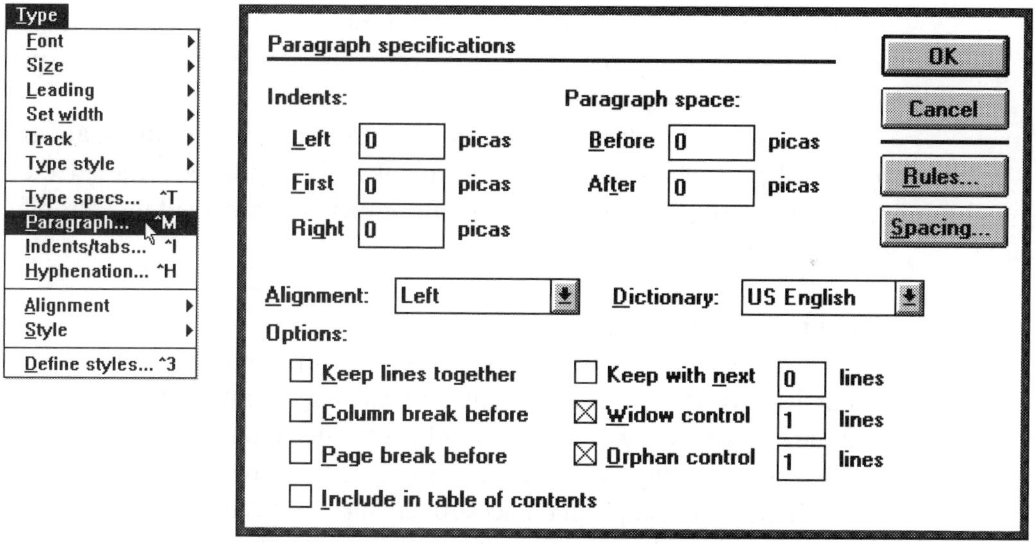

```
Type
 Font              ▶
 Size              ▶
 Leading           ▶
 Set width         ▶
 Track             ▶
 Type style        ▶
 Type specs...    ^T
 Paragraph...     ^M
 Indents/tabs...  ^I
 Hyphenation...   ^H
 Alignment         ▶
 Style             ▶
 Define styles... ^3
```

Paragraph specifications

[OK]
[Cancel]

[Rules...]
[Spacing...]

Indents:

Left [0] picas

First [0] picas

Right [0] picas

Paragraph space:

Before [0] picas

After [0] picas

Alignment: [Left ▼]   Dictionary: [US English ▼]

Options:

☐ Keep lines together   ☐ Keep with next [0] lines
☐ Column break before   ☒ Widow control [1] lines
☐ Page break before   ☒ Orphan control [1] lines
☐ Include in table of contents

Figure 3-26. The Paragraph dialog box for specifying characteristics of paragraph formatting and dictionary selection.

(in some cases, two or even three lines are considered the maximum for a widow or orphan).

The maximum is used by PageMaker to determine whether or not a paragraph's ending lines form a widow, and whether or not its initial lines form an orphan. If, for example, you set two lines as the maximum for widows, then if a two-line segment appears at the beginning of a page, PageMaker considers the segment to be a widow because it falls short of three lines.

PageMaker automatically gets rid of a widow or orphan by changing the number of lines on the previous page. The use of widow and orphan control is especially well suited for pages that have only one column of body text, because there is no need to match the column with another column of body text on the same page. Reports are typically designed to have one column of body text per page.

Other options in the Paragraph dialog box also control how paragraphs are broken over columns or pages. The Keep lines together option prohibits the selected paragraph or paragraphs from breaking over a column or page, so that an entire paragraph is always together. If you select an entire story and check this option, no paragraphs will be split over columns or pages.

The Column break before option sets the selected paragraph to always begin at the top of a column. The Page break before option sets the selected paragraph to begin a new page. Other options are described in examples later in this chapter.

Scaling and Cropping Graphics

The narrow column is useful for displaying images and graphics. This example uses clip art in order to point out that there are numerous libraries of electronic clip art ready to use in some of your publications, and the use of clip art does not incur any royalty expenses and does not require graphics skill, thus making them excellent choices for enhancing business reports.

A selected graphic image can be *scaled*—that is, its size can be changed by enlarging or reducing the overall image.

You can scale an image proportionately by holding down the Shift key while dragging any corner handle.

Without holding the Shift key, you can scale the image disproportionately, stretching or compressing an image.

Figure 3-27 shows a graphic image placed in the narrow column, scaled to fit (with Control-Shift while dragging a corner), and positioned to intrude slightly into the text.

Another graphic image is placed below it in the same manner. Switch to the text tool and type the caption in the narrow column, then resize the caption block to fit a vertical line for emphasis (Figure 3-28).

The cropping tool is useful for showing only part of a graphic image. (This tool does not change the original image, but just hides part of it.) Cropping is a way of cutting out the edges, and it does not scale, stretch, or compress the image.

To crop an image, select the cropping tool and click on the image to display handles on the image. Figure 3-29 demonstrates how you can align the cropping tool over a handle, and Figure 3-30 shows the result of cropping the image. After adding a caption as in Figure 3-28, switch to the full-page display to see if the additional graphic elements are balanced on the two facing pages.

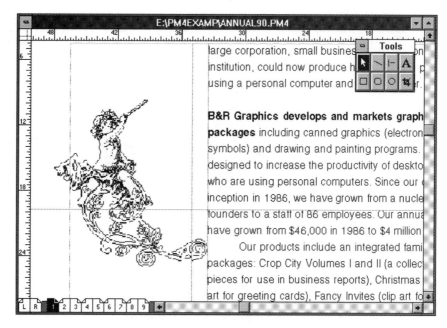

Figure 3-27. Place graphics in the narrow column.

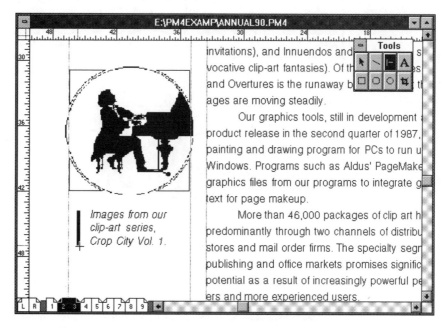

Figure 3-28. Add a caption and a vertical rule for emphasis.

Figure 3-29. Select a graphic image with the cropping tool.

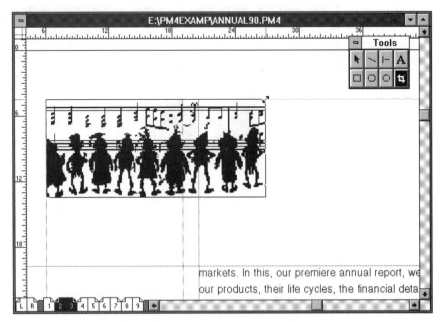

Figure 3-30. The result of dragging a handle to crop the image.

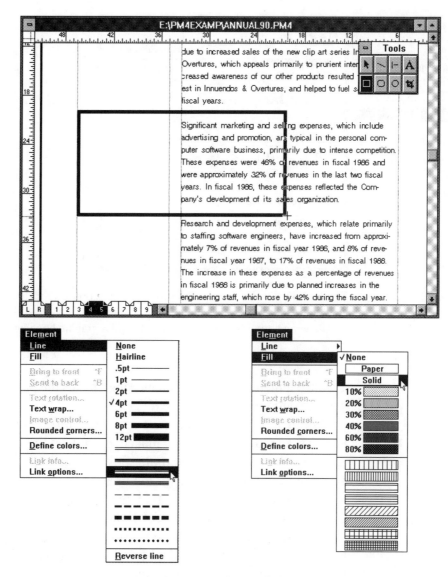

Figure 3-31. Draw a solid-filled box with a double-line style for a border.

Wrapping Text Around Rectangles

Even in a business report a picture may be worth more than a thousand words. You can add a compelling graphic image or photo in such a way

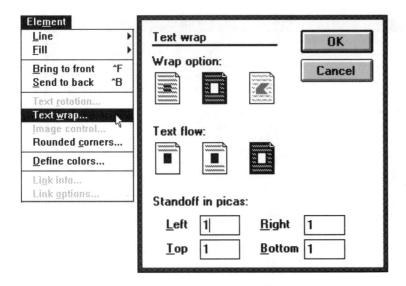

Figure 3-32. The Text wrap dialog box provides options for flowing text around graphics that intrude into text elements or are wholly contained by text elements. The middle wrap option is selected for a rectangular graphic boundary.

that the element adds visual balance and makes the page more interesting without detracting from the text.

For this example, if you have a scanned image, use it. If you do not have a scanned image, draw a placement box on the PageMaker page to represent the image. The example shows doing both: the placement box acts as a background frame for the image.

First, select a double-line style for the box edge from the Line pop-up menu in the Element menu. Select the box tool, click a starting point at one corner of the box, and drag the mouse to draw the box (Figure 3-31). While the box is still selected, set the box fill pattern to the Solid option in the Fill pop-menu in the Element menu.

With the box still selected, choose the Text wrap command from the Element menu. The Text wrap dialog box (Figure 3-32) lets you choose how to wrap text around shapes, and it allows you to turn off the automatic text wrapping feature if you wish.

Select the middle Wrap option and the right-hand Text flow option so that text flows around the graphic image with a rectangular boundary.

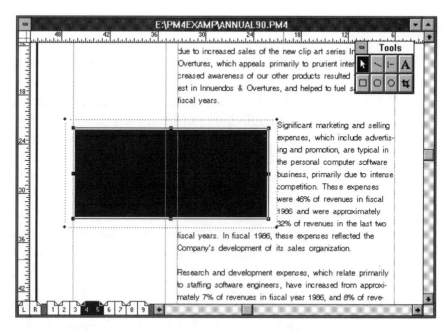

Figure 3-33. The result of choosing the middle wrap option to wrap text around a rectangular shape.

(The result of this operation is shown in Figure 3-33). Chapter 4 shows by example how to adjust the boundary of an irregularly shaped graphic image.

Standard business report elements, such as charts, graphs, and tables, will probably occupy larger sections of the pages and not have text wrapped around them. To make room in a text block for these elements, select the pointer tool and click anywhere inside the text block. Drag the bottom handle up to the top of the area to be reserved, and release the mouse button. You can continue text below a reserved area by clicking the bottom handle and clicking a starting point for the rest of the text.

Move a text block in the same way that you move a graphic—point in the middle, hold down the mouse button until you see the four arrows, and drag the text block into position. With Snap to guides on, you can attach a text block or a graphic to a column guide or a ruler guide. Use a ruler guide to help align text columns side by side.

Adding Tables and Charts

Reports usually contain financial or scientific data displayed in tables. The data elements come from a data base (a large file of structured information) or a spreadsheet (numerical information organized in rows and columns). In a spreadsheet, each number or text element is referred to as a *cell*. In many spreadsheet programs, such as Microsoft Excel, spreadsheets can have named cells, rows, and columns for easy reference. You can refer to, say, the "Total Expenses" row of an expenses spreadsheet.

With the supplied WKS and Excel spreadsheet import filters, you can import any WKS-type spreadsheet (such as ones created with Lotus 1-2-3 and Symphony) or any Excel spreadsheet, and place any named range in the spreadsheet (Figure 3-34). You can, for example, place a range that represents only the totals or subtotals of a spreadsheet. You can also place the entire printable area of the spreadsheet. The text of the spreadsheet is placed and assigned the WKS style definition, which you can then change as you wish.

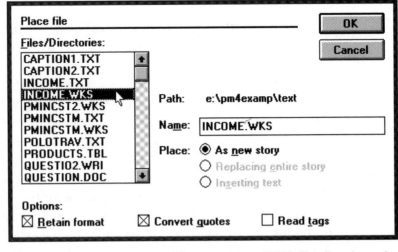

Figure 3-34. You can place a Lotus spreadsheet (WKS file) directly on the page with the WKS import filter dialog box, in which you can pick a range to place (such as the area defined for printing). The text is automatically set to have the WKS style.

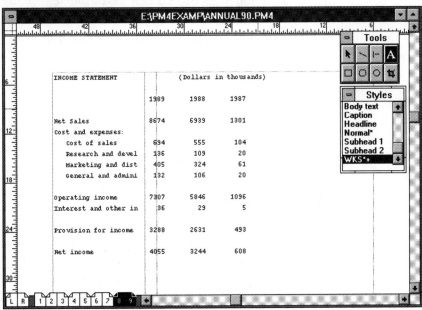

Figure 3-34. Continued.

An alternative, if the spreadsheet is in a file that is not compatible with PageMaker's filters, or if you plan to change the formatting of the spreadsheet, you can save the spreadsheet in a text format, PageMaker can import the text of the spreadsheet. Use the spreadsheet program to save the worksheet as a text file. If you create a table in a word processing program, use the same number of tabs to separate columns (do not use spaces), and use a carriage return (Enter or Return key) to end each row of the table. Then use the Place command in PageMaker to place the text file as a new story in the publication file. You can then edit the table in the Story Editor or in the layout view directly on the page. Usually this is the best method for handling simple tables with row elements that fit on one line.

Complex tables and tables with multiple lines per element can be built in a table editing program such as the Aldus Table Editor (supplied with PageMaker), or in Microsoft Word 4 (using its Table feature).

If the table is not in a final form and needs to have fonts and formatting added to it, you can save it as text using any of these table editing programs, and bring the table text into a PageMaker publication either by placing the text in layout view, or importing the text into a Story Editor window. You can then edit the table by adjusting the tabs (using Indents/tabs in the Type menu) and selecting fonts, sizes, and leading. PageMaker provides line drawing tools for adding lines to separate table elements.

If the table is already in a final form, styled and formatted properly using Aldus Table Editor or some other table editing program (such as Word for Windows), you can save it as a graphics file or copy it to the Clipboard. In PageMaker, use the Place command to place the file on the page, or use Paste to paste it from the Clipboard. You can then scale and crop the table image as you would any graphic image.

Importing Tables as Text

A table can be constructed in any word processor and saved as an ASCII text file. Some characteristics of ASCII text files can be changed during the importing into PageMaker step, by selecting options in the Smart ASCII import filter dialog box.

Tables prepared in word processing programs should be created with tabs between columns. Set the tabs so that the table columns line up in the word processor, with one tab between each column item. In PageMaker, you can change the tab settings to fit the column format or use the tabs already set in the word processing program.

After saving the table as a text-only file, you can use the Place command to place the text (Figure 3-35). Turn off the option to retain formatting, so that PageMaker displays the Smart ASCII import filter dialog box with its options. Choose the normal setting—no conversion—for spreadsheet data saved as text, because spreadsheet text columns are usually separated by a tab and consist of single-line cells.

However, if your spreadsheet text columns are separated by spaces, choose the option to replace one or more spaces with a tab. Select this option for tables justified in columns using spaces, so that those spaces between columns are replaced by a single tab space that PageMaker can adjust. You can also specify the number of consecutive spaces between columns, and the filter replaces that many spaces in a row (or more) with a single tab space.

Another option of the Smart ASCII import filter dialog box is to import the table using the monospaced Courier font, with the columns aligned to match the alignment of columns in a monospaced word processor. Using a monospaced font such as Courier, each character and space is aligned with a character and space on the previous monospaced line. To be sure that tables are formatted correctly, also select the option to leave the carriage returns in for tables and lists, if you select the option to remove carriage returns from each line.

With the spreadsheet text loaded into the text-flow icon, drag the icon across the page to define the text element. Then switch to the text tool, select the entire table, and change the tab settings in the Indents/tabs dialog box to align the columns (Figure 3-36). You can line up to the column the zero point on the ruler in the Indents/tabs box by clicking on the right and left arrows. Use the decimal-point tab, which lines up the decimal points of numbers. The decimal-point tab should be placed exactly where you want the decimal point to fall in your numbers (when using integers as in this example, the decimal point is the space after the rightmost number). You should be using only one tab between each column, to make it easy to adjust the columns.

Microsoft Word offers table formatting features that allow cells in a

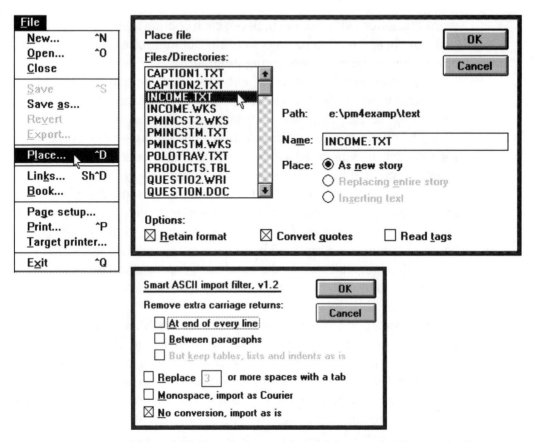

Figure 3-35. For other types of spreadsheets and tables, use the Place command without the Retain format option to import the text file. Set the Smart ASCII import filter dialog box to no conversion.

table to be formatted to be more than one line (or row) long. There are two ways to import Word tables into PageMaker: as text or as graphics. Use the text method for tables formatted with single-line cells (no more than one line per row).

To bring in Word tables as text, in Word type the character "T" on a line by itself before the table, and select Word's Hidden option in the Style box in Word's Character dialog box. This formatting step performed in Word changes the "T" into a hidden character that the PageMaker Word filter can interpret. When you place the Word text with PageMaker's

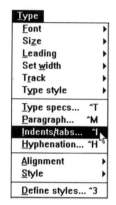

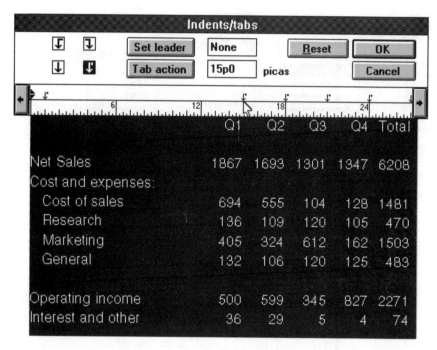

Figure 3-36. Change the column widths by adjusting the tab settings with the Indents/Tabs dialog box. The decimal tab lets you line up the decimal points of numbers.

Retain format option, PageMaker inserts tabs between each cell in the table. Each row of the table is formatted as a paragraph, and the styles you applied in Word are applied to each row. You can then adjust the table spacing by adjusting the tab settings in PageMaker's Indent/tabs dialog box as described previously.

Enhancing Text Tables

You can jazz up a text table created in PageMaker by drawing a rectangle as a frame and creating a drop shadow behind it. You can also use the line drawing tools to put lines in the table to visually separate table elements.

First, select a 1-point line and a Paper fill, then draw a rectangle around the table (Figure 3-37), and use the Send to back command in the Element menu to place the rectangle behind the text. Then, while the rectangle remains selected, choose the Copy command in the Edit menu to store a

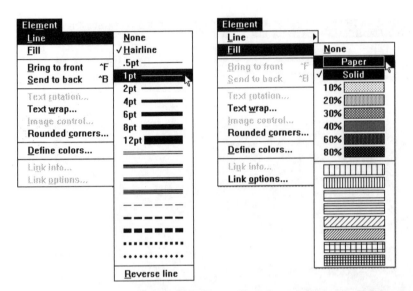

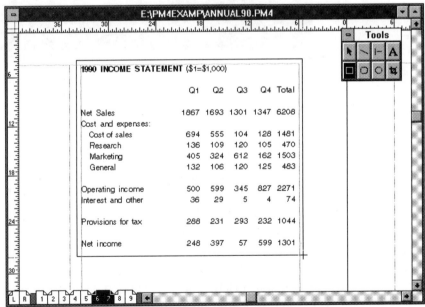

Figure 3-37. Set a 1-point line and a Paper (solid white) fill pattern, and draw a rectangle frame around the table.

copy in the Clipboard. Next, use the Paste command to paste the copied rectangle, and move the rectangle into position to be the dropped shadow (Figure 3-38). Set the fill pattern to Solid for the dropped shadow rectangle (which should still be selected after the Paste). Use the Send to

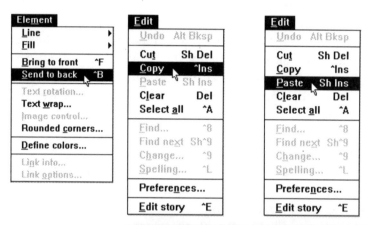

Figure 3-38. Use Send to back to place the white rectangle behind the text, then use Copy to copy it, and Paste to paste the new copy. Move the new copied rectangle into place.

back command again, to place the black rectangle behind the white rectangle (Figure 3-39).

To move the table along with its rectangle and shadow, select the text element and hold down the Shift key to select both rectangles. Shift selecting an object adds the object to the current selection. With the group of objects selected, click the center of the group until you see the four-arrow symbol, and then drag to move the entire group.

You may want to draw lines inside the spreadsheet to emphasize rows. You can do this with the perpendicular-line drawing tool (Figure 3-40). However, if you want clean borders for table elements, build the table using the Aldus Table Editor program, which provides automatic ways of setting up borders and text for a table.

Using the Table Editor

For complex tables, you should use the Aldus Table Editor program, which is a separate program supplied with PageMaker 4. To use the Table Editor, double-click the program's icon.

The Table Editor first displays a blank screen and its menu bar. Choose New from the File menu to create a new table. The program displays a dialog box for table setup, where you can specify the number of rows and columns, and the table size (Figure 3-41). The program then displays a blank grid representing the table's rows and columns.

With the "A" (text) tool you can type directly into the Table Editor's cells to start your table. The text automatically wraps around within each cell, and the rows grow wider as you type more text to accommodate the text (Figure 3-42). Press Tab to move on to the next cell to continue typing.

An alternative to typing the table text is to import the text from another program, such as Microsoft Excel or Lotus 1-2-3. Text to be imported into the Table Editor must be formatted to have each text element separated from the next by a tab (this is called a *tab-delimited* text file). The Table Editor can also import text files that use a comma as the delimiter rather than tab (a *comma-delimited* text file).

After typing or importing the text into the table, switch to the pointer tool to select cells, and select more than one cell by dragging with the pointer across the cells. You can change the type style to bold for all the text in the selected cells (Figure 3-43).

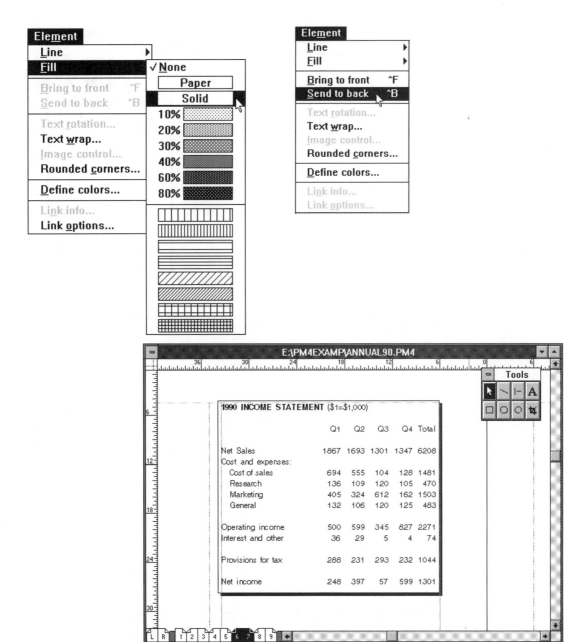

Figure 3-39. The dropped shadow rectangle, set to have a Solid fill pattern, is placed behind the other elements with the Send to back command.

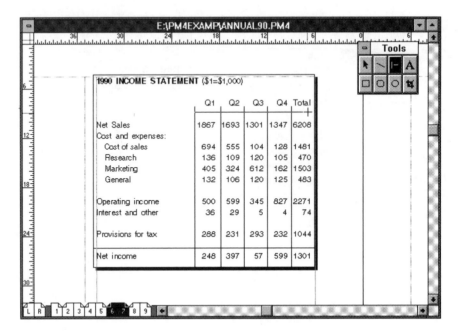

Figure 3-40. Lines are drawn in the table with the perpendicular-line drawing tool.

Drag a column or row divider in the outer label area of the grid to change the size of the row or column (Figure 3-44). As you change the width of a column, the other columns are adjusted automatically to preserve the table's size.

To set the headline of the table, drag the pointer tool across the top row of cells to select them, and choose the Group command in the Cell menu (Figure 3-45) to collect the cells into an unbroken group. You can then use the text tool to type the headline, setting its font size to 48 points and the bold style.

To make a table easier to read, it helps to add lines that separate rows and columns, or at least rows so that a reader can read across easily. To add lines, first select the rows by dragging down the row numbers in the left outer edge of the grid. Then select the Borders command in the Element menu (Figure 3-46).

The Borders dialog box (Figure 3-47) indicates that there are already lines on all four sides of the perimeter, and horizontal and vertical interior

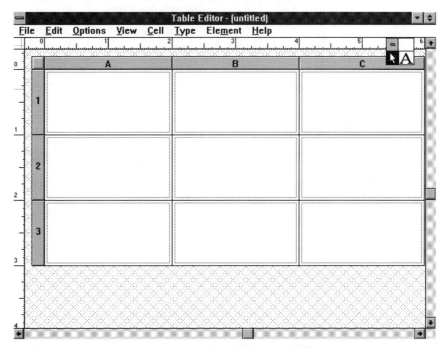

Figure 3-41. The Table Editor program's New command first displays a setup dialog box, and after you set the table size and click OK, it displays a grid representing the table's rows and columns.

lines. Leave all the options turned on, click OK, then choose the None style in the Line style pop-up menu. This applies the None style to all lines, so that none are left.

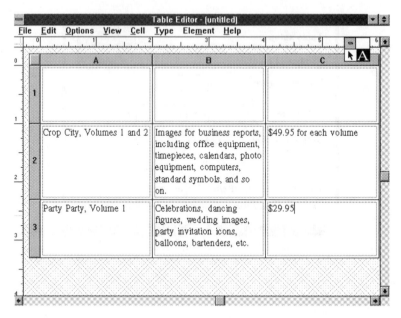

Figure 3-42. Type text directly into the Table Editor's cells, which grow vertically (increasing the width of the entire row) to accommodate the text.

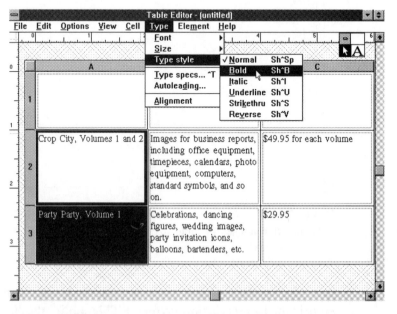

Figure 3-43. Select the cells in column one with the pointer tool by dragging down the column, and change the text type style to bold.

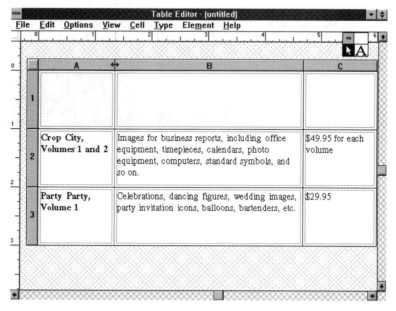

Figure 3-44. Drag a column divider in the outer edge of the grid to adjust the width of a column. The other columns are adjusted automatically to the new width, to preserve the table's size.

You can now add the lines you want to add, in a different line style. With the rows still selected, choose Borders again, and turn off every option except the Bottom option for Perimeter and the Horizontals option for Interior (Figure 3-48). Change the line style from None to a 2-point line in the pop-up menu. To see the result, turn off the grid lines and labels in the Options menu (Figure 3-49). Save the table with the Save command in the File menu.

To prepare a table for PageMaker, use the Export command in the File menu (Figure 3-50), and select the Windows Metafile option and the Entire table option.

Use the Windows Metafile option whenever you want to use the formatting and line styles set in the Table Editor. Use the Text only option (which uses tabs to separate items) to export the table text for use with another application (such as a word processor), or to import the unformatted text into PageMaker for editing and formatting as described previously.

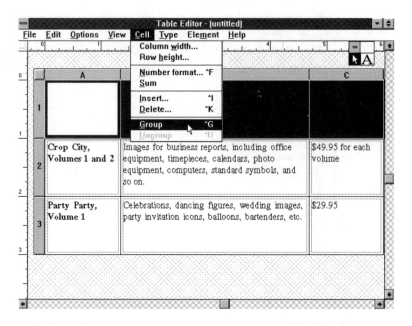

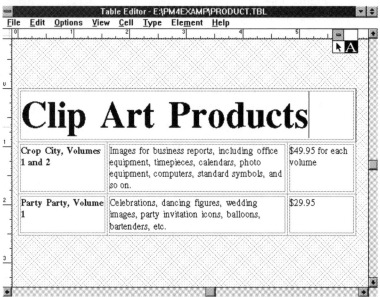

Figure 3-45. Use the Group command in the Cell menu to collect a set of cells into an unbroken group to hold the headline of the table.

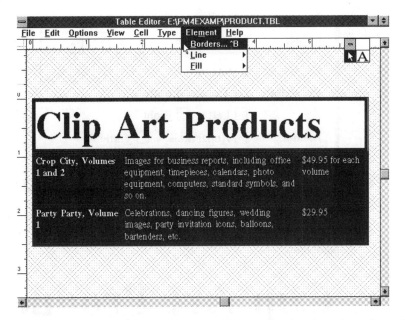

Figure 3-46. Select all the rows in the table by dragging the pointer down the row numbers on the left, and then select the Borders command to change the lines in the chart.

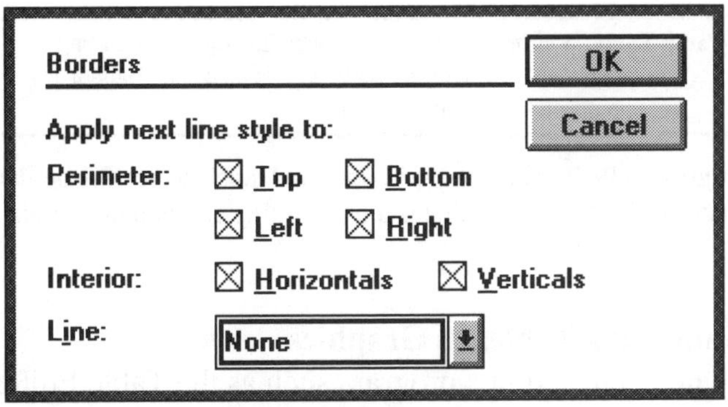

Figure 3-47. The Borders dialog box lets you apply a particular line style to the borders of the selected cells. The borders start with lines on all four sides of the perimeter, and horizontal and vertical interior lines. Select all, then choose the None line style in the pop-up menu to delete all lines.

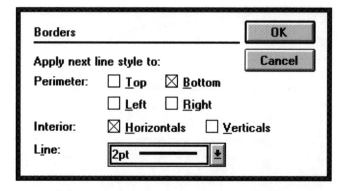

Figure 3-48. Set the next line style change to affect only the bottom of the perimeter and the horizontal lines in the interior. Then change the line style from None to a 2-point line.

Options
√ **R**ulers
Snap to rulers ^Y
Zero lock
Grid labels ^8
√ Grid **l**ines ^9
√ **T**oolbox
√ **S**croll bars
Transparent fills

Clip Art Products

Crop City, Volumes 1 and 2	Images for business reports, including office equipment, timepieces, calendars, photo equipment, computers, standard symbols, and so on.	$49.95 for each volume
Party Party, Volume 1	Celebrations, dancing figures, wedding images, party invitation icons, balloons, bartenders, etc.	$29.95

Figure 3-49. Turn off the grid lines and labels to see the borders created with the 2-point lines. The dotted line is a nonprinting cell boundary indicator.

Importing Tables as Graphics

A table created in a program such as the Table Editor, Microsoft Excel, or Microsoft Word can be saved as either a text file to be imported into PageMaker as text (described earlier), or as a Windows Metafile graphics file to be placed on the PageMaker page.

If the table is in final form in the table editing program, bring the table into PageMaker as a graphics file.

As described before, you can use the Table Editor's Export command to create a graphics file containing the table. You can then use PageMaker's

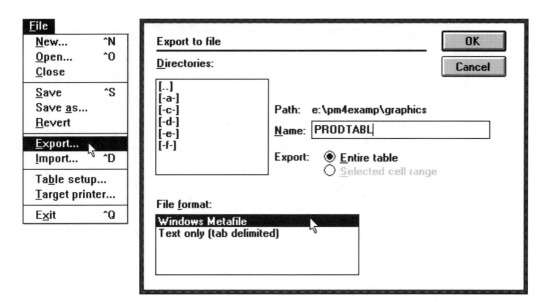

Figure 3-50. Prepare the table by saving it as a Windows Metafile (PRODTABL.WMF) using the Export command.

Place command to place the file as a graphic image on the page. After placement, the Metafile version of the table can be cropped and scaled like any other graphic image (Figure 3-51).

PageMaker offers another option for placing graphics files on the page: the *inline graphics* option. With this option, graphics can be placed *inside* the text so that it becomes part of the text. When the text is edited, the inline graphics are adjusted along with the text with the recompose operation. With inline graphics, the graphics move along with the text if the text associated with it falls on another page or appears in a different position on the page. Tables that must occur in a special place in the text should be placed as inline graphics. We describe how to place inline graphics later in this chapter in the example of a technical manual.

Adding Charts and Graphs
PageMaker can place the graphics files produced by some spreadsheet programs, such as the charts and graphs produced by Microsoft Excel and Lotus 1-2-3, and the business graphics produced by programs such as

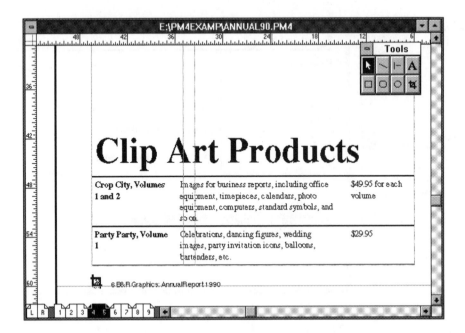

Figure 3-51. Place the table created in the Table Editor and exported as a Windows Metafile graphics file. You can then crop and scale the graphic image.

Harvard Graphics (Software Publishing Corp.), Micrografx Draw Plus, Micrografx Charisma, Micrografx Designer, Corel Draw, and various Macintosh graphics programs (such as Aldus FreeHand and Aldus Persuasion). PageMaker can place nearly any type of graphics file (see Appendix B for a complete description).

After using a spreadsheet program (such as Lotus 1-2-3), you can transfer the graphics to a better graphics program (such as Micrografx Draw Plus) in order to produce high-quality graphics with special effects (Figure 3-52).

If the graphics file is from an object-drawing program (as described in Chapter 1), you can scale the graphic image as desired without holding down the Control key. For instance, for Encapsulated PostScript (EPS) files, Windows Metafile files, and CGM files, just drag a corner of the image (hold down the Shift key to maintain the proportions) to the size that you need to fill. If the file is a bitmap image from a paint-type program such as Paintbrush, or a TIFF image (in a TIF file), hold down both the Control and Shift keys while dragging.

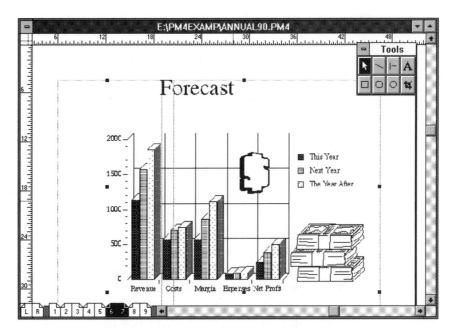

Figure 3-52. Place a chart that was created in a spreadsheet program, which can generate charts and graphs from spreadsheet data, and then enhanced in a graphics program.

Although paint-type graphics programs and drawing programs let you select fonts for text and these fonts are carried over into PageMaker when you place the image, the text may not look as good as when it is placed as text (or typed) into PageMaker. Text within a graphics file is reduced or enlarged with the image as you scale the image, but the fonts usually do not correspond directly to laser printer fonts (unless they are PostScript outline fonts defined in an EPS file). Besides, PageMaker gives you much greater control over text formatting.

Therefore, you should place just the graphics in PageMaker without the text and then add text with PageMaker, which gives you more control over text size and font styles within a text block. If the text is already part of the graphic image, you can crop the image to hide the embedded text, or draw white-filled rectangles (with line styles set to None) to hide the text. Then type new text (in PageMaker) in place of the embedded text.

If you want text to run vertically alongside a vertical axis, or to have any other orientation besides the usual horizontal orientation, use the Text rotation option in the Element menu to rotate text in 90-degree increments. First, select the text to rotate with the pointer tool (Figure 3-53), then choose the Text rotation option in the Element menu. This option presents a dialog box with icons representing the four angles for rotation (90-degree increments). Choose the angle you want, and click OK. The text is automatically rotated.

To edit the text after rotating it, you must choose the text element and open the Story Editor window (choose Edit story in the Edit menu, or type Control-E, or triple click the text element).

If you need to rotate text to an angle that is not an increment of 90 degrees, use a graphics program to create the text as an EPS or Windows Metafile graphics file that can be scaled without losing the quality of the font and type style.

You can draw an entire chart or graph using PageMaker's line-, rectangle-, and oval-drawing tools, and shape fill patterns. PageMaker's Snap to guides feature makes it easy to line up several distinct rectangles to form a bar chart. You can draw perfect circles by holding down the Shift key while dragging with the oval tool, or make perfect squares by holding down the Shift key while dragging with the rectangle-drawing tool.

Spreadsheet and business graphics programs can perform calculations and then produce a bar chart, a pie chart, or an x-y graph that is accurate in proportion to those calculations. It is therefore better to use the output of these programs, at least as a template for the purpose of tracing new shapes that are accurate. You can bring the template into a program such as Aldus FreeHand or directly into PageMaker, draw your own shapes based on the template, and then delete the template.

Producing the Report

PageMaker is best at preparing pages, and no word processor comes close to providing PageMaker's layout features and typographical controls. By using one program for both tasks, the complexity of having to keep track of multiple types of files by maintaining only a set of publication files is reduced. You also reduce the training that would be required for learning how to use more than one program. These benefits are useful when producing business reports.

PageMaker offers file management facilities including the ability to

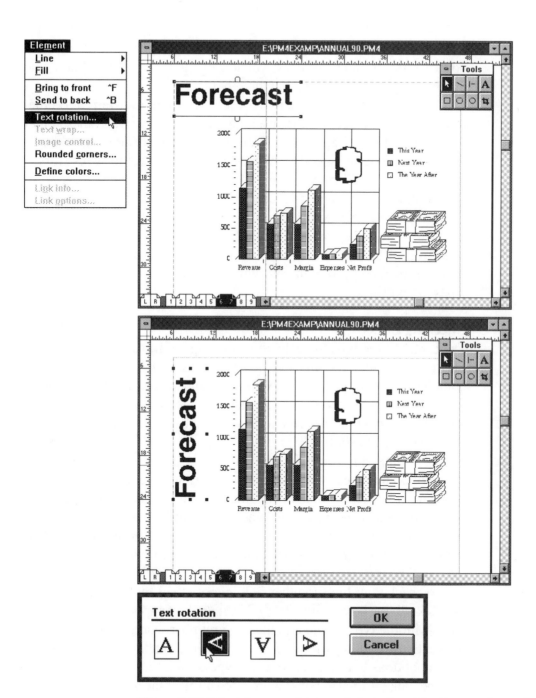

Figure 3-53. Select the text to be rotated, then choose the Text rotation option from the Element menu, and specify the angle (in 90-degree increments) for the rotation.

track revisions of text and graphics files used by PageMaker files, so that you can be sure that the latest version of the text, tables, charts, and graphics, have been included in the report.

As for exporting text, many reports have to be transferred to other locations or provided to other users in electronic form, and these other users may not have PageMaker. When exporting text from PageMaker's Story Editor, you can specify which word processing format to use for the text, and you can also export text in ASCII format, which is easier for telecommunications and file conversions. Thus, a report created in PageMaker could be exported to, say, a Microsoft Word text file, which can be transmitted by modem to another user and then incorporated into an entirely different publication. You can therefore use PageMaker as the central processing program, and with it create and use many different types of text files.

Checking Links

The Links dialog box, available by choosing the Links command in the File menu, offers file management features and lists each text and graphics file imported into a publication, indicating its file type and page in the layout. PageMaker forms a link to each imported text and graphics file so that changes to the original can optionally be passed automatically to the publication file.

For example, if you place in a publication file a Windows Metafile image of a table created in the Table Editor, and then later change that table and create a new image, PageMaker can automatically replace the older version with the newer one when you open the publication file. This active link between the publication file and the image file is accomplished with the Links feature and is available with any text or graphics file placed in a publication.

To check your links to other files, choose the Links command to see the Links dialog box (Figure 3-54). The linked files appear in alphabetical order with the type of file and the page number where it appears in the publication. Select any file and click the Link info button to see information, or Link options button to change the type of link.

The Link info dialog box (Figure 3-55) displays the path name, location, type of file, size, date and time it was placed in the publication, and the date and time of the last modification of the external linked file.

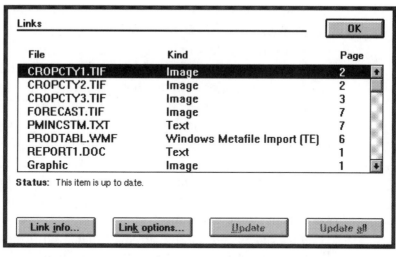

Figure 3-54. Use the Links command to display the Links dialog box, where you can establish active links with external files and check to see if a placed file is the most recent version.

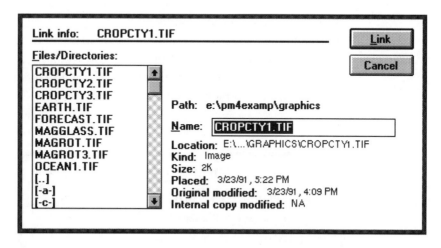

Figure 3-55. The Link info dialog box displays the path name, the location, the type of file, the size, the date and time it was placed in the publication, and the date and time of the last modification of the external linked file. You can update the link or change the linked file.

You can update the existing link with the Link button by selecting the same linked file. To re-establish links that have been broken (due to files being moved to other folders, or being renamed), or replace a link with a new link, change the linked file by selecting another file, then click the Link button.

The Link options dialog box (Figure 3-56) provides options for storing a copy of the file in the publication file, updating the file automatically, and displaying an alert message when automatically updating. With graphics and text created in the publication file, these options are grayed out. With graphics files, the linked file can be stored outside the PageMaker publication, making the publication files smaller. You have the choice to include the graphics inside the publication file, or keep them stored externally.

You can set up a publication so that if an original file is changed, PageMaker notifies you of the change in status and replaces the text or graphics element with the new version automatically. You have the option to set up a publication with automatic links, or just with notifications that original files have been revised so that you can update the links manually. Thus, you can keep the elements in a publication completely up to date automatically with the original files.

When the automatic update option is off, you have to update the link yourself with the Update button in the Links dialog box. After changing a file that is linked to the publication, the file appears in the Links dialog box with a link indicator next to its name (Figure 3-57). You can then

Figure 3-56. The Link options dialog box, called up from the Links dialog box after selecting a linked file, lets you store a copy in the publication file (or not), update the file automatically (or not), and provide an alert message when updating (or not). With no update options selected, you have to update the link yourself with the Update button in the Links dialog box.

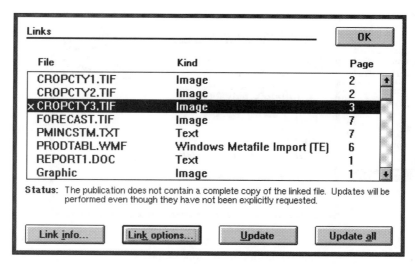

Figure 3-57. After changing a linked file and going back to PageMaker and running Links, the update symbol appears next to the changed file notifying you that it is not the most recent version. You can use the Update button to update the link.

update the link by clicking the Update button (or update all links at once with the Update all button).

You can decide in advance how you want your graphics files to be linked. Before placing the files, and without selecting any element, choose the Link options command from the Element menu. A dialog box appears (Figure 3-58) presenting the default settings for all text and graphics files to be linked to the publication. You can then set all graphics files to be stored outside the publication, all text files to be updated automatically, and so on.

Exporting Text

After creating text or importing text as a story, the story can be exported to a text or word processing file. The text of the report can be formatted in PageMaker, with font, size, and leading already set, and then exported with its formatting characteristics so that you don't lose the settings.

The exported file can also be brought into a PageMaker publication using Place and the Retain format option, and the text would still carry these formatting characteristics.

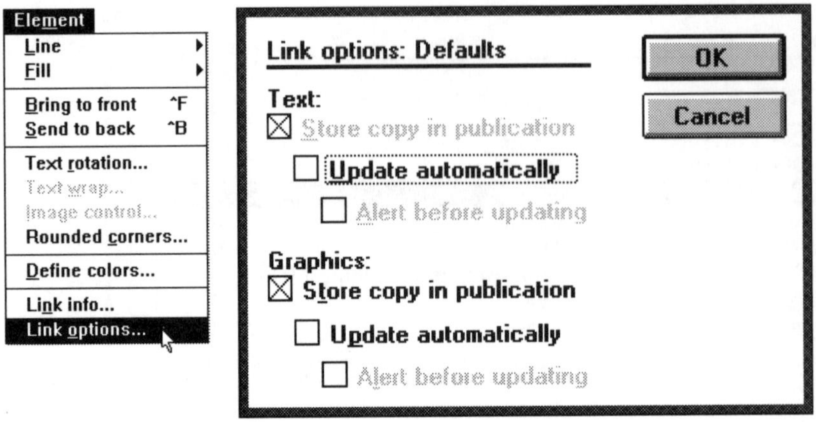

Element	
Line	▶
Fill	▶
Bring to front	^F
Send to back	^B
Text rotation...	
Text wrap...	
Image control...	
Rounded corners...	
Define colors...	
Link info...	
Link options...	

Link options: Defaults

OK

Cancel

Text:
☒ Store copy in publication
  ☐ Update automatically
    ☐ Alert before updating

Graphics:
☒ Store copy in publication

  ☐ Update automatically

    ☐ Alert before updating

Figure 3-58. Choose Link options before placing any files in order to set in advance the method of linking for your graphics files.

The Export command in the File menu is available when you click an insertion point in a story with the text tool, or when you open a story with the Edit story command. You can select an area of text to export, or export the entire story.

The export dialog box (Figure 3-59) provides a choice of word processor formats for the exported file (depending on which filters you've installed), and lets you export a selection of text or the entire story.

You can also export text with or without *tags*, which are style sheet names embedded in the text. The tags option is useful if you need to create ASCII text files and you want to preserve the style sheet assignments. PageMaker can place a text file containing tags and reassign the style sheet definitions. The book example later in this chapter shows how tags can be used.

Printing the Report: Using Different Devices

If you use the same printer with your business report that you specified as your target printer, you will obtain optimal results. However, it is often the case that the printer you are using now is not the same as the target printer for the final version of the report.

If you use the same *type* of printer (such as a PostScript printer) in both cases, there should be no problems with the output. For example, you may

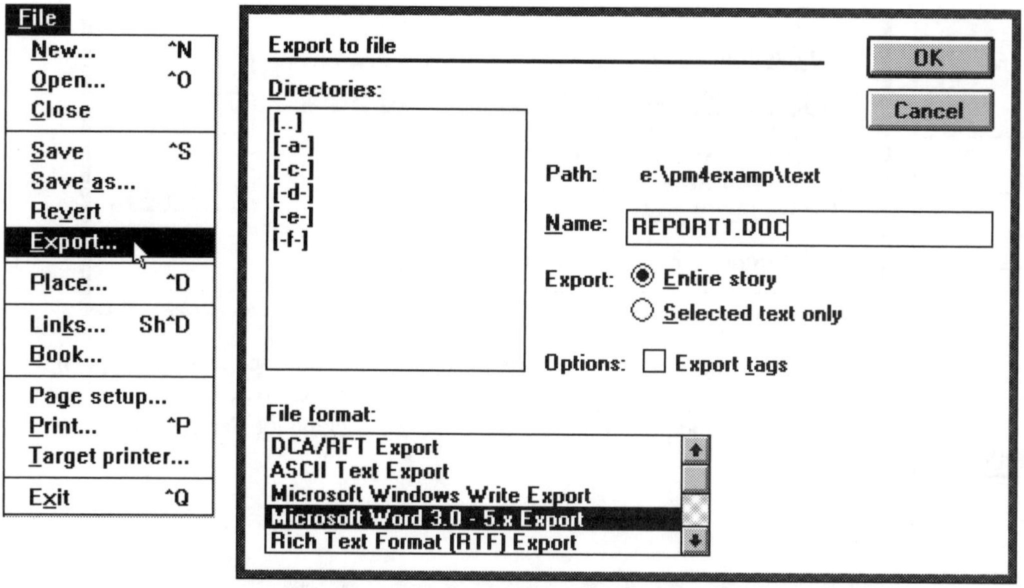

Figure 3-59. The Export dialog box lets you choose the word processor format for the exported file (depending on which filters you've installed), and lets you export a selection of text or the entire story, with or without tags (style sheet names embedded in the text).

have specified a high-resolution PostScript imagesetter as the target printer (Figure 3-60), but you want to print draft copies on a lower-resolution PostScript laser printer. Switching from one to the other is usually no problem.

Use the Print command in the File menu to change the printer and to start the print operation. In the Print window (Figure 3-61), you can select options such as printing the pages in reverse order, automatically collating the pages, printing thumbnail sketches of the pages for layout purposes, printing a range of pages, and printing crop marks so that the printing press operators can line up the pages. Click the Setup button to see the options for the type of printer already chosen as the target printer, and use the pop-up menu to display each printer model for that type of printer that has been installed for your system.

When you select the actual printer model, the paper options for that printer are displayed in the pop-up menus (Figure 3-62). For example,

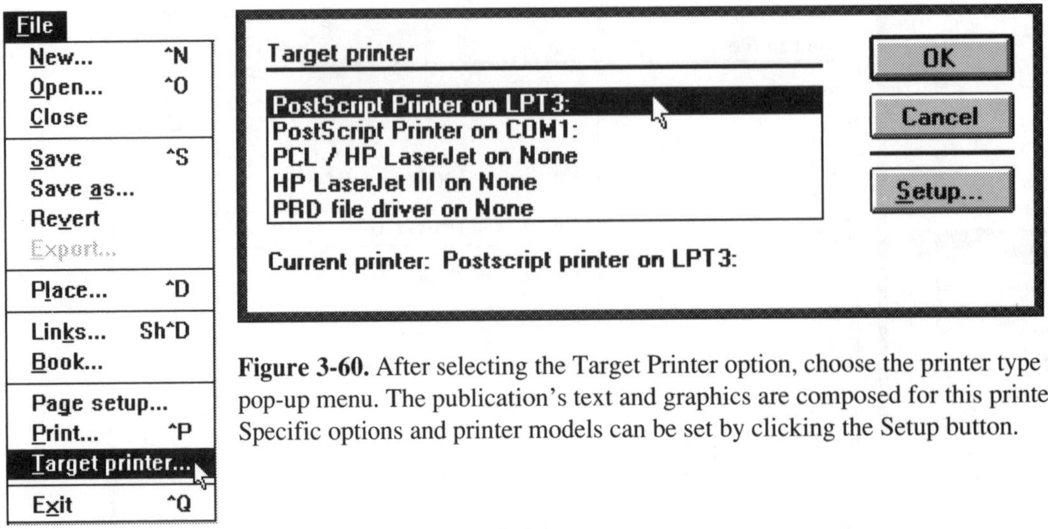

File

New...	^N
Open...	^O
Close	
Save	^S
Save as...	
Revert	
Export...	
Place...	^D
Links...	Sh^D
Book...	
Page setup...	
Print...	^P
Target printer...	
Exit	^Q

Target printer

PostScript Printer on LPT3:
PostScript Printer on COM1:
PCL / HP LaserJet on None
HP LaserJet III on None
PRD file driver on None

Current printer: Postscript printer on LPT3:

OK
Cancel
Setup...

Figure 3-60. After selecting the Target Printer option, choose the printer type in the pop-up menu. The publication's text and graphics are composed for this printer type. Specific options and printer models can be set by clicking the Setup button.

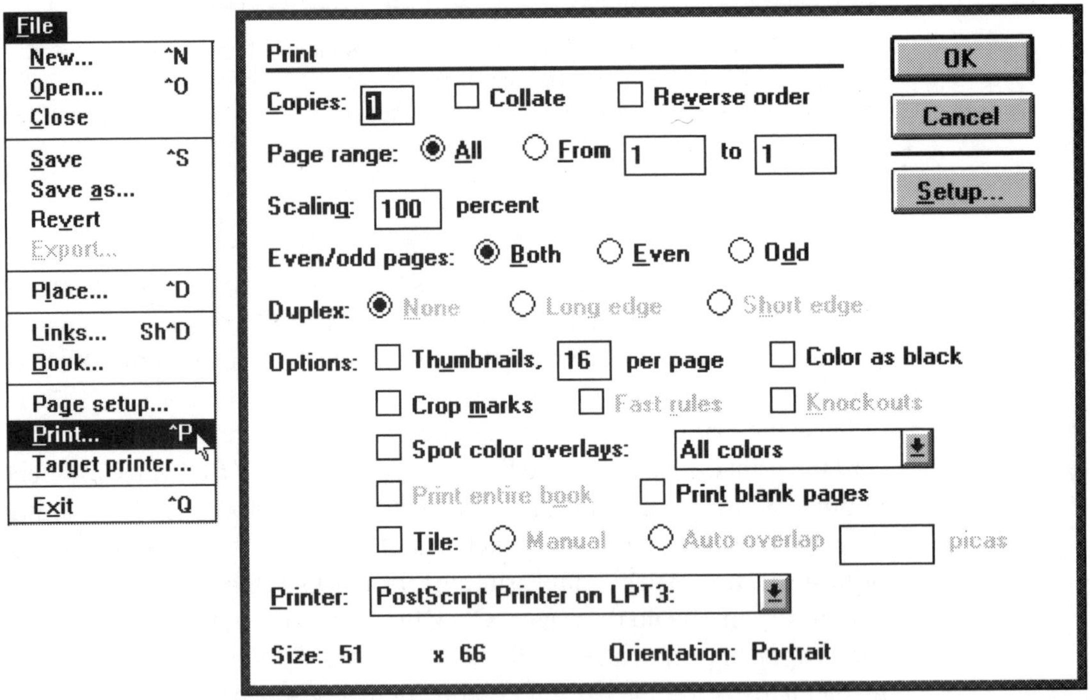

File

New...	^N
Open...	^O
Close	
Save	^S
Save as...	
Revert	
Export...	
Place...	^D
Links...	Sh^D
Book...	
Page setup...	
Print...	^P
Target printer...	
Exit	^Q

Print

Copies: 1   ☐ Collate   ☐ Reverse order

Page range: ⦿ All   ○ From 1   to 1

Scaling: 100 percent

Even/odd pages: ⦿ Both   ○ Even   ○ Odd

Duplex: ⦿ None   ○ Long edge   ○ Short edge

Options: ☐ Thumbnails, 16 per page   ☐ Color as black
☐ Crop marks   ☐ Fast rules   ☐ Knockouts
☐ Spot color overlays: All colors ▼
☐ Print entire book   ☐ Print blank pages
☐ Tile: ○ Manual   ○ Auto overlap [   ] picas

Printer: PostScript Printer on LPT3: ▼

Size: 51   x 66   Orientation: Portrait

OK
Cancel
Setup...

Figure 3-61. After choosing the Print command, click the Setup button to change the specific printer model and options.

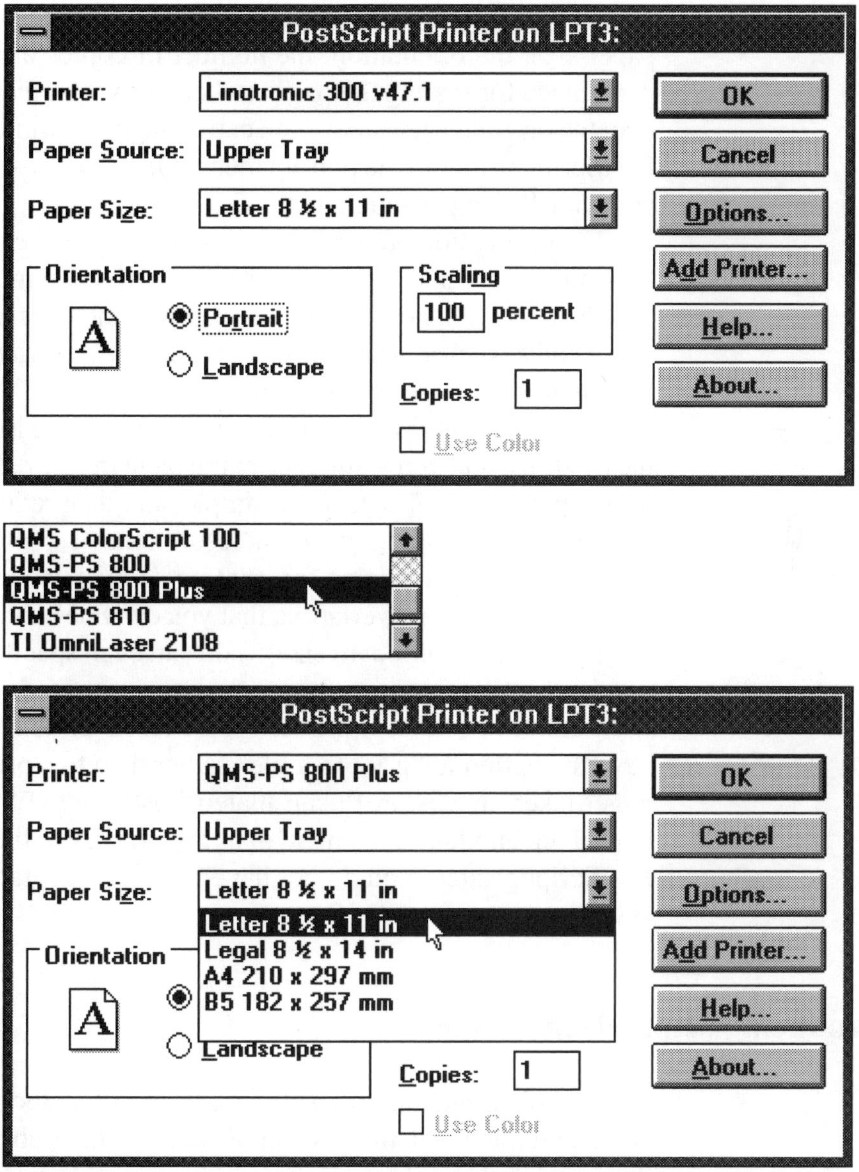

Figure 3-62. You can choose a specific model of printer, and then make choices among the options for that printer, in the Setup window.

with the Linotronic PostScript-based imagesetter you can change the paper size, the orientation, the number of copies of each page, and the percentage for scaling the pages (whether to print them smaller or larger than the original page size). You can change the printer model to another PostScript printer in the pop-up menu. Other options, such as paper size, are available in pop-up menus.

The orientation option lets you print tall or wide pages. The orientation you choose in this dialog box has no effect on the page design—it is simply a convenience for printing pages on devices that have very wide paper paths (such as a Linotronic). To change the orientation for the page design, use the Page setup command.

Scaling is useful when you design pages that are larger or smaller than the final size and you want to print the page in its final size. You can also print a page at 200% size, for example, and then reduce it with a camera to regular size, gaining twice the resolution.

Tiling is also available for printing an oversize image on a standard laser printer with an overlap, so that you can line up the pages to form the large page (up to billboard size). You can even specify the amount of the overlap for tiling.

With the PostScript printer-type chosen as your target printer, you have the option to "print to a file" rather than to a printer (Figure 3-63). PageMaker creates an Encapsulated PostScript (EPS) file that can be placed in another document that imports EPS files, or output to a PostScript printer. You do not have to have a printer connected to your system.

Producing Manuals and Books

The technical manual, the software tutorial handbook, the coffee-table book, and the novel are all examples of lengthy publications that can be produced by PageMaker. The Aldus PageMaker manual itself was produced with PageMaker, as was this book.

In many such projects the goal is to produce a publication in which all of the pages have a similar format, but contain certain differences, such as illustrations, photos, or footnotes. All such publications can be produced

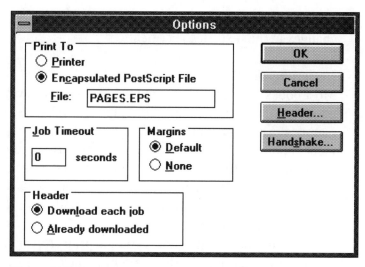

Figure 3-63. You always have the option to create an Encapsulated PostScript file to use with any PostScript printer, whether or not you have a printer connected to your computer.

with the techniques described in this chapter for business reports, and with the techniques described next.

It is very important to keep the design of a manual or book simple for many reasons. One important reason is the need to attract and hold the reader's attention without too many distractions. Another reason, particularly for technical manuals, is the need to streamline the production process to be able to produce many pages periodically and to update those pages quickly.

It is not only possible to produce a book with PageMaker, it may be the preferred method, so that the book's pages can be flexible in layout. Books can be produced in such a way that they are visually more interesting and more readable, especially in the case of a book that contains many illustrations (as this book does).

Books are like manuals in that both involve the use of long text files, are usually separated into chapters, and use a single column on each page (although some large books are laid out with two columns). A book is usually completely written before it is produced. In the case of some books, the ability to update the pages at the very last minute and save those changes in the text files is critical.

Designing the Pages

Most books and manuals are not 8.5 by 11 inches, which is the standard page size in the United States for letters, newsletters, and some technical manuals. Although you can lay out a smaller book size (such as 6.5 by 9 inches) on pages that are standard size (8.5 by 11 inches), and you can adjust margin settings to create an image area the size of the book's pages, it is much better to change the page size in the Page setup dialog box (displayed when you start a new publication file with New, or by choosing Page setup in the File menu).

With the changed page size, you can print crop marks on the 8.5 by 11-inch paper (which print outside the defined page size). *Crop marks* are marks recognized by the volume printer or print shop as the marks that define the edges of the page. They are printed automatically by PageMaker if you select them from the Print dialog box.

Start a new publication file for each chapter of the book or manual, and change the default settings for the page to have the dimensions of the book pages. This book, for example, was set to have a custom page that is 45 picas wide by 55 picas and 6 points high, with tall orientation and double-sided pages. The image area is defined by margins that are 4 picas and 6 points in from the binding, in from the edges of the page, down from the top of the page, and up from the bottom (Figure 3-64).

The master pages for this book (Figure 3-65) define the layout for all left and right pages. A horizontal guide is used for placing text at the top of the page, and a different page number header is used for the left and right pages. The layout is set to one column, but with a vertical rule guide on the left master page at the 33-pica marker, and another vertical rule guide on the right master page at the 12-pica mark. Vertical rule guides help in the placement of icons next to the body of the text, which will be indented.

A rectangle with None set for line style and pattern fill appears at the top of each master page, to reserve space between the headers and the body text for auto-flowing the text. Both master pages have the same general layout.

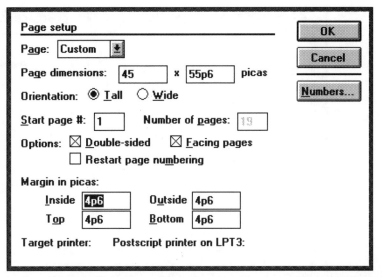

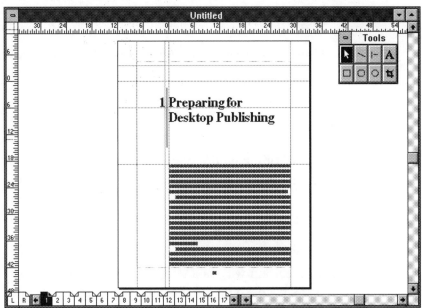

Figure 3-64. The Page setup for this book, which was produced with PageMaker.

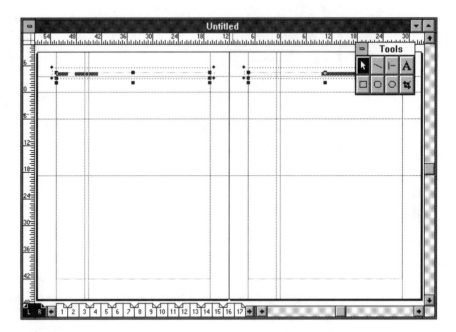

Figure 3-65. The master pages for this book, which is a one-column layout with a vertical ruler guide that defines the body text indent and narrow space for icons and menus. Rectangles with no line style and no pattern fill appear at the top of the master pages to reserve space for auto-flowing the body text.

All of the guides on the master pages are displayed on each regular page. You can modify them on each page without affecting the master page guides or the guides on other pages. To restore guides on a page to the guides used on the master pages, use the Copy master guides command in the Page menu.

You may want to save a version of a publication with guides and rulers set a certain way as a template so that you can start new chapters with blank pages, but with the page layout and ruler guides in place.

Similar to the Aldus manuals for PageMaker, you can design with a custom page setting of 48 picas wide by 52 picas tall, with a tall orientation and double-sided pages. The image area can be defined by margins that are 6 picas in from the binding, 5 picas in from the edge of the page, 1 pica and 6 points down from the top of the page, and 1 pica and 6 points up from the bottom (Figure 3-66).

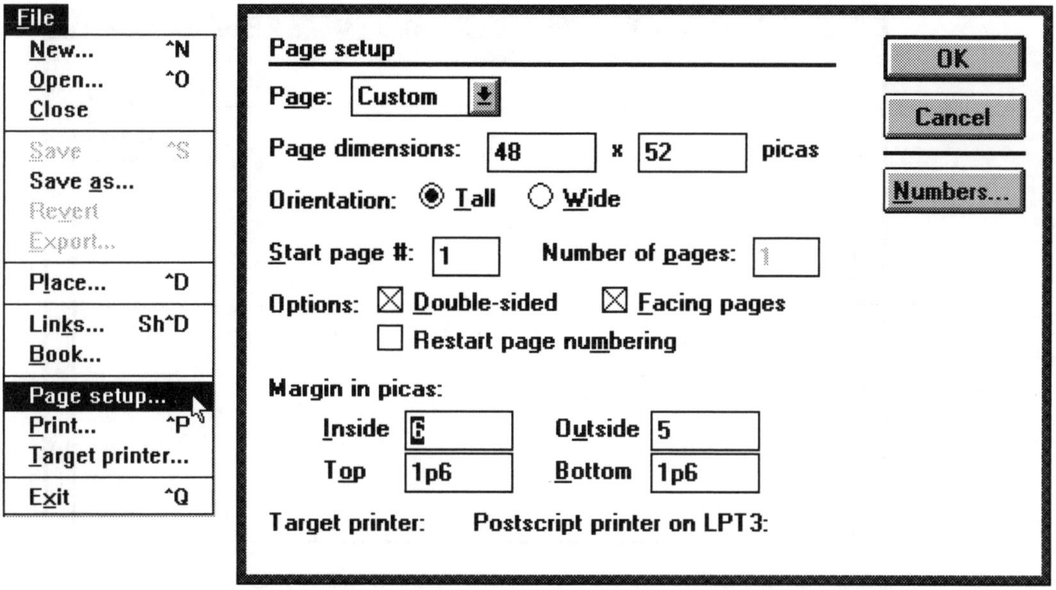

File	
New...	^N
Open...	^O
Close	
Save	^S
Save **a**s...	
Revert	
Export...	
Place...	^D
Lin**k**s...	Sh^D
Book...	
Page setup...	
Print...	^P
Target printer...	
E**x**it	^Q

Page setup

Page: [Custom ▼]

Page dimensions: [48] × [52] picas

Orientation: ● **T**all   ○ **W**ide

Start page #: [1]   Number of **p**ages: [1]

Options: ☒ **D**ouble-sided   ☒ **F**acing pages
         ☐ Restart page nu**m**bering

Margin in picas:
   Inside [6]   O**u**tside [5]
   T**o**p [1p6]   **B**ottom [1p6]

Target printer: Postscript printer on LPT3:

[OK]
[Cancel]
[Numbers...]

Figure 3-66. The Page setup for a technical manual that is about the same size as the PageMaker manual.

In the master pages (Figure 3-67), specify a two-column format with 1 pica space between the columns. If the guides are not locked (see the Options menu), you can drag the column guides to where you want them (one column for body text, the other for special tips, menus, icons, and so on).

Producing Text

In the report example, you learned how to use the Story Editor to write the entire report, or to import the report text from a text file. In single-person book and manual projects, PageMaker's Story Editor may be the best choice for writing, editing, and producing the project. You can divide chapters into separate publication files.

In multiple-person projects that require a great deal of passing information around, you can use PageMaker's Story Editor to create the text and pages of the book or manual and then export the text of each chapter into word processing files.

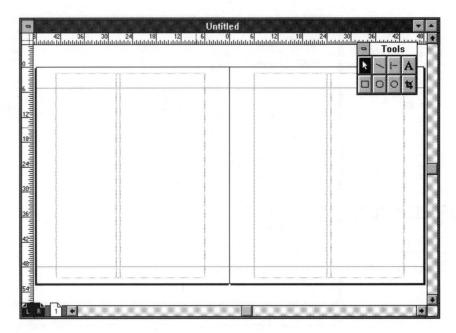

Figure 3-67. The master pages for a technical manual with a layout similar to the Aldus manuals for PageMaker.

PageMaker has a close relationship to Microsoft Word and other word processing programs, such as Word for Windows, Ami Professional (Lotus), and WordPerfect. PageMaker recognizes formatting, and with Word in particular it recognizes Word's style sheet definitions and index entries. In addition, PageMaker exports text, including style sheet definitions, to Word files. PageMaker also exports formatted text into a variety of other formats, including WordPerfect and IBM's DCA format.

Microsoft Word was used to create the manuscript of this book, and styles were assigned to sections of the text before placing the text in PageMaker. The style sheet definitions were edited in PageMaker, and include font, size, style (italic, bold, etc.), leading, paragraph spacing, tab settings, indents, and even color. When you change a style sheet definition, all sections of text defined by that style sheet change automatically to adopt the new definition.

When preparing text for a book or manual using another word processor, you can format the text in advance to have italic and bold styles, with the tabs already set, so that you can bring tables and formatted text into PageMaker with styles intact (using the Retain format option in the Place dialog box).

Use a tab if you want to indent the first line of each paragraph. (In Microsoft Word, you can use the first line indent for a paragraph format instead.) PageMaker recognizes the left margin setting as a starting point, but disregards the right margin. (PageMaker breaks lines according to the column settings.) PageMaker also recognizes the first-line indent of a paragraph in Microsoft Word and other word processors (see Appendix A), whether that indent is positioned to the left of the left margin (a *hanging indent*) or to the right (a regular indent).

If your text is not preformatted, you can still do some preparation work, even in an ASCII text file, that will help speed up the process. When you press the Return key in a word processor, you generate a carriage return. Use carriage returns only at the ends of paragraphs and fixed lines. Do not use extra spaces (such as the extra word space after sentences, which is usually inserted by typists).

In the Place dialog box, select the Convert quotes option so that PageMaker converts any instance of a double-hyphen to an em dash (–), and converts quotation marks and single quote marks into the proper open and closed quote symbols.

ASCII text brought in without formatting takes on the characteristics of the Type specs dialog box (in the Type menu). It makes sense to choose the text font, size, style, and leading before placing the text. If you place the text first, choose the text tool, click somewhere in the text, employ the Select all command (Command A) to highlight all of the text, and make changes in the Type specs dialog box.

The need to make last-minute changes is prevalent in book publishing because the printing and distribution process takes so long that many books are out of date before they show up on bookstore shelves. The export feature makes the updating process a lot easier if you make last-minute changes to the text in PageMaker. Books can be archived in PageMaker publication files, as well as in word processing files. You can export a story from PageMaker as a text-only file that can be read by any word processor. With the Export tags option in the Place dialog box, you can export the style sheet names as tags embedded in the text.

Style Sheet Definitions

This book uses a design in which the body text is indented from the left margin, while the first-level subheadings are flush with the left margin. Second-level subheadings are designed to be indented along with the body text. You could select all the body text and change its indent in the Indents/tabs dialog box, but this would take too much time for a lengthy book or manual.

It is much better and faster to define one style sheet for the body text, and a different style sheet for each of the the level one and level two subheadings. The text should be placed to fill the entire width of the page. By changing the style sheet definition of the body text to have an indent, you can indent the body of the text while leaving first-level headings out flush to the left margin.

It is preferable to assign the style sheet to the body text while you are writing and editing the body text. You can use the Story Editor to assign style sheet definitions. For example, if a Normal (or Body text) style is already defined, you can assign it to the body text in the Story Editor window. First, select one or more paragraphs (Figure 3-68), then choose the Normal style in the Style pop-up menu in the Type menu. We usually define a Normal style and then use that style as a basis for defining other styles.

Style sheets can be defined in PageMaker, or in a word processing program such as Microsoft Word. To define a style sheet in PageMaker, choose the Define styles command in the Type menu. A dialog box appears, listing the already-defined styles and a button to Edit any style sheet definition as well as a button to create New style sheets (Figure 3-69). When you click the New button, a dialog box appears for you to type the name of the style sheet (Figure 3-70). You can then click the Type button to set the type specifications, the Para button to set the paragraph specifications, the Tabs button for indents and tab settings, and the Hyph button for hyphenation controls.

You can edit any style sheet definition by clicking the style sheet name in the Define styles dialog box and then clicking the Edit button. This method was used to change the Normal style sheet definition to have an indent of 7 picas and 6 points (Figure 3-71). After clicking OK in the definition box and in the Define styles dialog box, the body text is indented throughout the entire publication file.

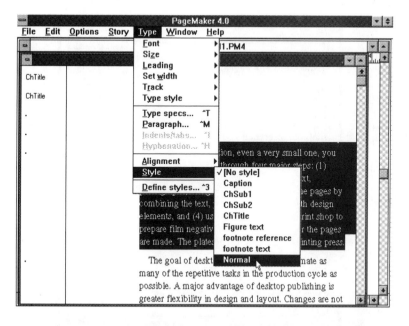

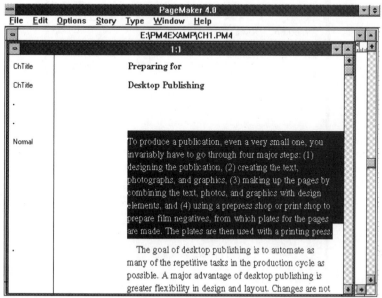

Figure 3-68. Select paragraphs to assign a style sheet definition, and use the Style pop-up menu in the Type menu.

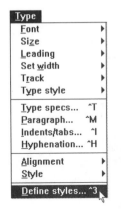
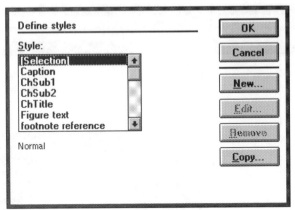

Figure 3-69. Use Define styles, and click the New button, to define a new style sheet.

Figure 3-70. Provide a name for the style sheet, then click the Type button to set the type specifications for the style sheet.

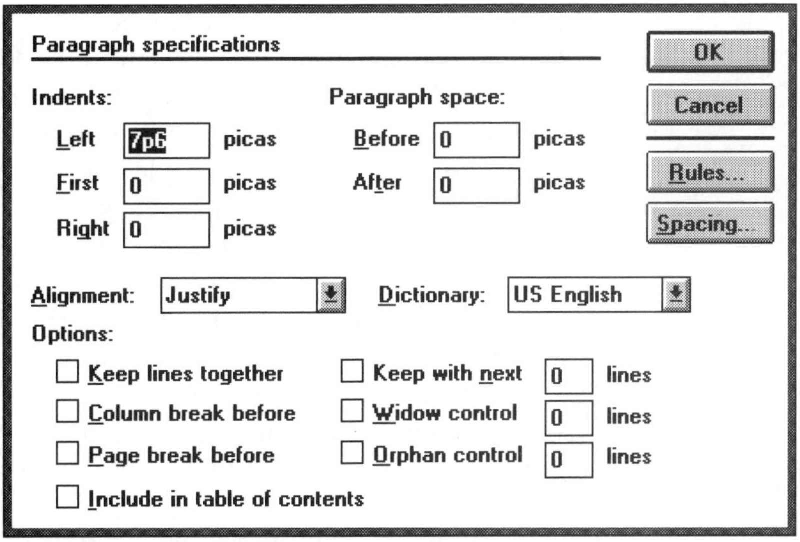

Figure 3-71. The Paragraph button shows the paragraph specifications (in this case for the new style sheet, which is based on Normal with its indent of 7 picas and 6 points).

When you create a new style sheet definition, PageMaker asks for its name, and you can base the style's definition on another style, and still add more unique characteristics.

For example, if you create a style sheet called Special, and base it on the Normal style sheet, you can change the font in the Normal definition and the change will also occur in the Special definition. You could then change Special without affecting Normal.

If you are placing Word-formatted text with style sheets, place the text with the Retain format option and the Convert quotes option turned on. Do not turn on the Read tags option, since Word does not require tags. With Word, PageMaker imports only the style sheets that are used in the text. Style sheets that were defined in Word but not applied to text are not imported. After a style is imported, PageMaker displays an asterisk (*) next to the style name in the Styles palette for each imported style.

If you are placing a text file that contains embedded tags, and you have already defined the style sheets in the PageMaker document using the same names as the tags, use the Read tags option.

When assigning style sheet names to the text, it helps to display the *style palette* (a floating tool box of style names). To do so, select the Style palette option in the Windows menu. The style sheet names appear in a scrollable box (Figure 3-72) on the page so that you can easily select text with the text tool and then select a style name (Figure 3-73). In this manner, you can go through the text body, select the headings and subheadings, and assign them a style sheet defined to not have an indent (so that they are not indented with the rest of the body text).

Style sheets are an important innovation because you can change the formatting of your entire publication by changing a few style sheet definitions. The use of style sheets is another reason why a template file is valuable—it contains predefined style sheets that can be assigned to incoming text without any need to remember the specifications of a design.

If you are using Microsoft Word, assign styles with the same names to the text so that when you bring the text into PageMaker, you can change the style sheet definitions in PageMaker. The style names should define the font, size, style, and leading, and include tab settings, indents, and any other formatting characteristics that are appropriate. The simple assignment of style names to appropriate sections of text is all you need to do, because you can edit the style definitions in PageMaker. The more you can set in advance, however, the faster the production process will be. Use the Retain format option in the Place dialog box to bring Word-formatted text into PageMaker with style sheets included.

Using Style Sheet Tags

If your word processor does not offer style sheets that are recognized by PageMaker, you might as well not waste time formatting the text in a word processor, because you want to control all formatting (for long documents such as a book) by using style sheets. You can create the style sheets in PageMaker later and place unformatted text, so *don't* use the Retain format option.

However, you can still speed up the process immensely by assigning style sheet definition *tags*, which are the names of the style sheets enclosed in angle brackets (such as **<ChSub1>**). Tags are embedded into any text file in order to define a section of text that follows it. Tags must be placed at the beginning of a paragraph, and a paragraph that is not

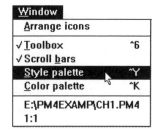

Figure 3-72. The Style palette for assigning style sheet definitions to selections of text. You can use it either in layout view or in Story Editor view. Scroll the list to see more style names.

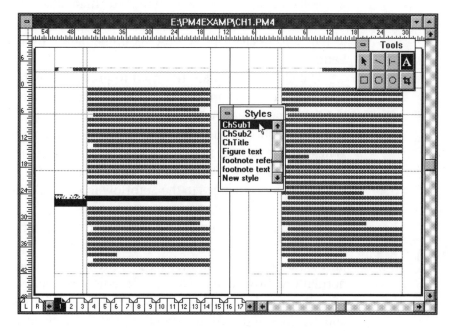

Figure 3-73. Select the ChSub1 style so that level-one subheadings are not indented with the body text.

tagged adopts the formatting settings of the previous paragraph.

With tags in the text file, you can use the Read tags option with the Place command to import the text and assign the tags to style sheets already defined with the same names in PageMaker. (You must first define style sheets with those names in the PageMaker document.) Tags are not necessary when using a word processor with style sheets that are recognized by PageMaker (such as Microsoft Word).

To transfer text from one PageMaker publication file to another, you can export the text with tags, so that when you place the text in the other publication file, the tags correspond to predefined style sheets (with the same names) in the new publication file. The new file's definitions take effect on the tagged sections of text.

Placing Text with Autoflow

The quickest way to place text is to use the Autoflow option. PageMaker lets you mix automatic text flowing with manual text flowing, so that you always have control. Even when text is flowing automatically from page to page, you can stop the process immediately by pressing the mouse button.

The chapter template file used to produce this book was set up for using the Autoflow option. This is why we placed blank rectangles, with the Text wrap option, in the master pages as described earlier—so that the Autoflow option would flow text below the rectangles. A ruler guide is provided to guide the placement icon into place on the first page. Switch the Autoflow option to on in the Options menu (Figure 3-74), and the placement icon changes to the autoflow icon. Click the autoflow icon to start the flow process.

PageMaker automatically pours text from column to column, page to page, stopping when it runs out of text in the file. You can also stop the process by clicking the mouse, in which case the icon changes to the normal text flow icon, ready for placement manually.

When the Autoflow option is on, PageMaker jumps over existing text and graphics and continues pouring text. You can also switch to manual text flow by pressing the Control key, or to semiautomatic text flow by pressing the Shift key. With semiautomatic text flow, PageMaker stops at the bottom of each column, but leaves the icon on the screen ready for you to place the next column. To switch back to automatic text flow, release the Shift key.

You can place text almost as rapidly as the fully automatic method by using the semi-autoflow feature, because it lets you place text in the wide column of each page without having to click the bottom handle. (Select the Autoflow option and hold down the Shift key when placing.)

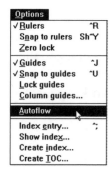

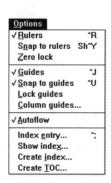

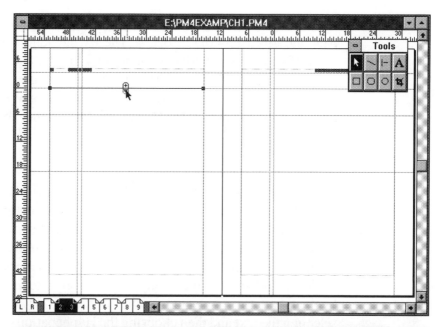

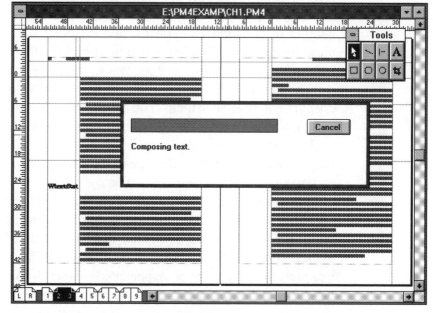

Figure 3-74. Click the text autoflow icon to place text with the Autoflow option, which continues to place text (creating pages as it goes) until the story is finished.

After placing text with the Autoflow option, you can go back to any page and adjust any column of text. The text elements remain linked in one story. If you use Cut with the pointer tool to cut a text element, and then use Paste to paste it somewhere on the page or pasteboard, that element is cut from the story and turned into a separate story. To keep a story linked, move the elements by dragging them rather than using Cut and Paste.

Adjusting Hyphenation and Spacing

The setting of type is a complicated process of deciding how many words can be fit on one line. PageMaker does everything automatically, but you can control the way type looks by adjusting certain factors, such as the amount of hyphenation, the way certain words are hyphenated, and the amount of spacing between words and between letters.

To avoid having too many hyphens in a row, you can turn off hyphenation for a selected section of text. This is accomplished by selecting the text and then choosing the Hyphenation command from the Type menu (Figure 3-75). You can turn hyphenation on or off, limit the number of consecutive hyphens, and establish a hyphenation zone (3 picas by default). With hyphenation turned on, PageMaker can decide how to hyphenate words in three ways.

The first way, Manual only, hyphenates only words with discretionary hyphens inserted in them. You can insert a discretionary hyphen when editing text in PageMaker by typing Control-hyphen (typing hyphen by itself inserts a real hyphen that prints every time). Discretionary hyphens only appear in print or on the screen if the word falls at the end of a line and manual hyphenation is turned on.

The second way, Manual plus dictionary, hyphenates words according to hyphenation breaks stored in the hyphenation dictionary, as well as words with discretionary hyphens. You can add new hyphenated words to the dictionary with the Add button, so that PageMaker remembers how you wanted the word to be hyphenated (Figure 3-76). You can add new words to the dictionary or change the way existing words are hyphenated. Type a new word into the Word entry box, and use tilde symbols (~) to indicate the hyphen locations. You can rank the locations by using the least number of tildes in the location that is most preferable, and the most

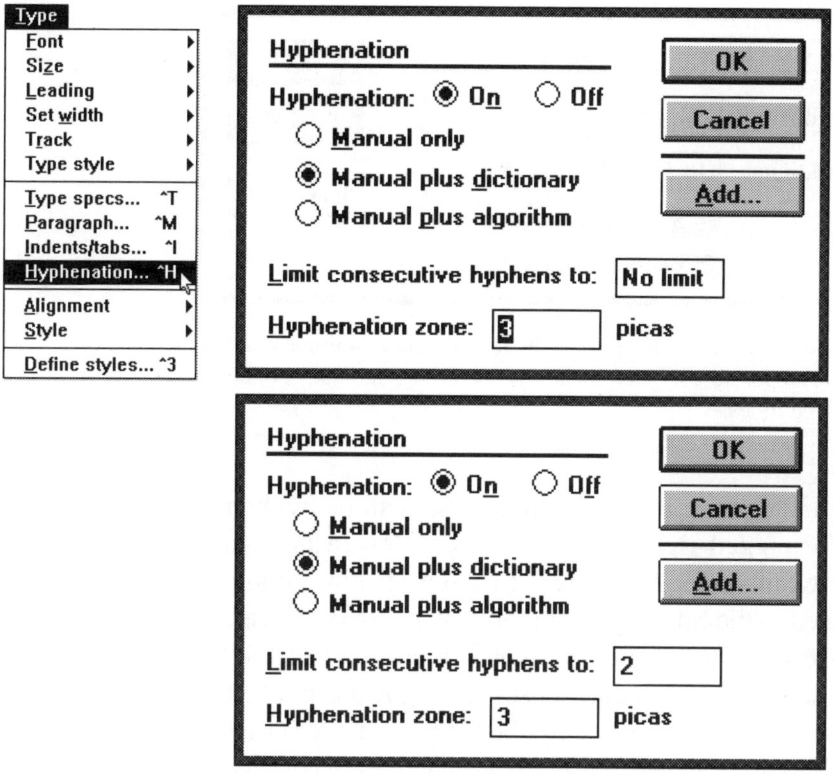

Figure 3-75. The Hyphenation dialog box has an option for turning the automatic hyphenation feature on or off. You can also limit the number of consecutive hyphens (this example limits them to two).

number of tildes in the location for the least preferable.

The third way, Manual plus algorithm, provides the most hyphenation. Discretionary hyphens are used, the dictionary is consulted, and algorithms are also used to insert hyphens in words that fall at the ends of lines.

You can limit the number of consecutive hyphens and dashes in a paragraph to prevent the ladder effect of stacked hyphens and dashes. Enter a number or the words **No limit**. The hyphenation zone measures the end-of-line space in which hyphenation should occur—the number 3 indicates 3 picas in from the right margin. Any word that starts before this

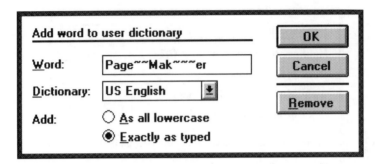

Figure 3-76. Add a new word to the hyphenation dictionary. The tilde symbol indicates a possible hyphen location—two tildes indicate a better hyphen location than three tildes.

zone and doesn't fall within that space can be hyphenated.

For ragged-right (unjustified) text, PageMaker first applies the desired word spacing and built-in letter spacing amounts, which can be changed in the Spacing dialog box available from the Paragraph window (Figure 3-77). It then uses the hyphenation zone to determine if hyphenation is needed. A larger zone causes the right margin to be more ragged; a smaller zone causes more hyphenation and a less ragged look.

You can change the word spacing values to get rid of the river of white effect that can occur with justified text (rivers of white seem to flow down the page). Spacing changes can be applied to an entire story or to one or more selected paragraphs. For optimal spacing for justified text, leave hyphenation on and set the word spacing range at 50% for minimum, 100% for desired, and 200% for maximum. Leave the letter spacing at 5% for minimum, 0% for desired, and 25% for maximum. Remember that narrower ranges of word spacing cause more hyphenation to occur. Letter spacing, by comparison, should be as close to zero as possible, which is the font designer's optimal spacing.

Letter spacing (the space between letters) is derived from information built into each font about the width of the characters (called the *pen advance*, which is the distance from the left edge of a character to the start of the next character). It changes from character to character, from size to size, and from font to font. PageMaker tries to use Desired spacing but will stay within the range to vary the spacing for justification. Word spacing is based on the size of a spaceband in that particular font and size (the

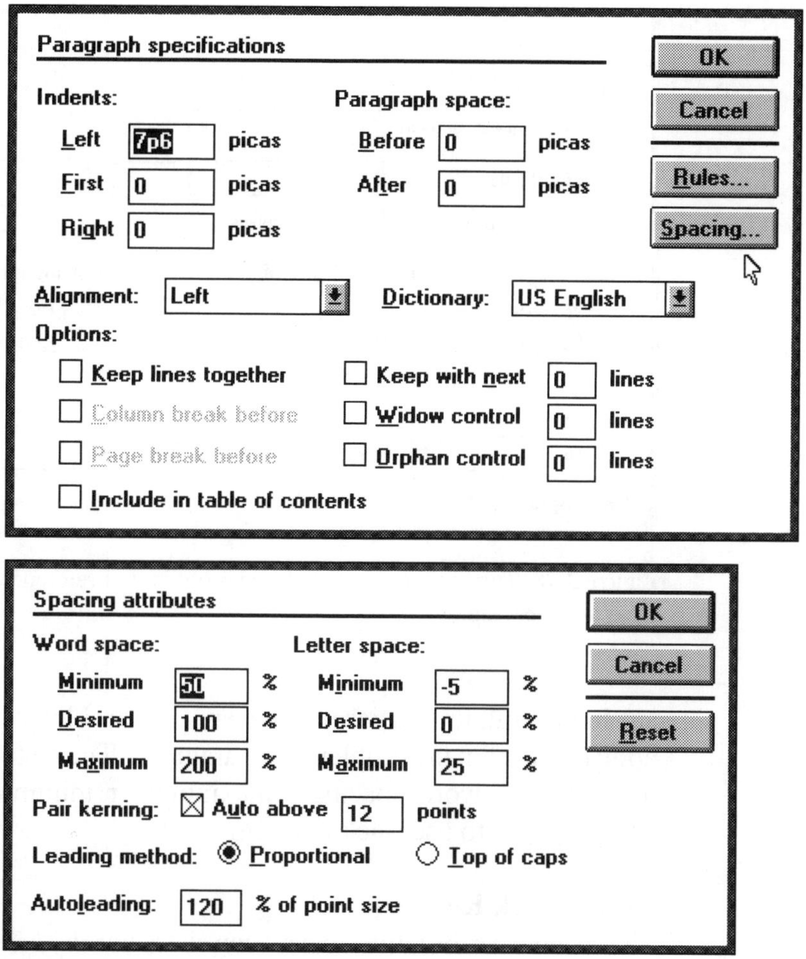

Paragraph specifications

Indents:

Paragraph space:

Left [7p6] picas   Before [0] picas

First [0] picas   After [0] picas

Right [0] picas

OK

Cancel

Rules...

Spacing...

Alignment: [Left ▼]   Dictionary: [US English ▼]

Options:

☐ Keep lines together   ☐ Keep with next [0] lines

☐ Column break before   ☐ Widow control [0] lines

☐ Page break before   ☐ Orphan control [0] lines

☐ Include in table of contents

Spacing attributes

Word space: Letter space:

Minimum [50] %   Minimum [-5] %

Desired [100] %   Desired [0] %

Maximum [200] %   Maximum [25] %

OK

Cancel

Reset

Pair kerning: ☒ Auto above [12] points

Leading method: ● Proportional   ○ Top of caps

Autoleading: [120] % of point size

Figure 3-77. The Spacing dialog box, available by clicking the Spacing button in the Paragraph window, lets you change the word and letter spacing values used to set type.

space from pressing the spacebar on the keyboard).

It is sometimes hard to see where spacing problems may occur, so you can have PageMaker notify you of spacing problems. Turn on the Loose/tight lines option in the Preferences dialog box (Figure 3-78), so that PageMaker can highlight any text where justification has pushed word or letter spacing outside the acceptable limits.

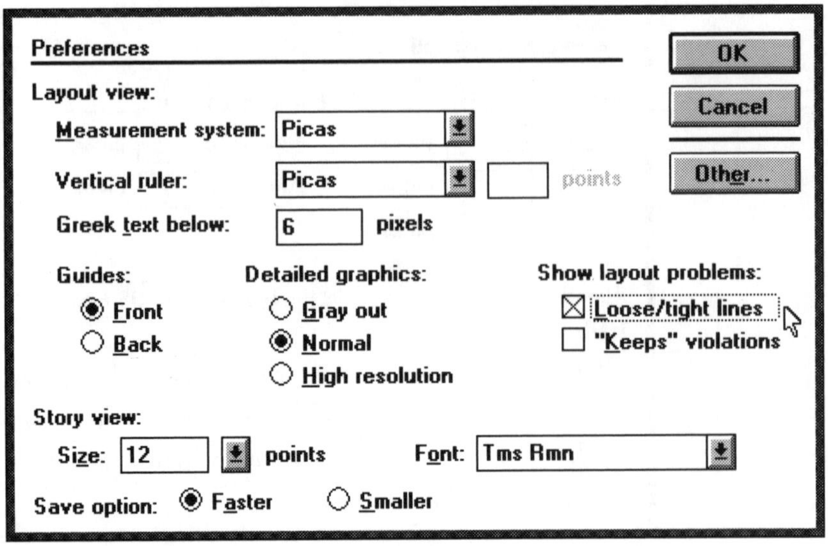

Figure 3-78. Turn on the Loose/tight lines option in Preferences to display problem areas with spacing.

In general, it is easier to solve spacing problems by turning hyphenation on or off in the problematic paragraph. The next easiest operation is to adjust the word spacing's maximum or minimum in the selected paragraph, or to use track kerning.

Using Track Kerning

The spacing can be adjusted between characters by *kerning* the characters. PageMaker offers several ways to change the spacing between selected letters: spacing controls (the previous section), automatic pair kerning, manual kerning, and track kerning. Manual kerning is for adjusting two characters closer together or farther apart, and is described in Chapter 4 (in the fancy titles discussion). It is unlikely that you would need to use manual kerning techniques with a lengthy document.

With automatic pair kerning turned on, PageMaker kerns character pairs that have been specified by the font designer (P., To, Tr, Ta, Tu, Tw, Te, Ty, Wa, WA, We, we, Wo, Ya, Yo, and yo are common pairs). By default, this option is turned on for text above 12 points. You can turn it off, or change the minimum point size, in the Spacing dialog box shown in the previous section.

Track kerning is a method of deriving the appropriate kerning amount by calculating along a curve in order to obtain less space between characters at high point sizes and more space between characters at low point sizes. Track kerning is supplied because linear-style kerning (in which you reduce the space between letters proportionately from low to high point sizes) can cause too much space to occur between letters at high point sizes and too little space at low point sizes.

You can apply track kerning to a section of text or to an entire story (by using Select all first). To apply track kerning, select the text (or Select all) and choose the tracking method from the Track pop-up menu in the Type menu (Figure 3-79). PageMaker provides five *tracks* (standard adjustment curves) to choose from that are derived from tables of kern values for specific fonts. The Normal track reduces the space for high point sizes and enlargens the space for small point sizes, but has little effect on median sizes. The other tracks (Very loose, Very tight, Loose, and Tight) are generally used for special effects with titles, as shown in Chapter 4.

Producing Graphics

Technical manuals usually require many illustrations comprised of line art. Drawings of equipment and schematics are called *line art* because they consist of lines, curves, and geometric shapes, without rough edges and blurred details. You would use a drawing program, rather than a painting program, so that the fine lines and curves will be reproduced with the highest possible resolution (and, therefore, the highest quality). You should create the graphics at the size that is most comfortable for you and most accurate in detail; draw-type graphics can be scaled in PageMaker to any size after they are drawn.

Technical manuals may also include photographs of equipment, which can be scanned into the computer using a desktop scanner. Existing line art can also be scanned to turn it into electronic form, but scanned images are paint-type graphics and are subject to the same restrictions as paint-type graphics (described in Chapter 1). You will obtain the best results from scaling scanned images if you use PageMaker's built-in scaling percentages (by holding down the Control key while scaling).

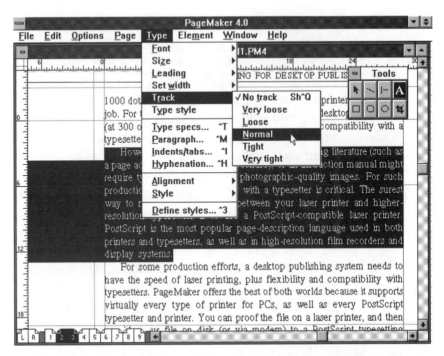

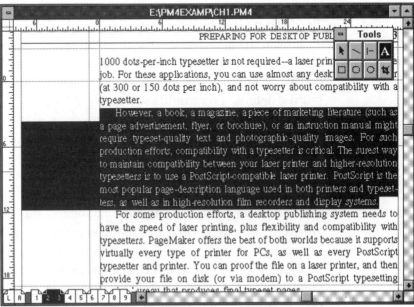

Figure 3-79. Select the text, and choose a form of track kerning to adjust the space between characters.

Books usually have all types of graphics, including gray-scale photos. It is still rare for books and manuals to use color photographs, but not so rare to use spot color. (Color is described in Chapter 4).

With scanned images and paint-type graphics, hold down the Control key while scaling them to fit the page, to use PageMaker's built-in optimal sizes for the selected printer (also hold down the Shift key to retain the same image proportions). Be sure to choose the right printer first in the Target Printer dialog box.

If you use Microsoft Word or another word processing program that provides automatic footnotes, you may find it useful to type figure captions as numeric footnotes, so that when PageMaker places the files, the captions (acting as footnotes) end up at the end of the story. You can then click the text element handles to move the captions into new positions alongside the figures. The numbered references in the text are intact, as are the numbered captions.

An alternate way is to store the captions in a separate file and place that file alongside the page in the empty pasteboard area. You can, of course, type the captions directly into PageMaker in layout view or in Story Editor view. Keep them linked rather than as separate captions, so that you can export all captions into one file. After placing an illustration that requires a caption, drag the captions block and click its handle to leave only one caption in place, and then place the rest of the caption block back where it was on the pasteboard. Continue with each figure until you have used all of the captions.

A large publication (such as a manual and a book) usually contains references to the publication's illustrations and photos, and you should place the illustrations and photos as close to their references as possible. However, how do you know where the references will occur without placing all of the text? Although you would start a short publication (such as a newsletter, brochure, or magazine article) by placing the graphics first, you probably would not start a manual or a book that way.

PageMaker's Autoflow and Text wrap features make it easy to place all of the text first, and then go back and adjust the text to accommodate illustrations and graphics. You don't have to adjust the text—simply place the graphic image and then select Text wrap from the Element menu. After setting the Text wrap for the graphic object, you can drag the object to another location in the text or even scale the object, and the text continues to flow automatically around it.

Placing Inline Graphics

PageMaker offers the *inline graphics* option for placing any graphics file. The Inline graphics option lets you place graphics directly in the text so that the graphics move with the text as editing changes are made. Inline graphics are associated with a particular text reference, and if that reference falls on another page or appears in a different position on the page than before, the inline graphics are also moved to the new page or new position.

Inline graphics (sometimes called "anchored" graphics) can be scaled, stretched, and cropped like any other graphics, but they can also be selected as text, scaled in point size, and aligned on the type baseline. This last feature is useful for special graphical elements that are the same size as the type.

To place inline graphics, select the text tool and click an insertion point in the text. Then use the Place command and select the graphics file (Figure 3-80). Be sure that the Inline graphics option is turned on in the

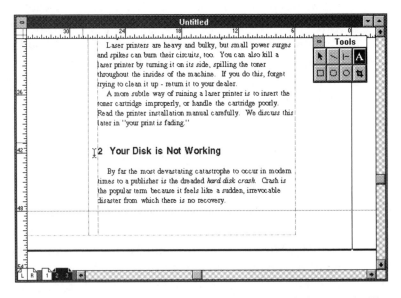

Figure 3-80. Click an insertion point with the text tool, then use the Place command. The Place dialog box lets you place graphics as inline graphics in the text.

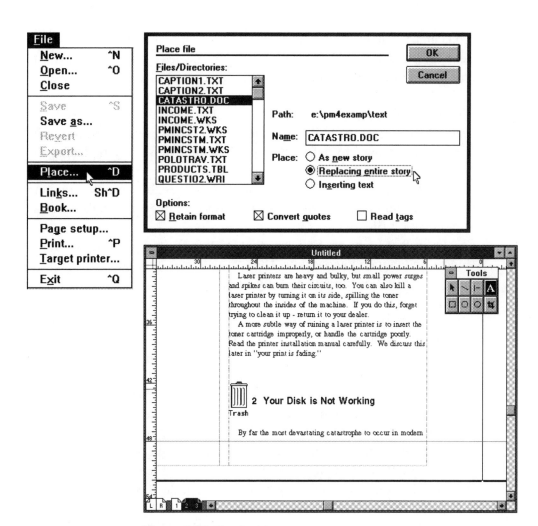

Figure 3-80. Continued.

Place dialog box.

Inline graphics remain with the text around it even after a recompose operation. The graphics can't be seen in the Story Editor window—a marker is used to show its place.

If you Place a graphics file when another tool is active, or without a text insertion point, the graphics file is placed separately. However, you can use Cut to cut the graphics into the Clipboard, then switch to the text tool and click an insertion point in the text, then use the Paste command to paste the graphics as an inline graphic image.

Saving and Using Templates

PageMaker offers the ability to save a publication file as a *template* file, which can be used to define new publications simply by replacing the contents of the template file with new contents.

You can do this with any publication. First, use the Save as command to save the publication under a new name as a template file, rather than as a publication file.

From that point on, you can double click the template file from the Finder and launch PageMaker. The template file automatically opens as a new, untitled document, leaving the original template file intact and untouched.

You can, of course, use the Open command and dialog box to open a *copy* of any publication as a new, untitled document, leaving the original intact. Creating a template file makes this operation automatic so that you can open a copy of the file, rather than the original file.

The use of a template to create publications is perhaps the easiest way to produce a publication. After opening the template as an untitled file, select the first column of the first story, then call up the Place dialog box. Choose the file that contains the story to replace the selected story, and select the option to replace the entire story (Figure 3-81). PageMaker replaces the text of the old story with the text of the new story in place on the page, using the same layout. Thus, if the text from the old story wrapped around a graphic image, the new text also wraps around the graphic image (if there is enough new text to reach that point in the layout). You can use this technique to start a new chapter of a book or section of a manual by saving a copy of a finished chapter, then replacing the text with the new chapter text and saving it as a new chapter.

You can also use the Place command to replace graphics with new graphics. When you replace a graphic element, the new graphic element occupies exactly the same space, distorting the graphic image if necessary. (You can adjust the image to be sized proportionately by holding down the Shift key while scaling.)

As shown earlier with the Links command, you can establish new

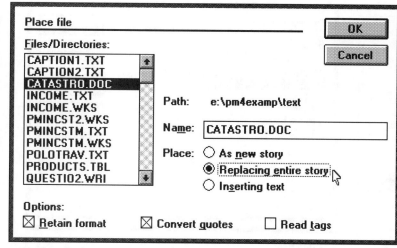

Figure 3-81. Place the new story with the Replace entire story option turned on, so that the new story completely replaces the old story in the layout.

links with external files to replace either text or graphics in a publication file. By clicking a new link (with the Link info command in the Element menu or the Link info button in the Links dialog box), you effectively use the Place command with the Replace option automatically.

Creating a Table of Contents

PageMaker can automatically create a table of contents of entries from one publication file, or from several publication files that are linked as a book. The table contains the text elements whose style sheets are defined to be included in a table of contents.

The best way to plan for a table of contents is to first define style sheets for the elements (such as chapter titles and subheadings) that will be included in the table. For the book chapters, we defined the style sheets in the template file, so that every chapter would automatically have styles defined to be in the table.

For each style sheet, you define in the Paragraph settings the option to include the style with the table of contents (Figure 3-82). For this book, we included the chapter title, and first- and second- level subheadings. If you like, you can include in the table of contents any selected paragraph by choosing the Paragraph command and turning on this same

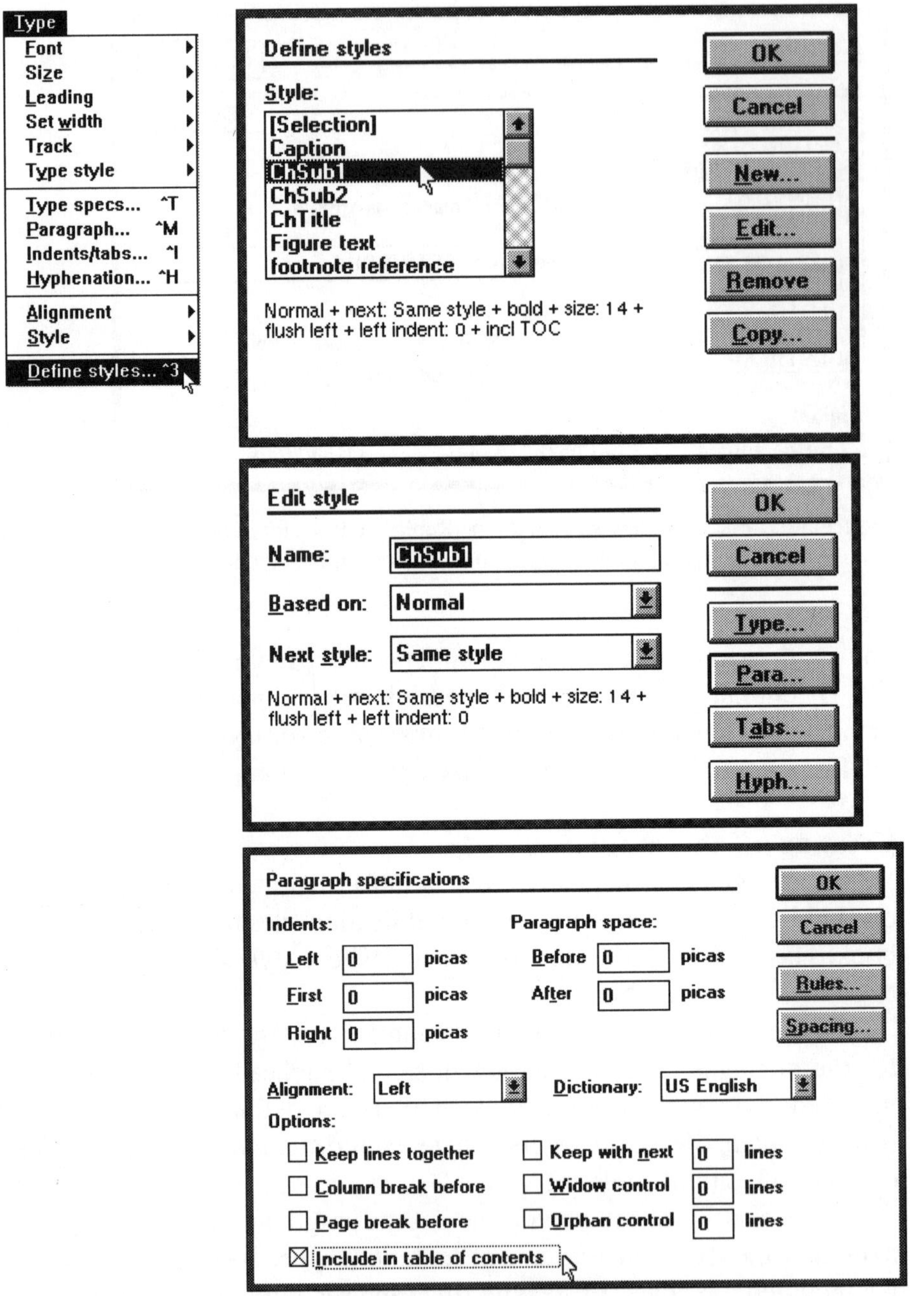

Type
Font ▶
Size ▶
Leading ▶
Set width ▶
Track ▶
Type style ▶

Type specs... ^T
Paragraph... ^M
Indents/tabs... ^I
Hyphenation... ^H

Alignment ▶
Style ▶

Define styles... ^3

Define styles OK

Style:
[Selection]
Caption
ChSub1
ChSub2
ChTitle
Figure text
footnote reference

Cancel

New...

Edit...

Remove

Normal + next: Same style + bold + size: 14 +
flush left + left indent: 0 + incl TOC

Copy...

Edit style OK

Name: ChSub1

Cancel

Based on: Normal ▼

Type...

Next style: Same style ▼

Para...

Normal + next: Same style + bold + size: 14 +
flush left + left indent: 0

Tabs...

Hyph...

Paragraph specifications OK

Indents: **Paragraph space:**

Cancel

Left 0 picas Before 0 picas

First 0 picas After 0 picas

Rules...

Right 0 picas

Spacing...

Alignment: Left ▼ **Dictionary:** US English ▼

Options:
☐ Keep lines together ☐ Keep with next 0 lines
☐ Column break before ☐ Widow control 0 lines
☐ Page break before ☐ Orphan control 0 lines
☒ Include in table of contents

Figure 3-82. To set up table of contents entries, first define styles that will be included in the table, then turn on the option to include the style in the table (the Paragraph settings dialog box from the Define styles dialog box).

option.

The next step is to get the publication files ready, and link them into one book. The Book command in the File menu lets you add or remove publication files from the book list (Figure 3-83). Click a file name on the left side, then click the Insert button to insert the name in the book list on the right side.

If you add publication files to the book list in the wrong order and you wish to change it, select a file to move down the list and click the Move Down button (Figure 3-84), or select one to move up and use the Move Up button.

When the publication is finished, you are ready to generate a table of contents. Start a new publication file based on the template that will hold the table of contents. Choose Create TOC from the Options menu, and turn on the Include book publications option (Figure 3-85) so that the table of contents is created from entries in all the files.

The finished table of contents is loaded into a text placement icon so that you can place it on the page. The final table (Figure 3-86) may need to have text changed in font and style from the original settings that were picked up from the chapter files. PageMaker creates new style sheet definitions for each type of table of contents entry; the style names begin with "TOC" and include the original style's name. You can modify these styles to adjust the formatting of all the entries of the table of contents.

Creating an Index

PageMaker can create an index of the publication files in a book list. This feature is powerful because you can edit the index entries and link cross references, as well as establish up to three levels for an index entry.

Index entries can be defined as you write, as you edit, or later, when the publication is finished. You can even define index entries in a word processor such as Word, and PageMaker can recognize them when you place the document. PageMaker continually builds an index so that at any time you can consult the index to see its list of topics and cross references.

To define an index entry, select the word or phrase to enter into the index, and choose the Index entry command in the Options menu (Figure 3-87). The Index entry dialog box appears, providing a way for you to change the actual index entry (Figure 3-88). If the word or phrase is not

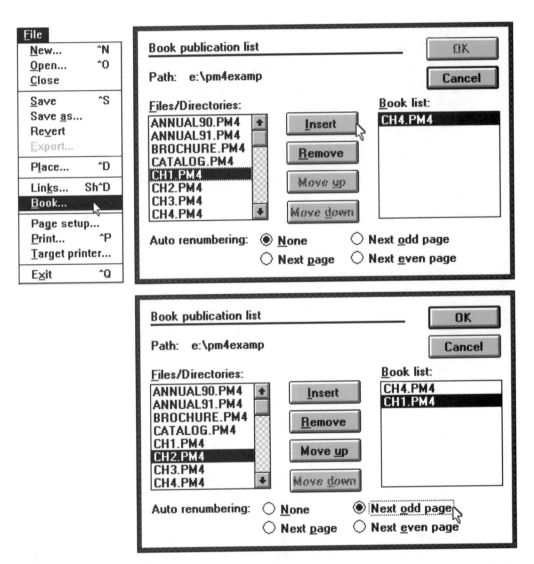

Figure 3-83. Link book chapters with the Book command, and use the Insert button to insert publication files in the book list. The automatic page renumbering feature is turned off for the first chapter (so that it begins on page 1), and is set to the next odd page so that the second chapter begins on an odd page.

exactly in the right format or sequence as it should appear in the index, you can change it. You can also click an insertion point in the text without selecting any word, and choose Index entry, then type a word or phrase in

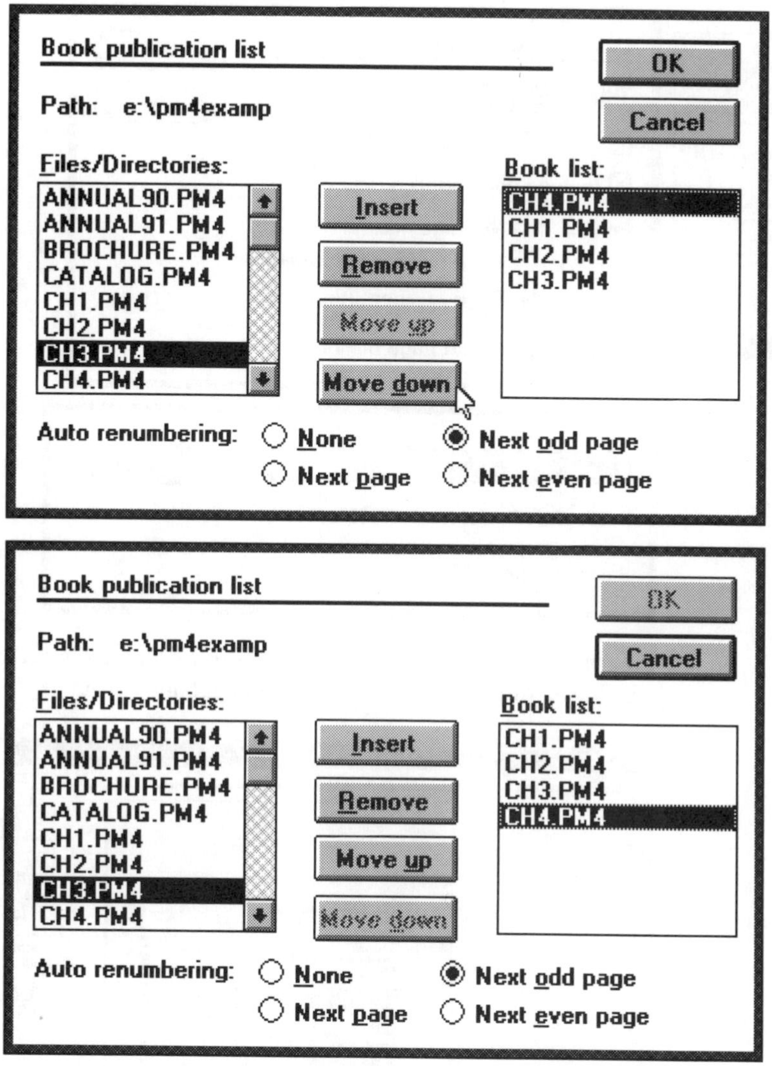

Figure 3-84. Move the CH4.PM4 file down the list by clicking the Move Down button three times, to change the order of files in the book list. You can move any file up or down the list.

the Index entry dialog box.

In the Index entry dialog box you can specify the page range for the index entry—the current page, for the next several paragraphs, or until the text reaches a different style sheet element. If the text you selected is in

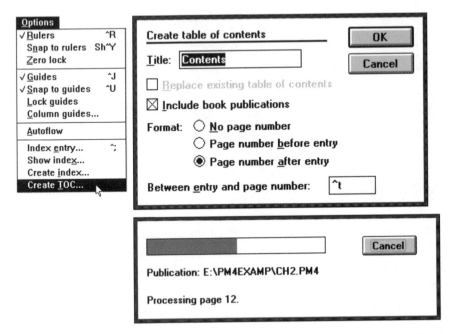

Figure 3-85. Create the table of contents using all the files in the book list. PageMaker displays a progress line while it builds the table.

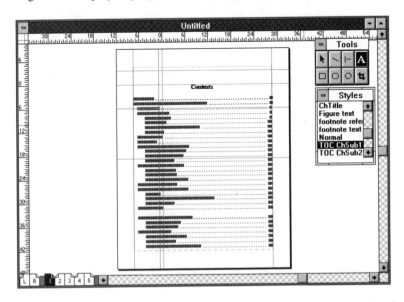

Figure 3-86. Adjust the formatting of the table of contents after placing it on the page by modifying the style definitions for the table of contents entries, or by directly changing the text on the page.

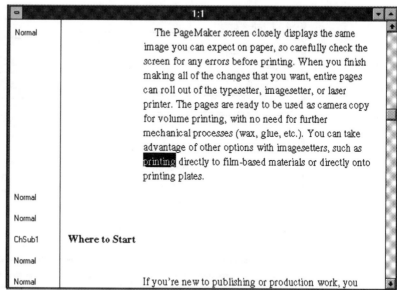

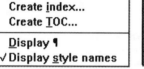

Figure 3-87. Select the word or phrase to include in the index, and choose the Index entry command.

italics, underlined, or in bold, you can override these styles for the index entry. The index entry appears in the Story Editor window as a marked word, although the mark does not print or appear in the layout view (Figure 3-89).

The index entry can have one or two levels below it (Figure 3-90), as in "mouse, pointing" and "mouse, dragging." Enter the index entry levels in the Topic entry boxes. You can click the Topics button to see other index entries (Figure 3-91).

To plan an index, keep in mind the important topics and think of each entry as capable of having two or more subentries (a two-level entry) and two or more sub-subentries (a three-level entry). For example, "printer, PostScript" is a two-level entry ("printer" is one-level), and "printer, PostScript, EPS file" is a three-level entry.

Cross references are also important for directing readers to similar or related topics. The Xref button also displays the topics window, and with it you can select a topic to use as a cross reference for the current index entry. The Import button imports topics from all the publications in the book list, so that you can establish a cross reference to a topic in another

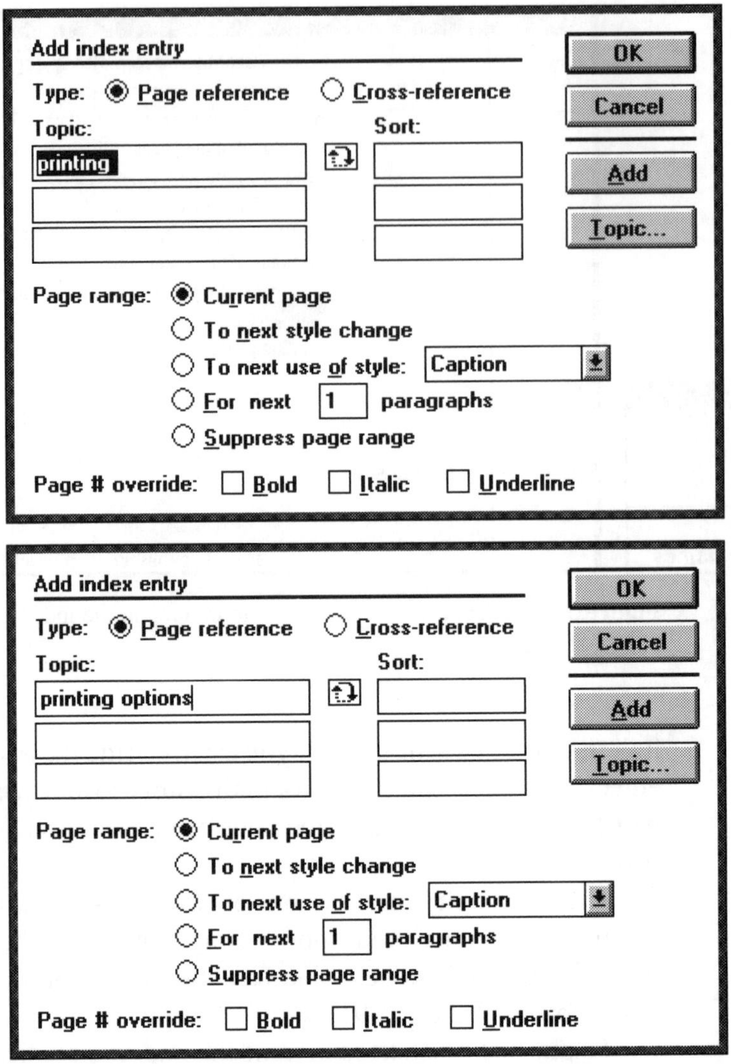

Figure 3-88. You can accept the index entry as is, or change it in the Index entry dialog box.

chapter.

The Sort entry boxes tell PageMaker how to sort the entry, and are used only if the index entry has an abbreviation or some other reason why it doesn't sort properly. For example, if the topic reference starts with "Dr." and you want it to sort under "Doctor," type Doctor in the Sort entry box across from

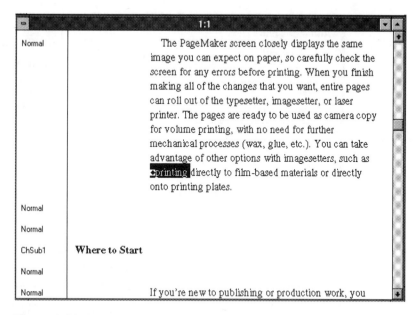

The PageMaker screen closely displays the same image you can expect on paper, so carefully check the screen for any errors before printing. When you finish making all of the changes that you want, entire pages can roll out of the typesetter, imagesetter, or laser printer. The pages are ready to be used as camera copy for volume printing, with no need for further mechanical processes (wax, glue, etc.). You can take advantage of other options with imagesetters, such as printing directly to film-based materials or directly onto printing plates.

Where to Start

If you're new to publishing or production work, you

Figure 3-89. The index entry appears as a marked word in the Story Editor window.

the entry. You can specify sort words for all levels of the index entry.

Those of you who want to create index entries quickly can press the keyboard shortcut Control-semicolon (;) to go directly to the Index entry dialog box. To bypass this dialog box and create an index entry with the default settings, use Control-Shift-colon (:).

As you create index entries, you can see the index at any time by visiting the Index entry dialog box and clicking the Topics button.

To generate a final version of the index, you can first review and edit all the entries, then format the index in advance, then create the final index. Use the Show index command in the Options menu to review and edit the index.

Next, create a new publication file from the template file to use for the index, just as before with the table of contents. The index is created as a story for placement, so you can always edit the text after placing the story.

Then choose Book from the File menu to check your book list to be sure that all the publication files are in the list in the proper order. (See the previous section for including publication files on the book list.)

Before generating the final index, choose whether you want to format

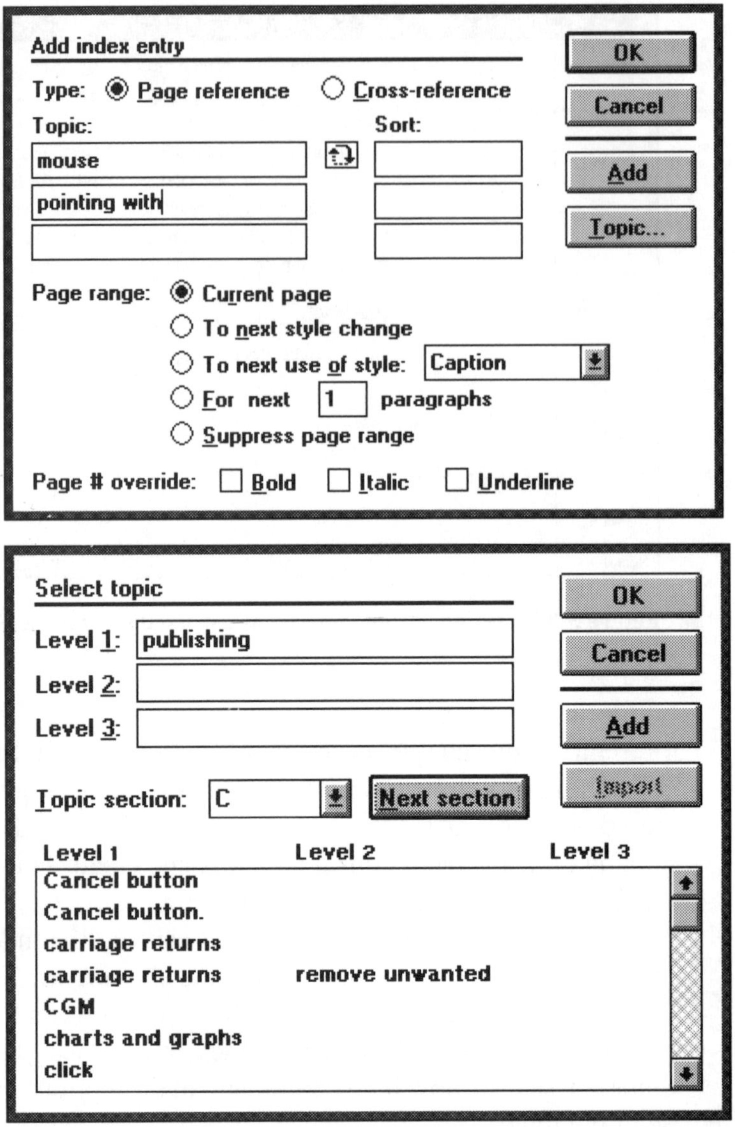

Figure 3-90. Create a two-level index entry by typing a second level in the Index entry dialog box. You can see other topics already in the index by clicking the Topics button, or link this entry to another entry by clicking the Xref button.

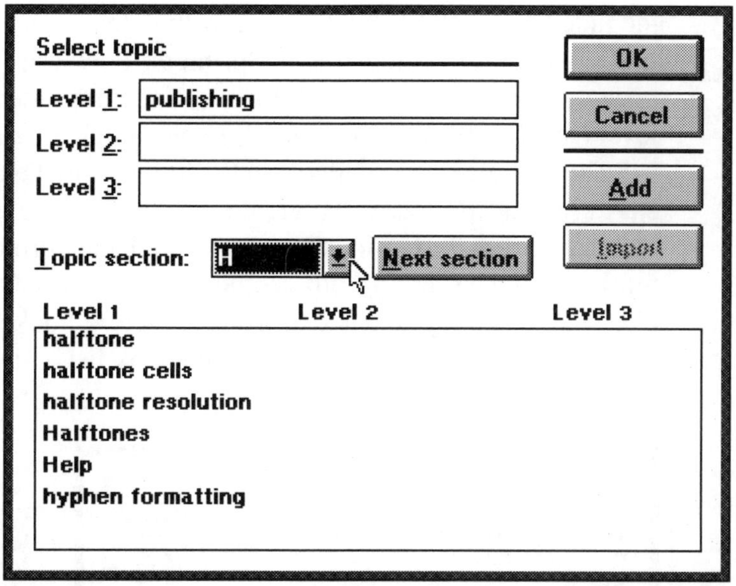

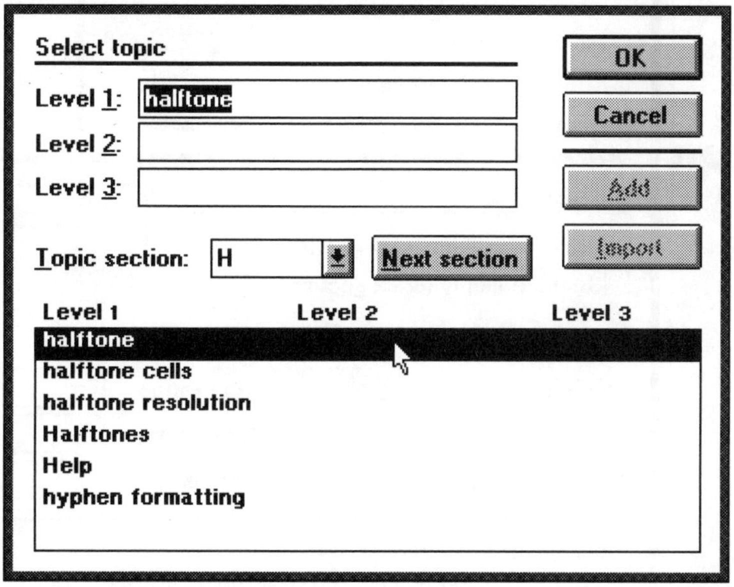

Select topic

Level 1: | publishing

Level 2: |

Level 3: |

[OK]
[Cancel]
[Add]
[Import]

Topic section: [H ▼] [Next section]

Level 1	Level 2	Level 3
halftone		
halftone cells		
halftone resolution		
Halftones		
Help		
hyphen formatting		

Select topic

Level 1: | halftone

Level 2: |

Level 3: |

[OK]
[Cancel]
[Add]
[Import]

Topic section: [H ▼] [Next section]

Level 1	Level 2	Level 3
halftone		
halftone cells		
halftone resolution		
Halftones		
Help		
hyphen formatting		

Figure 3-91. The Index entry's Topics button shows you the topics under each letter of the alphabet that have already been included in the index. A similar window appears when you click the Xref button, and the topic you select becomes the cross reference. The Show index command also displays a similar window for editing the index before generating a final index.

the index as Nested or Run-in. A run-in index includes all levels on one line separated by colons (as in "printers: PostScript"). A nested index places second and third levels on separate lines indented under the first level (see the index of this book for an example of a nested index).

These choices are available in the Index format dialog box when you start creating the index. To create the index, choose the Create index command from the Options menu, and click the Format button to display the Index format dialog box (Figure 3-92). Click OK to return to the Create index dialog box, and turn on the Include book publications option so that the index is generated from the book list. Click OK to create the

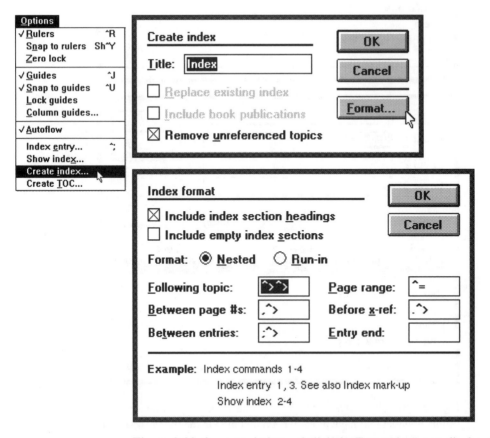

Figure 3-92. Create an index and click the Format button to display the options for formatting the index. The index in this book was created as a nested index.

index.

The index is generally the last thing you do before printing a finished publication. If you change any pages after creating the final index, you have to recreate the index to get accurate page references.

Printing Chapters

If you use separate publication files for chapters, include all those files in the book list (available by choosing the Book command from the File menu). You can print all the files in the book list with one Print command.

Set the starting page number of a publication file in the Page setup dialog box; the automatic renumbering feature in the Books dialog box (described earlier) controls how the pages are numbered when printing the entire book. PageMaker automatically numbers pages up to 9,999 (starting with whatever number you want), using arabic and composite page-numbering systems.

To change the numbering system, click the Numbers button in the Page setup dialog box (Figure 3-93). Several numbering systems are available, and you can set a prefix for page numbers used in the table of contents and index (such as "A-" for Section A).

If you turn on crop marks in the Print dialog box, crop marks will print at the page boundaries to be used as trim marks. You can also print the book's pages in reverse order, for use with printers that send pages out face-up (and backward in sequence).

Summary

This chapter presented the steps that you can follow to successfully produce a business report, a technical manual, and a book with PageMaker.

In this chapter you learned how to design these kinds of publications and set up the master pages. You also learned how to add a company logo, set up templates, and use the Story Editor to write and edit text.

In the Story Editor, you learned that you can import and create stories, place stories in the layout, use find and replace to make global changes to text, and check spelling.

You also learned how to enhance a report with a drop cap, with

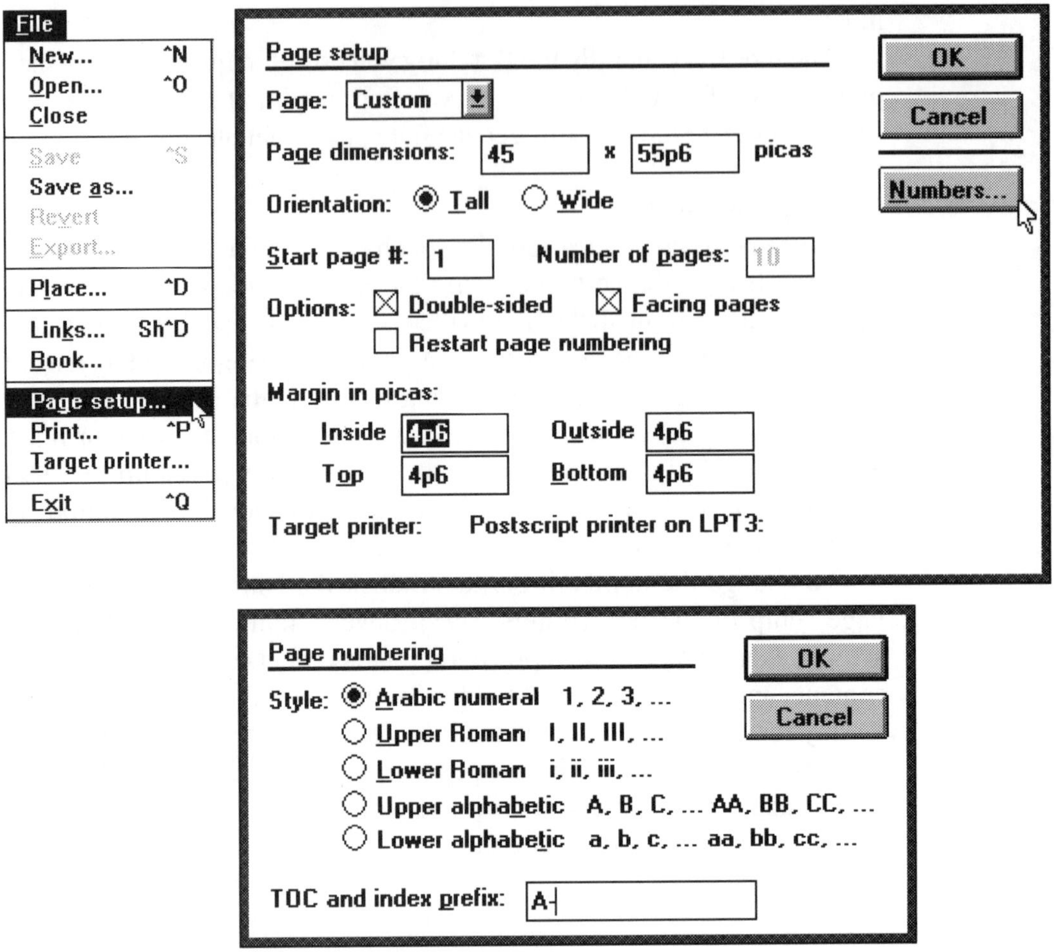

Figure 3-93. Change the page numbering system by clicking the Numbers button in the Page setup dialog box. A prefix can be added to page numbers in the table of contents and index.

graphics, and with charts, graphs, and tables. You learned about the Table Editor in this chapter, and how to import tables as text or as graphics files. In addition, you learned how to import spreadsheets, charts and graphs from other programs. Finally, you learned about printer options for printing reports.

You then learned how to design books and manuals, or any lengthy structured documents. You learned about flowing text with the Autoflow option, and how to design nonstandard page sizes. Style sheets and tags are explained, along with hyphenation, spacing, and track kerning for adjusting the spacing in text. Inline graphics, which are attached to reference points in the text and move with those points, are also demonstrated.

This chapter explained in detail how to set up a table of contents and an index for a book, manual, or lengthy document. It also explained how to link separate publication files in a book list, and how to print those files.

You learned all about producing long documents with text and graphics. In Chapter 4 you'll learn techniques for making fancy headlines, rules and borders, and special layouts with colors.

4 | Graphic Design

Coffee-table books require pages that have a designed look, and page advertisements and flyers are designed purposely to attract a reader's attention. Magazine pages are designed to be visually exciting, but with a clear hierarchy that starts with the article's title and department heading and extends to the text headings and captions for photos or illustrations.

There are many rules in graphic design, and only a few of them are obvious. Most of them are subtle and subjective. For example, as a rule you should not mix more than three fonts (not including the italic and bold styles of those fonts) on a page, and you should not crowd the page with text and graphics. Of course, art magazines break these so-called rules on purpose, as part of a stylistic decision. Programs such as PageMaker are designed to be used by everyone, and so the program will let you do things that designers may consider heretical, depending on the reasons for doing them. You can, for example, mix as many fonts as you wish on a PageMaker page—the program offers no constraints.

For the most part, design decisions are subjective. If you are not a designer and you have not employed one to design a template for you, use one of the supplied templates with PageMaker. These templates are all examples of excellent design techniques.

PageMaker excels at providing tools for moving elements on the page and for customizing layouts. You can mix two or more column styles on one page (e.g., use a two-column format at the top of the page, and a three-column format at the bottom), wrap text around irregularly shaped objects, put reversed (white) type onto a black background, rotate text vertically or upside down, and so forth.

You can move letters closer together by using a manual kerning or track kerning function. These kinds of enhancements are necessary if you want your pages to have a designed look.

The trick to producing custom pages is to design the elements first (such as fancy line styles and boxes, or reversed-type-on-black headlines) and copy them for use on different pages. For example, if you design a black panel with reversed (white) text that will be used on many different pages (perhaps with different text), you can copy the panel and text and paste them onto another page, and then type new text and resize the panel to fit the new text without having to reinvent the element. The original elements remain the same, so that you can copy and paste them again.

The following special effects and techniques are by no means the only effects that you can achieve with PageMaker, but they serve as a representative sample of what you can achieve by using PageMaker's tools. This chapter also shows how to change the contrast and brightness values of scanned images with the Image control command.

Layout Techniques

A hallmark of PageMaker's flexibility is that you can use a number of different techniques to achieve similar results. For example, there is more than one way to wrap text around an object, and the best method to use is the Text wrap option, unless you are wrapping text around text (such as a drop cap, described in Chapter 3). In such cases you would adjust the sizes of the text elements to fit side by side.

Layout can be assisted by the rulers, and you can change the zero point of the rulers to make it easier to measure distance on the page.

You can combine articles with different column layouts on the same page. You may start with placing text in one layout, then switch the column layout and place text in the other layout without affecting the first layout. In fact, whenever you need to place a text element without regard to column rules, drag-place (drag the text flow icon) over the area to be filled with text. These are some of the many techniques you may find useful in graphic design with PageMaker.

Ruler Zero Point

One capability of PageMaker's rulers makes them even more useful for measuring distances on layouts. The rulers start at a *zero point* that corresponds to the top-left edge of the page, so that you can measure to the right of the left edge, or down from the top edge. This zero point does not change as you move around the page so that you can measure distances from a specific point.

In a double-facing page display, the zero point is on the edge between the pages (the top-left edge of the right-hand page); otherwise, each page has its own zero point.

You can move the zero point to be anywhere on the page for the purpose of measuring distances across or down the page. Many designers prefer to move the zero point to the top-left margin of the page, rather than to the top-left edge.

To move the zero point, point on the two dotted lines that cross in the upper-left corner of the display (Figure 4-1). Drag the crosshairs diagonally to change both rulers, or drag the lines horizontally or vertically to change one or the other ruler. The zero point is the base for both rulers.

After you position the zero point where you want it, lock it into place with the Zero lock option in the Options menu so that you do not accidentally move it. When you start a new publication, the zero point is unlocked so that you can change it or lock it.

Wrapping Text Around Graphics

PageMaker offers a very flexible method for wrapping text around graphics, even irregular shapes. You have already learned how to wrap text around rectangular shapes. However, suppose you want to place a graphic image in the middle of text in such a way that the text wraps around the irregular shape of the image. You can use PageMaker's automatic Text wrap feature.

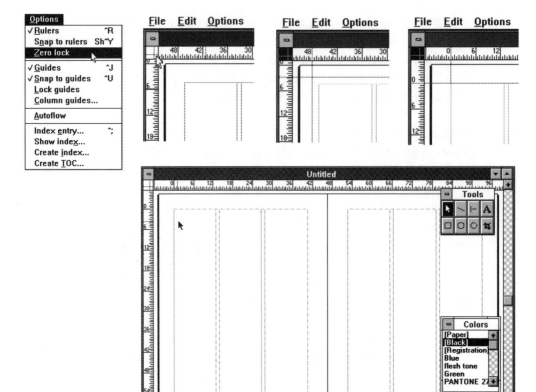

Figure 4-1. Click in the ruler intersection to get the crosshairs, then drag the crosshairs to a new location to set the zero point for the rulers. Lock the zero point so that it can't be moved accidentally.

First, place the image as an independent graphic image exactly where you want it on the page. Leave the image selected, or select it with the pointing tool (Figure 4-2). Then choose the Text wrap option in the Element menu (Figure 4-3), which displays the Text wrap dialog box. Choose the middle wrap option (the right one is grayed out until after you've created an irregular wrap), and the right-hand text -flow option, to define a standard wrap around the object. As a result, PageMaker displays a dotted line that acts as a wrap (or *text standoff*) boundary for wrapping

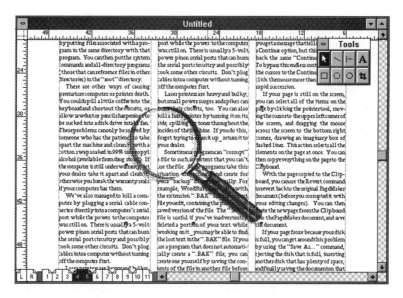

Figure 4-2. Select the graphic image to use the Text wrap feature.

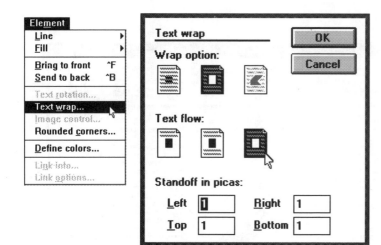

Figure 4-3. After selecting Text wrap from the Element menu, choose the middle wrap option, which automatically selects the right-hand text-flow option for flowing around the object.

the text around the graphic image (Figure 4-4). If you move or resize the image, the wrap boundary line moves or scales with it (Figure 4-5).

You can adjust the boundaries of the wrap by dragging the dotted line with the mouse, and thereby control the amount of white space between the text and the image (Figure 4-6). You can add points to the wrap boundary by clicking on the boundary line; then you can adjust the shape of the text wrap even further (Figure 4-7). The final wrap can be made very smooth by adding more points to the boundary and adjusting the boundary (Figure 4-8).

The wrap boundary provides the flexibility to wrap text around part of an image while overlaying text over another part, and lets you vary the amount of white space between the image and the text. You can enter the standoff amounts for the left, right, top, and bottom edges independently. Use a negative amount for allowing text to overlap graphics (or adjust the wrap boundary as described before). If you make editing changes later, the text flows naturally around the graphic image, as defined by the wrap boundary.

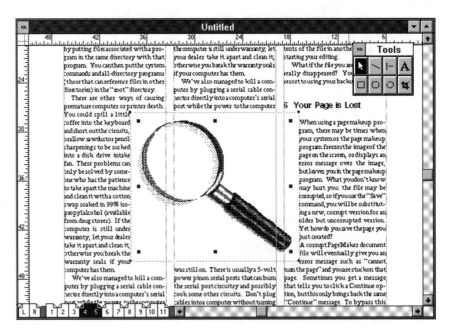

Figure 4-4. PageMaker displays a wrap boundary for customizing the shape of the wrapping of text around graphics.

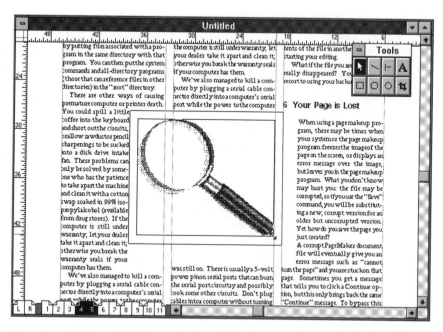

Figure 4-5. The wrap boundary scales automatically with the graphic image.

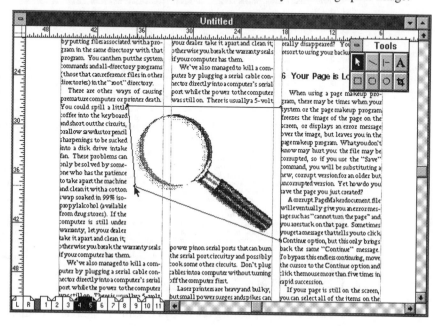

Figure 4-6. Drag a point along the wrap boundary to adjust the boundary's shape and thereby adjust the white space between the graphic image and the text.

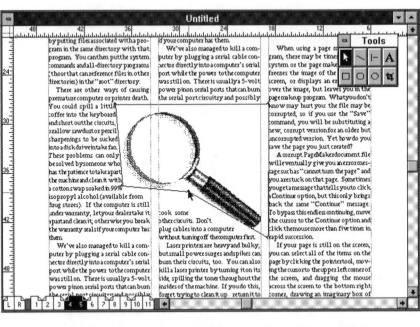

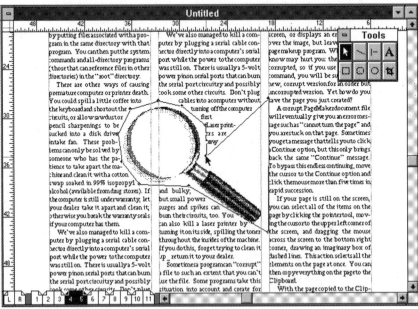

Figure 4-7. After adding points by clicking on the boundary line, you can fine tune the wrap boundary.

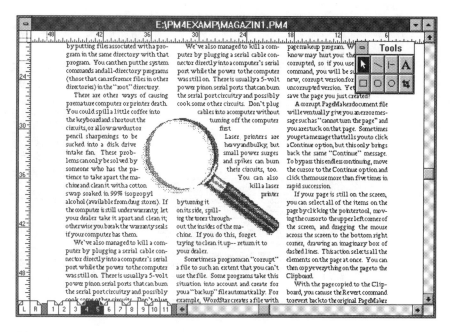

Figure 4-8. The finished text wrap.

If you want to create a caption after setting up the wrap boundary, and the caption should fall within the boundary, you should type the caption as a separate text element, and place the caption inside the graphics boundary so that it does not wrap around the boundary with the body text.

Mixing Column Layouts

You can combine one type of column layout (such as a two-column layout) with any other type of column layout on the same page. It is easier to combine column layouts when you first separate them with a rule (line) or with white space, so that readers are not confused about the flow of text.

A typical combination of layouts may be a two-column layout at the top of a page, and a three- or four-column layout at the bottom. The publication file should have master pages set to the predominant column layout (in this case, the three-column layout). Draw a line to separate the layouts (Figure 4-9), then change the number of columns with the Column guides option (Figure 4-10). You can now place the two-column text

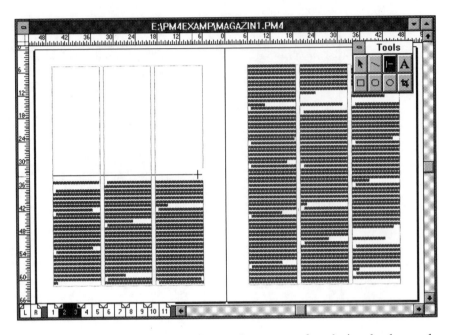

Figure 4-9. Draw a line across the three-column page after placing the three-column text, but before placing the two-column text.

Options	
✓ Rulers	^R
Snap to rulers	Sh^Y
Zero lock	
✓ Guides	^J
✓ Snap to guides	^U
✓ Lock guides	
Column guides...	
Autoflow	
Index entry...	^;
Show index...	
Create index...	
Create TOC...	

Column guides

OK

Cancel

Both

Number of columns: 2

Space between columns: 1 picas

☐ **Set left and right pages separately**

Figure 4-10. Change the number of columns for this page after pouring the three-column text; changing the column layout has no effect on already-placed text.

(Figure 4-11). Leave the same spacing between columns, or use less spacing if the columns are very narrow.

Continue placing the text in the two-column layout. When you finish, you may want to replace the rule with a stylized border, or draw a box around the three-column layout to separate it from the two-column layout.

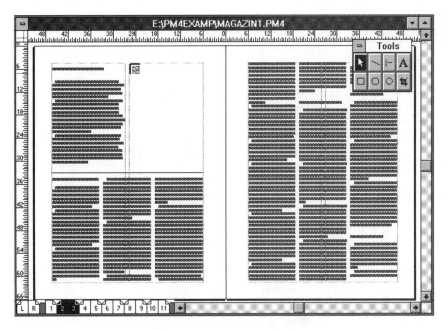

Figure 4-11. Place the text in a two-column layout after changing the layout.

Rules, Borders, and Boxes

The judicious use of *rules* (horizontal and vertical lines on a page), borders, boxes (rectangles), and line styles for these elements can make your page design more interesting and serve as helpful separators to preserve the hierarchy of headings, subheadings, text body, sidebars, pullquotes, and other elements.

Use a rule to divide one kind of text from another, such as a headline from text, one article from another, or an article from a sidebar. Vertical rules are often used to separate columns of text, especially when the text is aligned on the left margin and ragged on the right margin. Thick rules are often used to identify department headings in a magazine or to create black banners for reversed type. (You can reverse type—white type for a black background—by selecting the text and choosing the Reverse type style.) Figure 4-12 shows a thick rule used as a text banner, and a rule of dashes used to separate articles.

Use the appropriate thickness for the rule—don't use a thick rule to separate text in the same article; instead, use a thin rule (perhaps a hairline

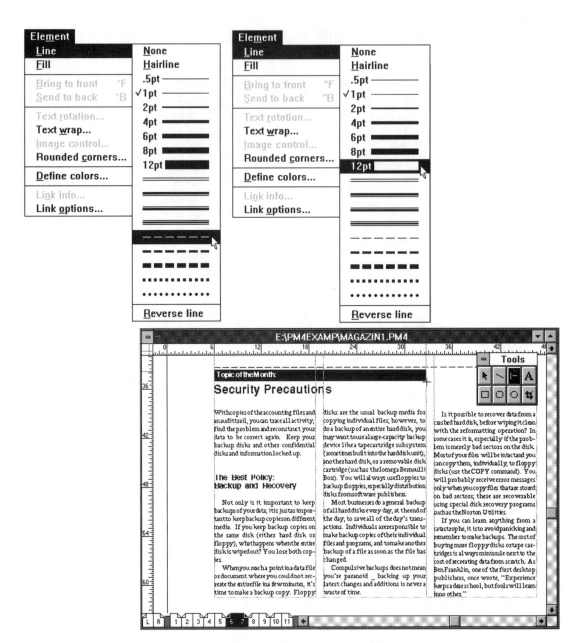

Figure 4-12. A thick rule with reverse type (a banner), and a dash rule separator.

rule). To draw attention to a headline, use a thick rule. Double rules tend to resemble picture frames, so use them only when they add emphasis to a headline or graphic or serve as an appropriate frame. Above all, be consistent with the use of rules in a publication.

Different line styles can enhance the appearance of the page. The dotted line is used in some popular magazine styles, as are the line of dashes. Figure 4-13 shows how you can mix a 12-point line (which looks like a solid vertically oriented box) and a dotted line in the same article title.

If you want a line style that is not available in the Line pop-up menu, try creating a rectangle that is only one line wide, and use an appropriate pattern. For example, you can create a much thinner line of dots by first selecting the rectangle tool, selecting no line style and parallel lines for the rectangle pattern fill, and drawing a rectangle the length of the line you want (Figure 4-14). The next step is to resize the rectangle, overlapping the long edges of the rectangle (Figure 4-15) until they disappear from the

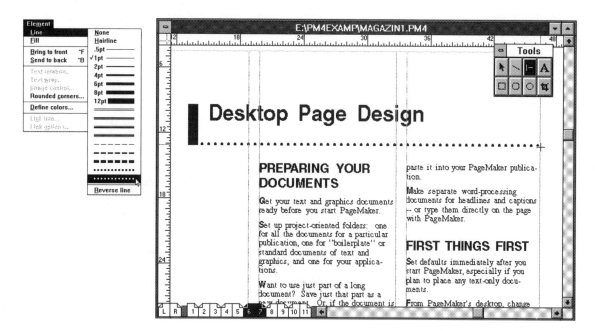

Figure 4-13. Line styles, such as a line of dots, can improve the appearance of the page.

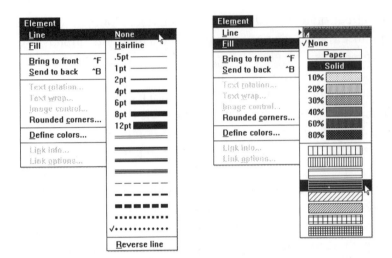

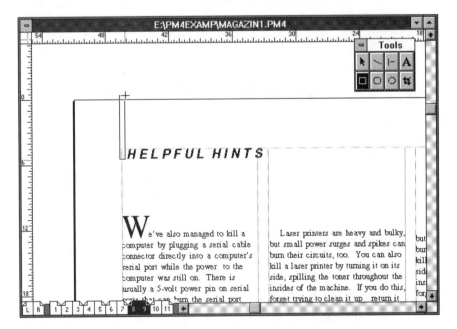

Figure 4-14. Select no line style for the rectangle, select parallel lines for inside the rectangle, and then draw the rectangle.

Figure 4-15. Change the width of the rectangle to be only as wide as a line. By selecting the parallel lines pattern, you change the very thin rectangle into a very thin line of dots.

display. The result is a thin vertical line of dots.

A box can be useful as a border around text that is separated from the main article, or as a border around an entire page that is different (perhaps because it uses a different column layout). Use thin line styles for borders around text, graphics, or a photo, with an equal amount of white space on all sides from the edge of the graphic or text to the box. To put a box inside a column, make the box line up with the margins of the column, and resize the text block inside the box to be narrower than the column (Figure 4-16).

Text Effects

Common techniques for creating fancy headlines and article titles include *spreading* a headline (stretching it or adding space between the letters), kerning the letters in a headline to be closer together, and printing white

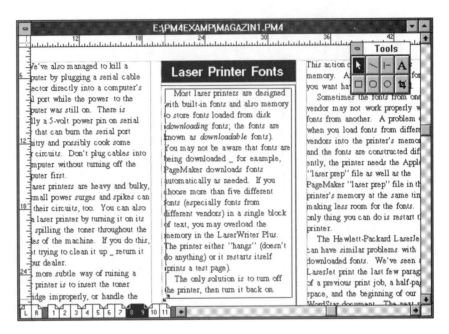

Figure 4-16. Resize the boxed text block inside a column.

characters on a black or colored background (reverse type).

You have already learned (in Chapter 2, the newsletter title) how to set text to have the reverse type style. You should use reverse type on a 100% black or a gray background with a 60% or 80% gray shade, because these contrasts provide the best results. If you want to reverse type on a colored or a patterned background, experiment to see which colors and patterns provide the best results.

Note that you will have a crisper white type if you use a sans serif font, such as Helvetica. Although you can use a very light or italic font reversed against a black background, don't use reverse italic type in a gray-shaded box. Always check that your printer can reproduce your master page for the press without breaking or plugging up the type.

Kerning is a process of removing or adding space between two characters using either a manual method, or by applying track kerning (described in Chapter 3) to a selection of text. Manual kerning is useful, for example, if the first letter of a headline is plain text or bold and the second letter is italic, or if the title is larger than 18-point type size. PageMaker handles both effects and many others.

Spreading and Distorting Text

There are several ways to spread text, such as headlines, across the page to fill the space. You can stretch (distort) the characters so that they are wider, or tighten them to make them thinner. You can add space evenly between characters to force-justify text to the margins of the text block. Or you can add space to a headline by simply typing a space between each character. You can type an em space by pressing the Control, Shift, and M keys simultaneously. To type a nonbreaking space, hold down the Control key when you press the space bar.

To spread a headline so that it fills a specific width without distorting the characters, first isolate the headline as a separate text block by cutting the headline from the rest of the article text and pasting it elsewhere on the page, or by simply typing the headline separately.

After setting the headline's font, size, and leading, select the headline with the text tool (Figure 4-17). Select the Force justify option of the Alignment command in the Type menu to spread the headline across the entire text block (Figure 4-18). The result is a justified, evenly spread headline without distorting the characters.

If you instead want to spread the headline to a specific width, you can first adjust the width of the text block, then use Force justify. Another method is to use the space bar to add one regular space between each letter (two spaces between each word), and one regular space at the end of the headline, then hold down the Control key while pressing the space bar to add enough nonbreaking spaces to fill the line until the cursor jumps to the next line.

To distort the characters by stretching or condensing (tightening) them, use the Set width pop-up menu in the Type menu. First, select the text to be stretched or condensed (Figure 4-19), and use the Set width values to experiment (Figure 4-20). To change it to a higher or lower percentage than available on the menu, use the Other option and specify a percentage. If you are using PostScript (Type 1) outline fonts, type can be stretched or condensed from 1/10% up to 250% in 1/10% increments as you wish to fill space, without detracting from the quality of the type (Figure 4-21).

Manual and Automatic Kerning

You can adjust the spacing between letters manually (by kerning) or control the automatic spacing. PageMaker performs automatic kerning with predefined pairs of characters (called *pair kerning*), using infor-

Figure 4-17. Select the second part of the title after cutting and pasting it as a separate text block, and choose Force justify from the Alignment submenu.

Figure 4-18. The result of using Force justify to spread the headline across the entire text block, adding space evenly between the letters.

Figure 4-19. Selecting the headline without using Force justify so that you can stretch the characters without adding space.

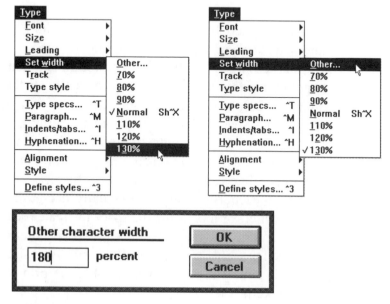

Figure 4-20. To distort (stretch or condense) text, select the text and use the Set width options in the Type menu. You can choose an appropriate width percentage, or select Other to enter your own percentage.

Figure 4-21. The result of using Set width to stretch or condense the headline.

mation supplied by the designer of the printer font. The degree of automatic kerning depends on the font you use.

Pair kerning is usually turned on for all text that is set to larger than 12 points in size, but you can change this setting in the Spacing dialog box (Figure 4-22), which is available from the Paragraph dialog box by clicking the Spacing button. If automatic kerning is used for text point sizes smaller than 12 points, the text flowing and placement functions slow down. You can turn on automatic kerning for selected areas of the text, rather than kerning the entire text.

Kern the letters in headlines manually, decreasing the space to tighten any two letters or increasing the space to create breathing room between any two letters. You may not notice the space increasing or decreasing on your display—although at the 400% viewing size (Figure 4-23), the change is almost always apparent—but the printed page should show properly kerned letters.

To kern manually between two characters, click an insertion point the text tool between the two characters. Press the Control and Backspace

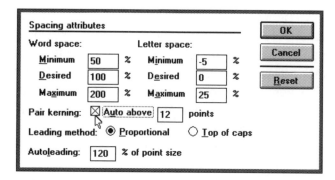

Figure 4-22. The Spacing dialog box lets you turn on automatic pair kerning with a minimum point size before pair kerning is activated. You can thereby turn off kerning pairs for that point size and lower.

Figure 4-23. Use 400% view to kern between two characters in a headline. Press Control and Backspace simultaneously (or Control and minus on the numeric keypad) to decrease space, or Control, Shift, and Backspace (or Control and plus on the numeric keypad) to increase space.

keys to tighten space in increments of 1/25th of an em space. You can alternatively press Control and the minus (-) key on the numeric keypad. If you need more precision, press Shift, Control, and minus (-) on the numeric keypad to tighten in increments of 1/100th of an em space.

To increase the spacing in increments of 1/25th of an em space, press the Control, Shift, and Backspace keys, or the Control key and plus (+) key on the numeric keypad. To increase the spacing in increments of 1/100th of an em space, press Control, Shift, and the plus (+) key on the numeric keypad.

To manually kern a selection of text at once, select the text and use the same key combinations described above. You can remove all kerning from a selection of text by pressing Control, Shift, and zero (0).

Adjusting Leading

Leading is the vertical distance between lines of text. You may want to adjust leading to improve a design so that text is more readable and less distracting. Too much leading can distract a reader by making it hard to follow the text from line to line. Too little leading can also distract by causing lines to look cramped.

With body text, it is usually best to use enough leading to separate lines but not too much to be noticeable. A general rule is to use a leading value that is at least 20% greater than the font's point size (120% of the point size). Body text is typically 10 points with 12 points of leading, or as in the case of this book, 12 points with 14 points of leading. You can adjust the leading amount in increments as small as 1/10 of a point.

When you select text in layout view, PageMaker displays the highlighted text in a bar that is called a *slug*. The slug (Figure 4-24) is a measure of the leading amount (it is useful to switch to 200% or 400% page view).

Inside each slug the characters are aligned to an invisible baseline. The bodies of characters rest on this baseline, while descenders drop below it.

In the Spacing dialog box (shown in Figure 4-22), you have a choice of methods for measuring leading: Proportional or Top of caps. The proportional method places the baseline two-thirds of the way down from the top of the slug. With the top-of-caps method, the baseline is placed

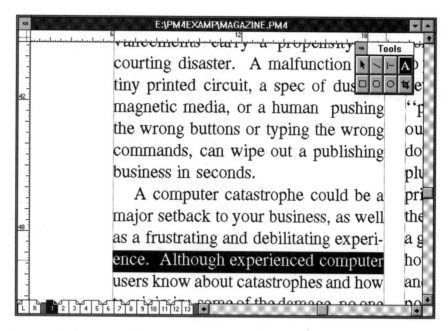

Figure 4-24. When you select text in layout view, the slug (a measure of leading) is displayed (shown at 200% view).

after calculating the height of the tallest ascender (the vertical stroke of a lowercase "b" or "h") in the largest font on that particular line.

With either method, PageMaker can calculate the leading as 120% of the font's point size with the Auto setting in the Leading pop-up menu. You can also set the leading to any positive point size number in the Other dialog box.

If you set the leading of one or more characters in a line to be larger than the line's leading amount, the entire line's leading is adjusted automatically. If editing forces the higher-leading characters to the next line, the lines automatically change accordingly.

Rotating Text

It is often necessary to place text in a vertical orientation within a regular layout. For example, you may need to put photo credits alongside a vertical edge of a photograph.

Figure 4-25. Select the text element with the pointer tool, then use the Text rotation option.

To rotate text, select the text element with the pointer tool (Figure 4-25), and use the Text rotation option in the Element menu. Select an orientation for the text (Figure 4-26), and click OK to rotate the text.

If any object is next to the text when you rotate it, and if that object has been defined to have a text wrap boundary, the rotated text wraps around all sides of the object.

PageMaker can rotate text in 90-degree increments. To rotate text to any other increment, you should use a graphics program such as Corel Draw or Micrografx Designer. PageMaker also can't rotate a text element that contains an inline graphic image.

If you want to rotate a combination of text and graphics, or perform other special effects with type, use a graphics program. You should use one that can save an EPS (Encapsulated PostScript) graphics file containing the rotated text, which you can place on the PageMaker page. If you can't save an EPS file, save a Windows Metafile graphics file for placement on the page, or use the Clipboard (Copy or Cut in the graphics program, and Paste in PageMaker).

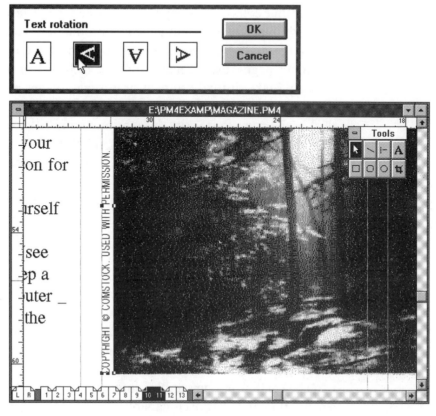

Figure 4-26. Select an orientation for the rotated text, and click OK to perform the rotation.

Image Control

PageMaker not only lets you place a scanned image, such as a photo, onto the page—it also lets you adjust the brightness, contrast, and halftone screen characteristics.

PageMaker prints scanned images at actual size or at reduced or expanded sizes with excellent results if you use the automatic resizing feature (by holding down the Control and Shift keys while resizing).

A *halftone* is a continuous tone image converted by the use of a screen to dots, or *halftone cells*, that simulate gray shades on a black-and-white printer, or colors on a color printer. The *screen density*, which is the frequency of cells measured in lines per inch (lpi), determines the size of the halftone cells in the image. This size can make the difference between a muddy reproduction and a clear reproduction. Newspapers typically need a 65- or 85-line screen. For advertisements, commercial work, and magazine pages, use screens with 120, 133, 150, or more lines per inch.

PageMaker initially screens gray-scale images at the target printer's default angle and line frequency, which is 45 degrees and 53 lpi with 300-dpi LaserWriter (PostScript) laser printers, and 90 lpi with high-resolution devices such as the Linotronic 100 or 300. With the Image control feature, you can change the angle and screen frequency as well as the contrast and brightness.

To make the equivalent of a halftone cell, the printer or typesetter combines several small dots (all of the same size) into one halftone cell dot (which can vary in size). You can raise the resolution of the image, but the result is a denser image with less gray levels or less colors.

To determine the number of gray levels that will be printed, divide the printer resolution (dpi) by the halftone screen density (lpi), and raise the result to the power of two.

Thus, a 300-dpi laser printer can print a 50-lpi halftone with 36 (simulated) levels of gray—suitable for a newsletter or an internal document.

The PostScript-compatible Linotype Linotronic 300 Imagesetter (with a resolution of 2540 dpi) is capable of reproducing a commercial-quality gray-scale halftone at up to 150 lpi with at least 256 levels of gray—suitable for a magazine.

Color images must be adjusted with Aldus PrePrint or a similar color retouching and balancing program, although PageMaker can print color images as separations on high-resolution equipment and as composite images on color printers.

PageMaker's Image control command gives you control over the frequency and angle of the line screen for gray-scale halftoning, and over the lightness and contrast values of gray scale images. Remember, however, that the more gray levels you specify (the higher the frequency), the longer it will take for the image to print.

Adjusting Lightness and Contrast

To use Image control, first place the image (usually a TIFF file) on the page. The Preferences dialog box (choose Preferences from the Edit menu) lets you set the display mode for graphics (Figure 4-27). Change it to the high-resolution setting so that the images appear in high resolution on the page.

Select one image (Figure 4-28), and choose the Image control command from the Element menu. PageMaker displays the Image control dialog box (Figure 4-29), which has scroll-bar controls for lightness and contrast, and options for specifying the type of screen, the screen angle, and the frequency.

To use the lightness and contrast scroll bars, click the arrows to reduce or increase the amount, or drag the scroll-bar boxes. The lightness value lightens (Figure 4-30) or darkens the image, and the contrast value lightens or darkens areas of the image in relation to their surrounding backgrounds. To see the result of any adjustment, click the Apply button.

Different combinations of lightness and contrast amounts can be used for special effects. You can adjust the contrast of an image to 100% and reduce the lightness to 0% to obtain a high-contrast image with no gray scales (Figure 4-31). You can also use a negative value for the contrast to produce a negative version of the image (Figure 4-32).

You can always reset the image to the way it was by clicking the Default button, and you can Cancel the operation with the Cancel button.

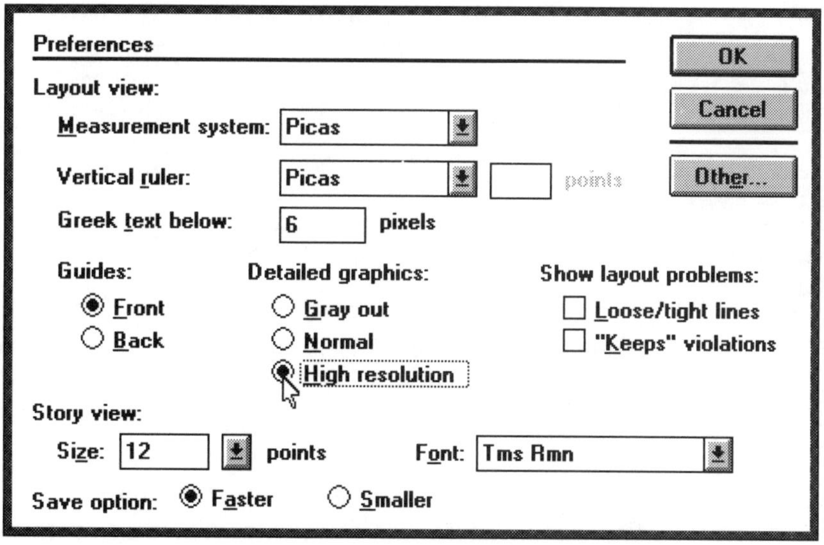

Figure 4-27. Use the Preferences dialog box (from the Edit menu) to change the graphics display mode to high resolution.

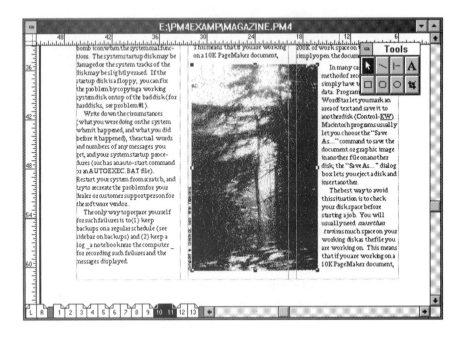

Figure 4-28. Select a scanned image on the page. (Image courtesy Comstock Desktop Photography, Copyright ©1988.)

Figure 4-29. Choosing the Image control option for the selected image. The Image control dialog box with default settings.

Adjusting the Screen Angle and Frequency

The screen angle and frequency are adjusted to optimize the printed results for different printing presses and papers.

The Image control dialog box lets you specify either a dot or line

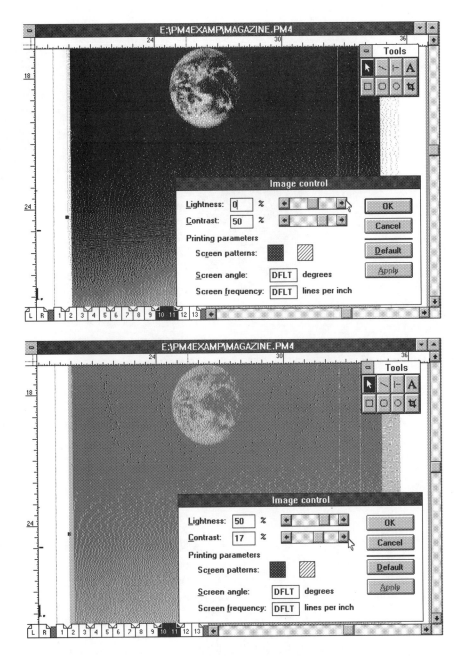

Figure 4-30. The image before and after changing the contrast amount.

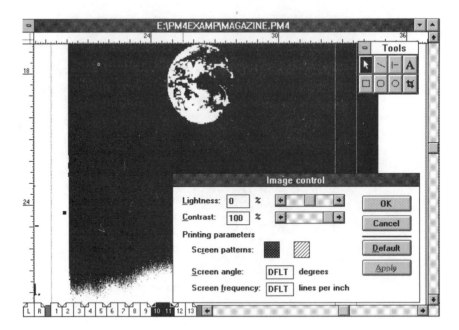

Figure 4-31. The result of increasing the contrast to 100% while reducing lightness to zero: a black-and-white image with no grays.

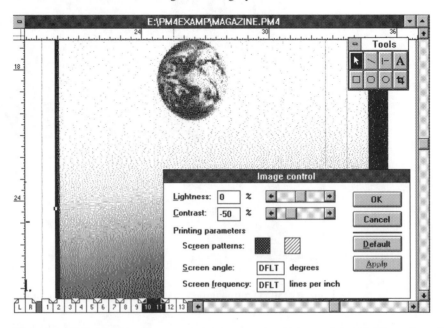

Figure 4-32. Reversing the amount for contrast to produce a "negative" version of the image.

pattern, along with the screen angle and the frequency (Figure 4-33). The type of screen (the default is dot) can be changed for special effects. The frequency is measured in lines per inch (such as 53 lpi).

You should consult your press operator before deciding on a line screen. Typically you work with lightness and contrast first, getting the right look for the image, and then use the default screen angle and frequency for the proof printer (usually a laser printer).

Then, when the final pages are ready, you should run a test page to see if the lines per inch and screen angle are set appropriately for the resolution of the output device. The imagesetter operator can tell you which settings are best for their equipment.

Using Color

Color is an essential ingredient in publications, and high-quality color reproduction is the hallmark of commercial magazines, advertising

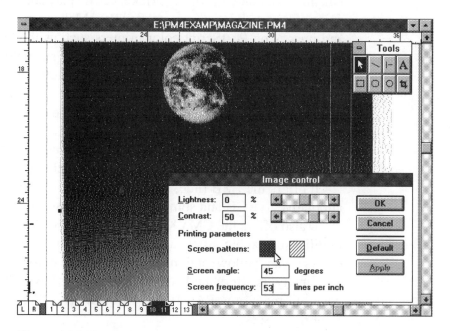

Figure 4-33. Use the Image control dialog box to set the screen pattern, angle, and frequency (dot pattern selected).

pages, and brochures. Color printing, however, remains a more expensive process than black-and-white printing, and the cost of printing is a limiting factor in producing commercial and in-house publications and documents with color graphics and photos. You always need to justify the use of color in economic terms.

Nevertheless, the cost of producing color publications is coming down, and the reason is that the cost of preparing color images and color graphics has come down drastically.

PageMaker offers full support for color on displays that support Windows 3, including the processing of full-color photographs scanned with color scanners and digitizers. PCs can offer from 4 bits per pixel (16 different colors or gray levels) with the standard VGA adapter to 8 bits (256 colors or grays) with a "super" VGA, or more with special color graphics display adapters. In PageMaker, you can assign any color to any page element, and you can import nearly any type of scanned or drawn color image, without regard to the type of display adapter (if you don't use color displays, you see black-and-white versions).

PageMaker lets you apply colors to text and drawn objects on the page (such as boxes and lines). PageMaker can display color images from color painting and drawing programs, and PageMaker can print color graphics and images on PostScript color printers such as the QMS ColorScript. You need a color display monitor in order to see colors displayed, but remember that the displayed colors do not match printed colors exactly.

PageMaker offers four different methods of defining color (called *color models*). You can switch from one to the other, depending on the type of color you are using.

PageMaker offers the familar RGB (red, green, and blue) model used by many graphics programs because it is suitable for displays.

It offers the HSB (hue, saturation, and brightness) model that is an alternative to RGB and sometimes easier to use to select a color.

It also offers the CMYK (cyan, magenta, yellow, and black) model familiar to graphic artists and press operators who work with process colors (cyan, yellow, and magenta) and make color separations.

Finally, it offers the PANTONE system of over 700 colors that are coded to match the PANTONE MATCHING SYSTEM inks used on printing presses.

Types of Color

Color is used in several different ways on printed pages, and PageMaker can prepare pages with spot color, color tints, and color halftones.

Spot color is an area of the page, or of a graphic image, that is set to a solid, consistent color such as a PANTONE color or a process color with the same luminosity, hue, and saturation over the entire area. Spot colors are often used as a highlight for thick page rules and bars, in logos, and in solid two- and three-dimensional models. PANTONE colors that directly correspond to PANTONE inks used in print shops are often applied as spot colors. A spot color can also be composed of a combination of process colors—cyan, yellow, magenta, and black. In addition, the RGB and HSB models can be used to specify process colors.

A *color tint* or *gray tint* is an area that has a percentage of a spot color (or of black, which produces a gray tint) less in density than a solid color. A tint is often used behind text in a boxed area, or as a shading behind an image. Tints are usually composed of percentages of PANTONE or process colors.

Color *halftones* (printed version of a continuous tone image) are scanned photos and digitized video images, which consist of continuous tones of color or gray, must be converted into halftones for the printing press. Four process colors are combined to make color halftones. Color photos must be separated into layers representing percentages of each of the four process colors (cyan, yellow, magenta, and black).

To print color on a printing press, you supply color pages with the colors separated onto different pieces of film—a separate film for each colored ink. The set of films is called a *color separation*. Many publications are printed in four process colors (cyan, magenta, yellow, and black, or CMYK), with perhaps a fifth colored ink (usually a PANTONE color) as an option. You can make a color separation of a PageMaker publication using the Aldus PrePrint color separator utility program (available for the Macintosh and used by technicians at PostScript output service bureaus). You can also print spot color overlays directly from PageMaker that can serve as a color separation for the spot color.

Spot colors, tints, and color illustrations (which are usually made up of spot colors and tints) are relatively easy to reproduce on a printing press with high-quality results. Magazine-quality photos, however, are much harder to reproduce and maintain a level of quality equal to conventional methods of color halftoning. One color halftone can occupy far more disk space than several pages containing spot-colored halftones. In addition, most desktop scanners' accompanying software is not yet capable of performing as well as million-dollar prepress systems.

You can produce inexpensive color separations, however, on PostScript imagesetters, such as the Linotype Linotronic 300 (used widely in service bureaus). PostScript-compatible color desktop printers can be used to print proofs of color images before starting the presses rolling. PostScript is the page description language that has become a standard file format for laser-printed master pages for publishing applications.

PostScript is also useful for transferring computer-generated color images directly to prepress systems in an all-digital color separation process in which color PostScript printers act as proofing devices along the way.

With PageMaker and a color page printer, you can create color mock-ups, also called *comps*, with the color images and elements in place on the page. PageMaker's color features are designed to make overlays for spot color (such as solid color areas, color screens or tints, and colored text). PageMaker can print color pages directly on a color printer, and print color pages directly to a film recorder to make slides. Color separations are not required for printing on a color printer and then copying on a color copier.

Using the Color Palette Window

Colors can be assigned directly to objects (text, lines, or PageMaker graphic objects) by selecting the object and choosing the Color palette command from the Windows menu, which displays the color palette (Figure 4-34). You can keep the color palette displayed so that you can assign colors to other objects. You can also resize the color palette, just as you can resize any window.

When you apply a color to a shaded box, the shade pattern changes color but remains a pattern. Boxes, circles, and ovals can be filled with a color, and the bounding line of the object takes on the same color. You can also apply color to text or to the black portions of a graphic image.

Defining Colors

Colors for a publication are defined in a color sheet, which is like a style sheet that holds the names of the colors and is saved with each publication.

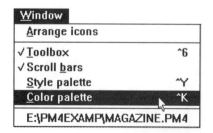

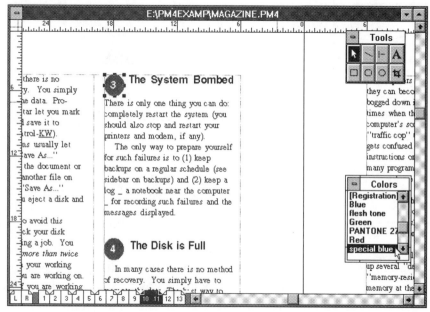

Figure 4-34. Assign a spot color to a circle on the page using the Color palette window.

You can copy colors from another publication (just as you can copy style sheet definitions), and edit color definitions as well as remove them. Each color has an associated name and value, with the value expressed in either percentages of cyan, magenta, yellow, and black (CMYK); in red, green, and blue (RGB); or in hue, lightness, and brightness (HSB). PageMaker also lists PANTONE colors, which you can assign other names to display in the Color palette window.

The Define colors option in the Element menu provides a dialog box for defining colors in any one of the four color models (Figures 4-35 and

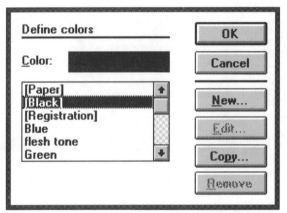

Figure 4-35. Choose Define colors to define color names for the Color palette window. Click New to define a new color, or Edit to edit an existing color definition.

4-36). The colors that you define appear in the color palette by name, so you can assign colors on a black-and-white monitor. Click the New button to define a new color, click the Edit button to change a color's values, or click the Copy button to copy colors from another publication. You can also remove a color from the color sheet for the open publication.

When you edit a color, you are changing the color of every object in the publication to which that color name is assigned. For example, if you edit the "special blue" color to be a different tone, the color of all items tagged as "special blue" changes to the new tone.

You can apply a color to a selected object from the Define colors dialog box. If you are applying a color from the color palette, you can modify the color's definition before applying it by holding down the Control key while clicking the color name. PageMaker takes you directly to the Edit color dialog box to make changes, and then returns you to the color palette. To close the color palette, select the Color palette again in the options menu, or press the Control and K keys.

Making Overlays and Separations

PageMaker is useful for separating the tinted areas of a page or spot-colored elements. To create overlay pages that contain the colored objects, choose the Print command, and click the Setup button in the Print

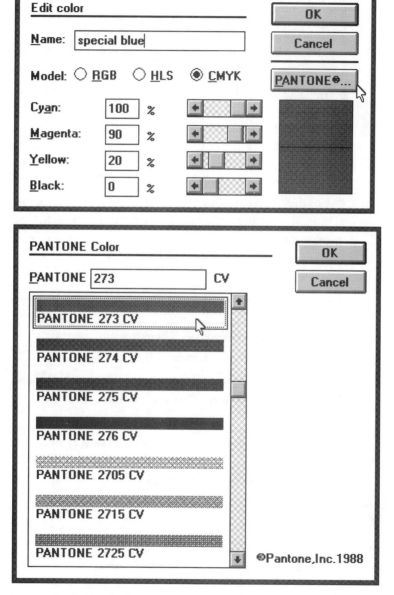

Figure 4-36. The CMYK (cyan, magenta, yellow, and black) model is easy to use to define a process color. You can define a PANTONE color to appear in the palette by clicking the PANTONE button.

dialog box to display the Setup dialog box for choosing the printer. Click OK to return to the Print dialog box, and select the Spot color overlays option (Figure 4-37).

PageMaker automatically prints color registration marks (for lining up overlays) and the name of each color on the overlay. A different overlay is printed for each color. You can specify a single color for an overlay in the color pop-up menu (Figure 4-38).

It is sometimes helpful to the press operator to use the Knockouts option to create a blank spot on the bottom (black) overlay where the colors overlap. The color objects are knocked out on each overlay according to the order in which they are stacked on the page (by previous use of the Send to back command). Be sure to check the Crop marks option if you are printing pages smaller than the normal 8.5 by 11-inch size. Crop marks only print if the paper (or film, in the case of imagesetters) is larger than the page size defined in PageMaker.

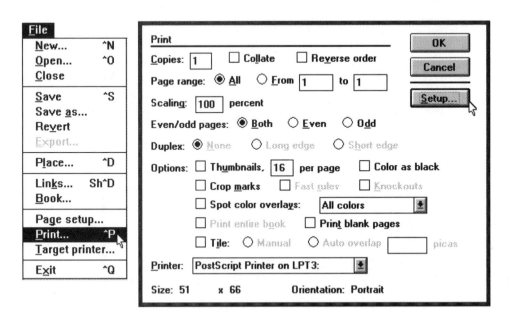

Figure 4-37. In the Print dialog box, click the Setup button to choose the appropriate printer in the Setup dialog box, and click OK to return to the Print dialog box, then select spot color overlays with knockouts.

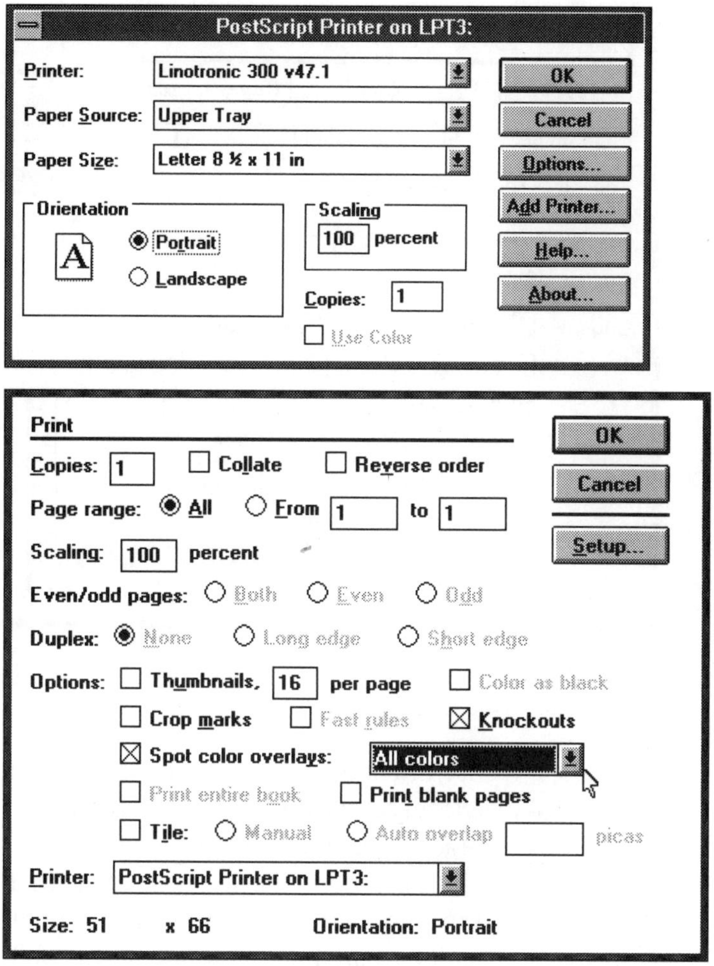

Figure 4-37. Continued.

You may want to use copier-certified acetate sheets to print the spot color overlays and print the black elements on paper, so that you can easily overlay the paper with the acetate sheets to match registration marks and so on. Your printing process will determine whether this is useful. Check with your printer to see if the final artwork should be printed on separate sheets of paper, or if acetate sheets can be used as final artwork. If your

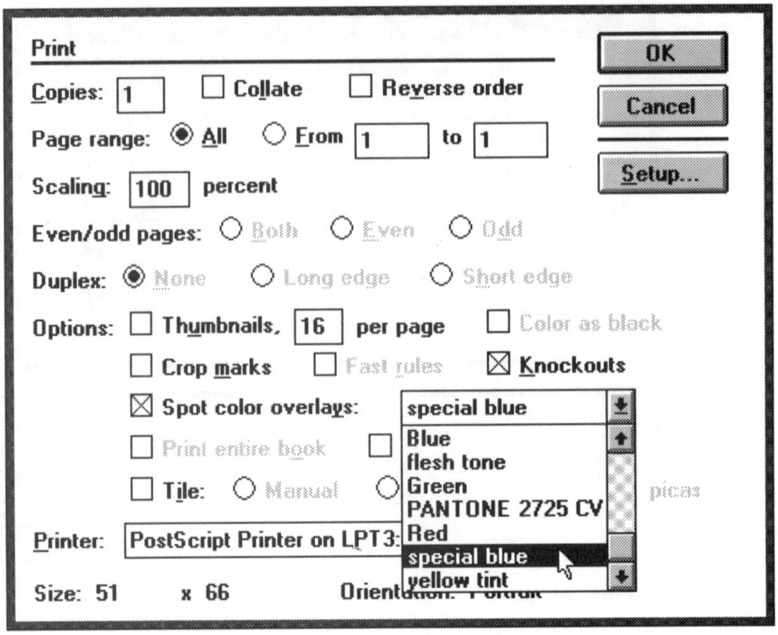

Figure 4-38. Specify a single color for an overlay with the color pop-up menu.

printer can work from both paper and acetate, check the text areas of your pages, looking closely at the type to see whether paper or acetate provides the crispest characters, and use the best medium.

Aldus PrePrint can modify the colors in a PageMaker publication's images to perform color correction operations for printing press inks before creating color separations. You can prepare an Encapsulated PostScript file for PrePrint by choosing the Options button in the Setup dialog box, and selecting the Encapsulated PostScript file option (Figure 4-39).

With PageMaker (and PrePrint for pages with halftone images), you can produce color separations that are near-magazine quality, and certainly excellent quality for newsletters and newspapers. PrePrint can also prepare pages for use with the Open Prepress Interface (OPI) to prepress systems for professional-quality all-digital halftone separations. From OPI information in the file, the prepress system can automatically find the color images on the pages, adjust higher-resolution versions (scanned on prepress scanners) with cropping and scaling, then create process color separations based on the higher-resolution versions of the images.

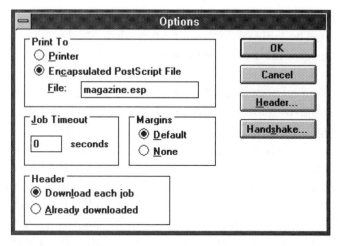

Figure 4-39. To prepare color separation files for a service bureau, click the Options button in the Setup dialog box, and select the option to create an Encapsulated PostScript file and specify its name.

Special Layouts

The role of PageMaker in the design of special layouts for publications is to provide boilerplate graphics, design elements (such as rules, boxes, and reverse text panels), and repeatable formats (such as indented paragraphs, dot leaders, and stretched headline or title blocks). Save all of the designed elements in a separate template file that can be opened whenever you need them. You can copy the elements to your publication via the Clipboard and the Copy and Paste commands, and save some of them on master pages to be repeated as necessary. Save also the column layout of each page without text and graphics, so that you can place new text and graphics without redrawing the column rules and reinventing other design elements.

Table of Contents Page

Publications usually include special pages, such as a table of contents or an index page, that require a special layout and elements not used in other pages. Catalogs and database listings may also require the use of special page elements and very narrow columns.

The table of contents feature, described in Chapter 3, can be used to design a table of contents page automatically. When the table of contents is generated and placed in a publication file, the table elements are assigned a special style sheet name. You can edit the style definitions to design the table with indented subheadings under the chapter headings, or indented descriptive text under the article titles.

To create dot leaders between headings, subheadings, and page numbers, use the tab settings and leaders in the Indents/Tabs dialog box. First, move the dialog box so that the ruler lines up with the text, then point on the ruler a tab setting to mark the end of the space for the dot leaders. Then select a leader pattern to fill the space (Figure 4-40). The result is a horizontal line of dots between the subheadings and the page numbers.

You can specify a different character to use for a leader, or use the dotted or dashed line leaders. You can also control the alignment of the characters within a tab space. (The arrows in the ruler define the endpoint of a tab space.) The tab spaces in the sample table of contents example are all left justified.

Catalog Page

A catalog page may contain many small items and one large item. Figure 4-41 shows a page from a publisher's catalog.

To prepare this page, use a four-column layout and drag-place the opening text blocks over two columns at the top of the page (leave the space between columns unchanged). Add the headings and images, then place the rest of the text. Use the Wrap text option to specify that text should jump over the images, and leave six points of space between the text and the images (Figure 4-42).

Advertisements, Flyers, and Brochures

A flyer or a handout is usually a standard 8.5 by 11 inches in size, and is designed to look like a one-page advertisement. Brochures can be almost any size and shape, depending on how they are folded. The simplest folding methods are done with standard 8.5 by 11- or 14-inch-long paper.

A helpful way to decide what size to use is to get samples from a printer. The type of fold you choose should be one that can be handled by the printer's machines, because hand-folding is expensive.

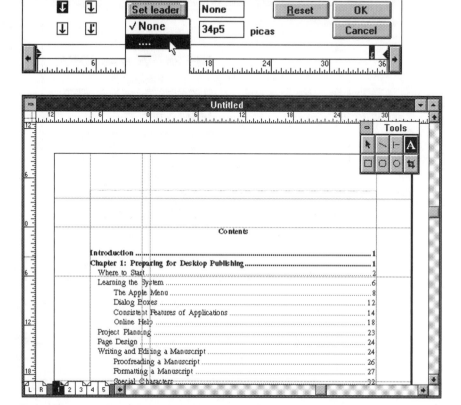

Figure 4-40. After setting the tab space, choose a leader to typeset a horizontal line of very small dots in the tab space.

There are many different ways to lay out information for a brochure or flyer. It is most helpful to first define the page setup to reflect the measurements of a folded and trimmed page of the brochure. Figure 4-43 shows the Page setup dialog box for a typical gate-folded brochure using standard 8.5 by 11-inch paper, defined to have a wide orientation rather than tall (using the 11-inch dimension as the width). The margins are reduced from the default sizes to avoid wide edges on the front panels when the brochure is folded. The selection is for two-sided facing pages in order to display both sides of the brochure.

Figure 4-44 shows how two pages in a publication file can produce a

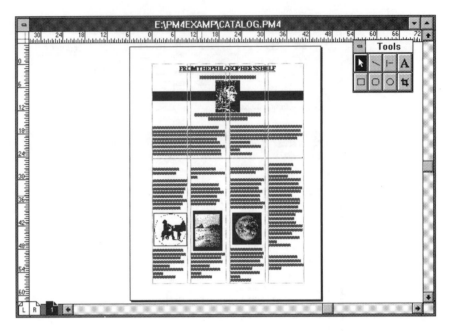

Figure 4-41. A page of a publisher's catalog, which uses a mixed-column layout, dotted rules, and images.

Figure 4-42. Use Text wrap to force text to jump over the placeholders or graphics, and leave at least 6 points of space between the text and each placeholder.

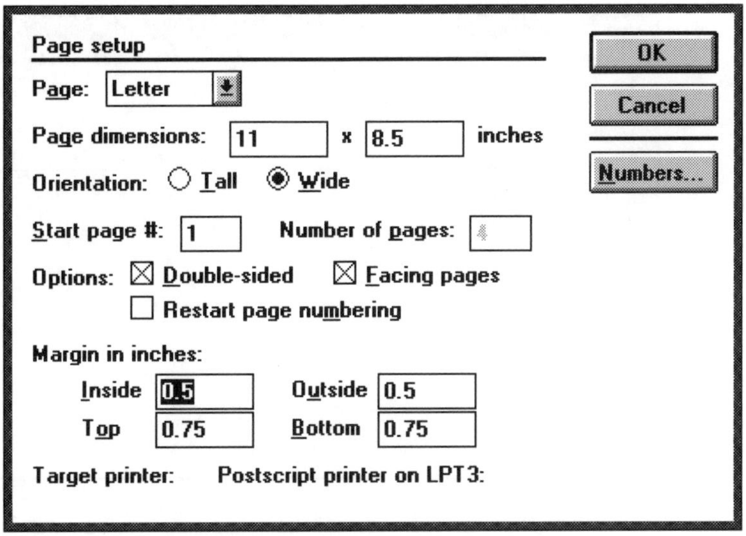

Figure 4-43. The Page setup for a gate-folded brochure.

gate-folded brochure, so that the panels are ready for folding. Graphics and text can bleed across the middle panels on the front and back of the brochure. (Experiment with page mockups on your printer before doing real production work, because laser printer models are different. Most laser printers can't print to the very edge of standard-sized paper, and leave about 1/8 inch or so of blank paper at the margins.)

Use special graphic effects on brochures and advertisements to attract the reader's attention. Enlarged initial capitals, dotted-line styles for rules, and four-color photos or other colored images can enrich the information in your brochure. Use a small font size for charts and diagrams, and a larger font size for headlines and attention grabbers. Banners with white or black type (with black or a specified background tint, as described previously) are especially useful as attention grabbers.

There are few rules for designing effective advertisements, but there are plenty of guidelines published in magazines and newsletters about advertising and design. These publications contain regular feature columns by the design experts that critique advertising. It helps a great deal to read about actual ads that worked or flopped.

Advertisements take up costly space in magazines, and direct-mail

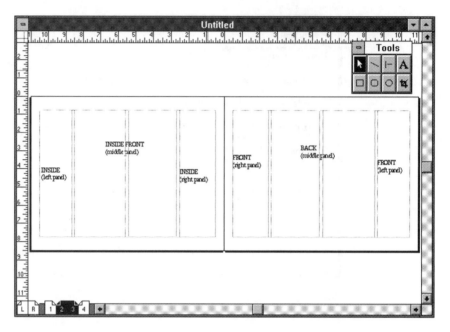

Figure 4-44. Pages 2 and 3 are used to define the several brochure pages in landscape mode, using 8 1/2 by 11-inch folded paper.

promotions are expensive to create, mail, and manage. Promotions and advertisements should directly generate income for your business.

Consult with a communications or design expert before finalizing your ad design to ensure that your ad looks as good as it possibly can.

Summary

This chapter presented some design rules and techniques for achieving various special effects with PageMaker. You learned how to adjust the ruler's zero point for accurate measuring.

In addition, the chapter covered several layout techniques such as combining articles with different column layouts on the same page, and wrapping text around a rectangular shape (such as a box), or around an irregular shape. It also explained how to make use of rules (horizontal and vertical lines), borders, and boxes around text.

Also described in this chapter were several text effects, including manual and automatic pair kerning, spreading and distoring characters, adjusting the leading (line spacing), and rotating text. You can spread the letters in story titles to fit a particular width by using fixed spaces or by stretching the characters.

PageMaker offers image control—the ability to adjust the brightness, contrast, and halftone screen characteristics of a scanned continuous-tone image (photograph). The Image control command also gives you control over the type of screen, the screen frequency (in lines per inch), and the angle of the line screen. By default PageMaker uses a dot screen at 53 lpi.

The lightness value lightens or darkens the image, and the contrast value lightens or darkens areas of the image in relation to their surrounding backgrounds. To determine the number of gray levels that will be printed, divide the printer resolution (dpi) by the halftone resolution (lpi), and raise the result to the power of two.

PageMaker automatically creates spot color overlays—a different overlay for each color—and lets you assign colors to text, drawn objects (such as lines, boxes, and ovals), and the black portions of graphic images. The Color palette displays the names of defined colors in the color sheet and lets you assign colors to objects.

The Define colors option lets you define color names for the color sheet (stored with each publication). When you edit a color name's definition, you change the color of every object in the publication to which that color name is assigned.

To create a different overlay page for each color, choose Print and select the Spot color overlays option. PageMaker automatically prints color registration marks (for lining up overlays) and the name of each color on the overlay. Select Knockouts to create a blank spot on the bottom (black) overlay where the colors overlap.

Crop marks are available in the Print dialog box, but only print if the paper (or film) is larger than the trim size defined in PageMaker.

By using PageMaker's publication files to hold design elements and boilerplate graphics, you can manage the production of magazine pages, catalog pages, and special pages such as a table of contents. Advertisements, flyers, and brochures can also be created in nonstandard page sizes. Use the techniques presented in this chapter to enhance your page designs. Consider consulting a design expert before you mass produce your masterpiece, or get feedback on the design from the intended audience in order to get the best possible result.

5 | Tips and Techniques

This chapter contains important tips, tricks, and techniques for working with PageMaker. Tips have been organized by topic, and the topics are listed in the same logical order in which you are likely to encounter them. This simple organization should provide easy access to the information without having to search through previous chapters. Should you want more information about a topic, or for topics not covered here, refer to the index of this book and to the PageMaker manuals.

Very Important!

There are two very important things you should know before starting a PageMaker project. One is that you should know in advance the type of printing device you will use for the final pages. This helps prevent unwanted patterns in your images and text recomposing operations when printing to certain devices. The other is that you should know how to use the Save and Save as commands to save your publication file.

Choosing a Printer
Before starting a publication, select a type of printer in the Target printer

dialog box that best matches the final output device you will be using, and if possible, select the actual printer driver in the Setup dialog box from the Target printer dialog box. You can change the target printer for a publication at any time. Every time you change the target printer, however, the composition of the publication may be altered, because different target printers use different fonts and options.

For example, if you are printing on a laser printer but you plan to use a PostScript Linotronic 300 for final output, you should choose the Linotronic 100/300 device as your printer in the Setup dialog box of the Target printer dialog box, before placing and scaling graphics. It is not necessary to actually print something (or even to have the device connected).

Your choice of printers determines how PageMaker will calculate the built-in "magic sizes" for scaling graphics with the Control (Ctrl) key to match the resolution of the printer. The magic sizes are important if you want to avoid unwanted patterns (such as moirés) that can occur with some paint-type graphics and with scanned images.

It doesn't matter if you print to a laser printer or any other type of printer later. It only matters that you have the appropriate printer selected when you are placing and resizing graphics. After resizing the graphics, no more calculations are performed that are based on the printer's resolution.

If you had chosen the wrong output device and had already placed and scaled the graphics, don't panic. Simply choose the right device, and then select each graphic image and scale it again while holding down the Control key (and the Shift key if you are scaling the image in the same proportions). The new magic sizes are calculated for the new printer.

The printer you choose remains in effect until you change it. You can change the printer for a publication anytime. After you change to a different printer with a different resolution, PageMaker uses the new resolution to calculate the magic sizes for scaling graphics.

Saving Publication Files

Don't wait for a catastrophe to happen—save now, and save often! Use the Save command to save a publication file immediately. Use the Save as command to save a file by another name, or to replace the old version with a new version that is more compact. The Save and Save as commands can also be used to create a template.

PageMaker performs a mini-save whenever you turn the page. You can revert back to the version of the publication file at the last full save operation, or you can revert back to the last mini-save operation by holding down the Shift key when selecting Revert.

Preparation

There is no better way to save time and money in any project than to be prepared. You must prepare text and graphics in advance, and you must prepare a design in advance.

The preparation for publishing consists of three steps: (1) develop an idea into a written and edited manuscript, (2) create and gather together illustrations and photos, and (3) design the overall look and the individual pages.

Editing Text

PageMaker allows you to type and edit words on the page in the layout view, or using the Story Editor. The Story Editor lets you write and edit text without having to wait for the page to be reformatted. You can import text from a word processing file into the Story Editor, or place word processing files into the layout. In addition, stories can be exported into a word processing file format for use with other programs.

You can edit text directly on the page in layout view, but PageMaker recomposes the text as you type it, making editing slower. If you plan to change only a few words, edit directly on the page, but if you plan to make a lot of changes, edit in the Story Editor window.

You could use PageMaker's Story Editor as a word processor, or you could use your favorite word processor for most of the writing effort, then use PageMaker's Story Editor for the editing phase. If you are already using a word processor, there is probably no reason to change tools—you can use PageMaker to finish your pages, because it can place on the page or import into the Story Editor virtually any kind of word processing file.

For those of you not yet using a word processor, PageMaker can be an economical choice for several reasons. You need only buy one program to do both word processing and page makeup, and you can prepare a text file in almost any word processor format by exporting the text from

PageMaker. Besides, you can check the spelling of all the text in the publication by opening a Story Editor window.

The Story Editor is a text-only window that uses a generic font and size for the text, but can display different styles, such as italic and bold. The original font information in the story is not changed; the generic font is used only for fast display in this window, which is optimized for fast editing and for applying styles to paragraphs. Once you've completed working in the Story Editor, the text is automatically poured back into its original location on the page, or loaded into the Place icon for automatic, semiautomatic, or manual placement.

In the Story Editor, you have the ability to search for and replace letters and phrases, fonts, point sizes, and paragraph styles. You can therefore make sweeping global formatting changes in a single operation.

Although you can change fonts, styles, and sizes for text in PageMaker's layout view, select them in the Story Editor while writing in order to save time. The text is formatted for placement when you close the window, and you can place text on many pages at once in the PageMaker publication file without stopping to select fonts. The Story Editor can open multiple stories at once, so you can copy and paste text from one story to another through the Clipboard.

You should make style sheet assignments to the text while writing or editing in the Story Editor or in another word processor that supports the use of style sheets. Doing this in advance greatly increases your productivity with PageMaker.

A style sheet definition is a set of text formatting instructions that can be applied to a single paragraph or to multiple paragraphs in one step. With style sheets you can change the text formatting of your entire publication by changing a few style definitions. PageMaker's Story Editor is useful for word processing due to its ability to assign style sheet definitions.

If your word processor is not listed in the PageMaker reference manual, then your file should be saved and placed with the Retain format selection turned off. In such cases, the text takes on the default font, style, size, leading, and tab settings that are already defined in PageMaker. These default settings can be set before opening a publication.

PageMaker recognizes tabs in a word processor file and uses them to align text or numbers in tables. You can change tab settings in PageMaker to fit the column width. The word processor file should already contain the tab characters, and each line of a table should end with a carriage return.

Typeset copy should not contain two spaces after any sentences. One formatting step that you should perform in the Story Editor with all stories, or with your word processor before you place stories, is to search for all instances of two consecutive spaces after a period and replace the two spaces with one space.

Captions, footnotes, and other independent elements can be typed directly onto the PageMaker page or into one or more stories in the Story Editor. If you use the Story Editor, for example, to type all the captions into one story, then the captions are linked from page to page, and you can export all the captions to a single file. When exporting text, you can export a selection of text or an entire story into one file.

Tabs and carriage returns, as well as spaces, are recognized by PageMaker in ASCII-only files, but no formatting settings from the word processor are used.

You can bring tables and paragraphs of text into PageMaker without retaining formatting settings (in other words, as ASCII-only text), and still retain paragraph endings and table column positions—as long as each table row ends with a carriage return.

After you select a file to place without retaining formatting, PageMaker displays a Smart ASCII import filter dialog box. You can choose to remove extra carriage returns from the file, which is a useful option if your ASCII file has a carriage return at the end of each line. After choosing to remove extra carriage returns from the file, you can select an option to remove carriage returns from the end of every line, from between paragraphs, or both.

PageMaker can rotate text to angles of 90-degree increments. If you want text to be rotated to an angle that is not an increment of 90 degrees (i.e., an angle other than 90, 180, 270, or 360 degrees), use a PostScript graphics program or a type manipulation program to rotate the text. Then save the text as an EPS or Windows Metafile graphics file.

Preparing Graphics

Use draw-type programs for logos, line drawings, business charts, graphs, and schematics, and use painting programs to create intricate designs and freestyle artwork. The highest resolution can be achieved with PostScript-drawing programs, which permit the creation of resolution-independent PostScript graphics.

Almost all painting and drawing programs can save a Windows Paintbrush or Bitmap file. Paintbrush and Bitmap images are stored as bits mapped directly to screen pixels. If the graphic image consists of line art, it can be resized into almost any proportion and size and still look good. Images with tight, regular patterns do not print well (they appear muddy). If you use the Control key while resizing, which limits you to sizes that print best at your printer's resolution, you can still get excellent results.

Most drawing programs, such as Corel Draw, Micrografx Designer and Draw Plus, and Aldus FreeHand, can save an EPS (Encapsulated PostScript) file, a CGM (Computer Graphics Metafile) graphics file, or a Windows Metafile graphics file, and many drawing programs can save all three types. Drawing programs give you precise tools for drawing geometric shapes. Usually, the drawing tools emulate drafting tools such as a compass, a T-square, a precise ruler, and a grid, and there are extra tools for quickly drawing perfect squares, circles, and geometric shapes. Drawing programs save graphics in a format that is independent of the resolution of the display and drawing device, so that when you print the graphics, PageMaker uses the highest possible resolution of the printing device. Draw-type graphics can be scaled in proportion, expanded, or condensed, with very little or no loss in quality.

When using graphics files, you may have to delete the text from the graphics first, place the graphics on the page, and then replace the text using PageMaker to get the best results. EPS (Encapsulated PostScript) files retain the quality of text styled in a PostScript font when you transfer them from one application to another, so you can create graphics with text when using the EPS format.

Using Scanners

Scanners are most useful for scanning line art and sketches that will be improved with drawing software, and for scanning photos and slides. At the very least, the scanned image can serve as a placeholder for a conventionally produced halftone. At most, it can serve as a substitute for the halftone, eliminating the need for the photographic halftoning process.

Scanners can also be used to scan text, but today's desktop scanners and OCR (optical character recognition) software only have high accuracy rates with typewritten text, or text printed in the Courier font on a laser printer, high-resolution dot matrix printer, or daisy-wheel printer. The OCR software can store text in simple ASCII format which can then be edited with a word processor. It almost always has to be edited, because the software makes many mistakes.

Text scanning works best either with clean, crisp originals that were printed using a Selectric-style typing element or a daisy wheel with carbon-film ribbons, or with clean copies of the originals. If a character is broken, or a bad photocopy is used, the software can't automatically recognize the character.

The text-scanning process is fastest when you use a clean original and place it flat on the glass platen so that the lines of text are parallel to the top of the platen. The OCR software reads slanted text (which results from the paper being placed askew on the platen), but the scanning speed is slower than usual.

Design

A newsletter should look interesting, and perhaps a bit informal (depending on the nature of the content). An annual report, however, should look sophisticated and important. You should lay out the text with enough white space surrounding it to make the text look very significant. In many book and manual projects, the goal is to produce a publication in which all of the pages have a similar format, but contain certain differences, such as illustrations, photos, or footnotes.

Although you can lay out a smaller page size (such as 6.5 by 9 inches) on pages that are standard size (8.5 by 11 inches), and you can adjust margin settings to create an image area the size of the pages, it is much better to change the page size in the Page setup dialog box. With the changed page size, you can print crop marks on the 8.5 by 11-inch paper (which print outside the defined page size). *Crop marks* are marks recognized by the volume printer or print shop as the marks that define the edges of the page. They are printed automatically by PageMaker if you select them from the Print dialog box.

You can bypass page specifications either by choosing the default specs (click OK) or by starting with a template. You can then replace the text and graphics in the template with new text and graphics by using the Place command.

Design Tools

You can print thumbnail sketches of the pages from the Print dialog box. Use gray boxes to represent text, black boxes to represent images, and white boxes to represent line art.

Use about 1/4 inch (0.25) for the column gap (space between columns) to open up more space, or use the PageMaker default of 0.167 inch (1 pica).

PageMaker usually displays a horizontal and vertical ruler unless you turn off the ruler display by selecting Rulers from the Options menu. You turn the ruler back on by selecting Rulers again. PageMaker automatically uses inches, but you can change the unit of measurement to centimeters or to picas with points by selecting Preferences from the Edit menu.

You may also want to use guides on the page because you can attach text and graphics blocks to them without the need to position a mouse exactly—the guide acts as a magnet so that when you move an element close to it, the element snaps to it. The Snap to guides command in the Options menu controls this feature, which is is on until you turn it off by selecting it. To turn it back on, select it again.

The master pages are designed to include the text and graphics that you want repeated on every left or right page (or both pages) of the publication file. For example, you probably want to have page footers appear on each page with the proper page number. You set this up by creating page footers on the master pages in order to repeat the footers on each page. Each footer can hold a marker for the page number that should be printed on each page.

However, the footer should appear not on Page one of the newsletter, even though it should appear on every other page. To turn off the footer (and any other master-page elements) for Page one, choose the Display master items option in the Page menu. If this option has a check mark next to it, the check mark disappears when you select it. The check mark means that master page items are displayed on the current page; with no check mark, it means that no master page items will be displayed for the current page. Therefore, you would turn this option off (no check mark) for a blank title page.

Design Rules

With body text, it is usually best to use enough leading to separate lines but not too much to be noticeable. A general rule is to use a leading value that is at least 20% greater than the font's point size (120% of the point size).

Don't mix more than three fonts (not including their italic and bold styles) on a page. Use white space so that the page is not overcrowded with text and graphics. You can use reverse (white) type in a black background or on a background with a 60% or 80% gray shade.

Above all, be consistent with the use of rules in a publication. Don't use a thick rule to separate text; instead, use a thin rule (perhaps a hairline rule). (If your printer can't produce a hairline, a thicker line will be substituted.) To draw attention to a headline, use a thick rule. Double rules tend to resemble picture frames, so use them only when they add emphasis to a headline or graphic, or serve as an appropriate frame.

A box can be useful as a border around text that is separated from the main article, or as a border around an entire page that is different (perhaps because it uses a different column layout). Use thin line styles for borders around text, graphics, or photos. Leave an equal amount of white space on all sides from the edge of the graphic or text to the box.

To put boxed text inside a column, line the box up with the margins/column guides of the column. Resize the text block inside the box to be narrower than the column.

Placing Text

PageMaker offers three ways to place text. To use manual placement, click the top of each column and then click the handle on the bottom of each text block to continue placing the text. To use semiautomatic placement, simply click the top of each column. There is no need to click the bottom handle because the program continues placement automatically.

To use fully automatic placement, use the Autoflow option, which pours each column and creates pages, if necessary, without your intervention. When placing text manually, you can switch to semiautomatic placement by holding down the Shift key, or switch to fully automatic placement by holding down the Control key. You can also turn on Autoflow in the Options menu for continuous automatic placement. To stop automatic placement at any time, click the mouse.

Another form of manual text placement is the drag-place feature. Instead of simply clicking the mouse button to place text, press down on the mouse button and drag diagonally to establish a bottom-right corner point before releasing the mouse button. This method is especially useful for placing headlines across more than one column on a page.

Retaining Formatting

You may place a text file and use the Retain format option so that PageMaker uses the formatting already specified in the word processing file. Alternatively, you may place a text file without retaining its formatting settings.

PageMaker does not use the right margin setting, page numbers, headers, or footers created by word processors. The program breaks lines to fit its columns, and treats carriage returns as paragraph endings. PageMaker recognizes most fonts, type styles and sizes, line spacing (leading), upper- and lowercase letters, left and right indents, first-line indents, and tab settings for most word processors.

If your word processor is not supported by PageMaker, or if you want to ignore formatting, place your file without the Retain format option so that PageMaker will apply its default type specifications.

If your word processor file contains a 1-inch indent from the left margin, and you place the file while retaining its formatting, PageMaker measures 1 inch from the left edge of the column.

PageMaker recognizes first-line indents in a word processor file that are either indented to the right (regular), or to the left of the left margin (a hanging indent). (See Appendix A for more information about how PageMaker treats text files from popular word processing programs.)

When you place a spreadsheet from Lotus 1-2-3, Lotus Symphony, Microsoft Excel, Borland's Quattro, or a variety of other spreadsheet programs, PageMaker displays named cell, row, column, and range references, as well as the print area. You may place any area of a spreadsheet by placing that area's name. You can also place the entire print area. Save other types of spreadsheets as text-only files and then place them.

With Excel, you have the choice of placing the spreadsheet (or chart) as an in-line graphic image embedded in the text (with formatting as set in Excel), or as text (with formatting controlled by PageMaker). When placed as text, each row is placed as a separate paragraph. Styles are applied so that you can change the formatting by redefining the appropriate styles.

You can place a dBASE or R:Base database file and select the fields of the database for importing into PageMaker. Two methods of placement are provided: directory format, in which each record is placed as a single paragraph with fields separated by tabs (as with spreadsheets), or catalog format, in which each field is a separate paragraph with a separate style definition.

Any kind of information can be imported into PageMaker (without retaining formatting) as long as the information is saved as a text file.

Without Retaining Formatting

Tabs, carriage returns, and spaces are recognized when you place text without retaining formatting settings, but no formatting settings from the word processor are used.

You can bring tables (with tabs) and paragraphs of text into PageMaker without retaining formatting, and still retain paragraph endings and table column positions in most cases. (See Appendix A for more information.)

You can place an ASCII text file and automatically delete carriage returns at the ends of lines. After selecting to place a file without retaining formatting, PageMaker displays the Smart ASCII import filter dialog box. You can choose to remove "extra carriage returns" from the end of every line, or from between paragraphs, or both. You can also choose to leave indents, tables, and lists as they are.

PageMaker recognizes tables and lists if each line of text has one or more embedded tabs but does not start with a tab, or if each line of text is followed by a line starting with a space or a tab. (For a complete description of importing ASCII text, see Appendix A.)

Converting Quotes

If you turn on the Convert quotes option, PageMaker automatically changes a double quote (") with a preceding space into an open quote ("), and changes a double quote followed by a space into a closed quote (").

The program also changes a single quote (') in the same manner, so that contractions, possessives, and quotes-within-quotes have the properly slanted punctuation symbols. PageMaker changes a double hyphen (- -) into an em dash (—), and changes a series of hyphens into half as many em dashes (creating a solid line).

Placing Graphics

PageMaker places graphics saved in a variety of file formats, including all Windows graphics formats (such as Windows Metafile, Bitmap, and Paintbrush files), TIFF (tag image file format), the PC Paintbrush (PCX) format, various vector graphics formats (such as AutoCAD files), the CGM format, Macintosh formats (MacPaint and PICT), and EPS (Encapsulated PostScript).

PageMaker offers a drag-place feature for images as well as text. Instead of simply clicking the mouse button to place the image, press down on the mouse button and drag diagonally to establish a bottom right corner point before releasing the mouse button. This sets the size of the image.

It is usually better to place the image without dragging so that the image appears at full size. You can then resize the image at any time. To do so, use the pointer tool to select the image, and click and drag any corner to make the image wider or more narrow.

Spreadsheet and business-graphics programs can perform the calculations that produce a bar or pie chart, or an x-y graph, that is accurate in proportion to the calculations. You can place these charts and graphs directly as graphics into PageMaker files.

Linking to External Files
PageMaker forms a link to each placed text and graphics file so that changes to the original can optionally be passed automatically to the publication file. The links are managed in the Links dialog box, which lists each text and graphics file placed in the publication.

When you place a paint-type graphics file or a scanned image (such as a TIFF file), you have the option to store the image inside the publication file, or leave it outside and establish a link to it. Since the linked file can be stored outside the PageMaker publication, publication files can be smaller.

In order for PageMaker's link to work automatically when printing graphics from external files, you have to leave the original graphics file in the directory that it was in when you placed it (i.e., not move it or delete it); otherwise, you must select the directory and file in a dialog box when you open or print the publication, or re-establish the link in the Links dialog box.

When you leave the graphics stored externally, PageMaker creates a lower-resolution version of the image for displaying on the page. It also establishes a link to the original, higher-resolution version of the file so that the program can use the higher-resolution version of the image when printing. PageMaker uses the lower-resolution image for display purposes in order to increase the speed of the program. You can move, resize, and crop the image, and PageMaker applies those changes to the original file when printing (although it does not change the original file).

Scaling Graphics

If the graphic is an EPS file, you can scale it by dragging a handle until the graphic is the right size for your layout. If it is a paint-type graphic with a pattern or fine detail, hold down the Control key to automatically display a selection of the optimal sizes for your target printer. In addition, hold down the Shift key while resizing in order to keep the same proportions; otherwise, you can distort the image by stretching or condensing from any of its sides.

By holding down the Shift key, you constrain any resized image to retain the same ratio. By holding down the Control key, you select only the "magic" image sizes that work well with the selected printer. Without holding down the Shift key, you can stretch or condense an image or graphic, as well as change its size. Without holding down the Control key, you can scale the image to any size, even to sizes that are not optimal for your printer. Remember to release the mouse button before you release the Shift and/or Control keys to achieve the desired result.

No matter how you stretch or condense an image, you can snap it back to a size equally proportional to the original by holding down the Shift key while resizing the image. If you hold down the Control key, the image snaps into the sizes that work well with the selected printer.

You can resize any paint-type graphic image in PageMaker by using the built-in resizing feature to obtain optimal sizes for the best results with your printer. If you change your printer, resize paint-type graphics with this built-in resizing feature if the graphics contain a tight pattern of dots (to avoid moirés). Select the paint-type graphic image and resize it by holding down the Control key while dragging one of the image's corners.

To reduce the size of a graphics file that contains text that doesn't print well (especially draw-type graphics), first use the graphics program to delete the text. Place just the graphics, and then add text with PageMaker for more control over text size and styles within a text block.

If the text in an EPS graphic image is printed as Courier by mistake, it is usually because the printer does not have that font. Download the appropriate font to the printer first.

Layout Skills

There are some skills that you should develop in order to be more productive with PageMaker. For example, you should know how to view pages at different sizes, how to move text and graphics elements with ease, how to select text, change a text column's width, and so on.

Perhaps the most important features to learn how to use to increase productivity, besides keyboard shortcuts, are style sheets and master pages. To find the keyboard shortcuts, look at each menu and remember the Control (Ctrl) key equivalent for the next time you use it. The Control key is abbreviated as "^" in the menu. We've introduced most of them in the previous chapters.

Viewing Pages
You can switch back and forth from actual size to reduced size by holding down the Control and Alt keys and clicking the mouse. To change the display quickly to a full-page view from actual size, click the right mouse button, or type Control-W (or pick the Fit in Window option from the Page menu).

When you hold down the Control and Alt keys and click the mouse while pointing to a spot on the page that you want to view, PageMaker jumps into actual size. When you repeat these steps, PageMaker jumps to full-page view; the command toggles the displays.

Actual size approximates the printed page size, but the 200% size (Control-2) produces the most accurate display for positioning text and images. You can also jump from actual size to 200% by clicking the right mouse button while holding down the Shift key.

Hold down the Control, Shift, and W keys to see the entire pasteboard. Hold down the Control and W keys to see all of the page or the spread that you are working on, plus some of the pasteboard (Fit in window).

An alternative to using the scroll bars is the grabber hand, available at all times, no matter which tool you are using. Hold down the Alt key, press down on the mouse button, and the pointer changes to the grabber hand. Drag the grabber hand, and the page moves in the window. Release the mouse button when the appropriate portion of the page is in view, and the pointer reverts to the tool you were using. If you hold down the Shift key as well as the Alt key, and drag the grabber hand up/down or left/right, the scrolling is constrained to vertical or horizontal movement.

Moving Text and Graphics Elements

Move a text or graphics element by pointing in the middle of the element and holding down the mouse button until you see the four arrows. Then drag the element into position. With Snap to guides on, you can attach a text or graphics element to a column guide or a ruler guide.

To move several objects at once so that they stay in position in relation to each other, select one object in the usual way, and then select the others in any sequence by holding down the Shift key and selecting each one with the pointer tool. Point in the middle of one of the objects, hold down the mouse button until you see the four-arrows symbol, and drag all of the objects at once into position. If a text block, graphic, or box disappears, select whatever is covering it and use the Send to back command in the Element menu.

By holding down the Shift key while dragging a graphics or text element, you can drag evenly, without moving up or down. You can drag text over a graphic image or drag a graphic image over text. If you want the text to appear (as text blocks are transparent), select the text and choose the Bring to front command in the Element menu.

Deleting and Combining Text Elements

To delete a text element but not the text that it contains, select the element with the pointer tool. Close the element by dragging its bottom handle up to meet the top handle. Do not delete the sole text element of a story, or you will delete the story. You can click the + symbol of a previous element's bottom handle to reflow the text. You can, of course, delete text elements by selecting them and then pressing the Delete or Backspace key, or by using Cut from the Edit menu.

To combine multiple text elements into one element (effectively deleting a layout so that you can start fresh and place the text again), close the text elements as described previously, but start with the last text element of the story and work backward to the first. Don't close the first element. Reflow the text by clicking the + symbol of the first element's bottom handle.

Selecting Text

There are several different ways to select text. Select a single word by double-clicking the word; you can then drag in any direction to select a group of words. You can extend a selection from an existing selection by holding down the Shift key and clicking a new ending point. (You can also use the cursor movement keys, rather than the mouse.) Another way to select a large area of text is to click a starting point at one end, and then Shift-click the ending point at the other end. The easiest way to select all of the text is to click anywhere in the text once, and then choose the Select all command from the Edit menu (or press the Control and A keys).

The same conventions work inside the Story Editor window. You can open the Story Editor window by triple-clicking a text element with the pointer tool, or typing Control-E with a selected text element.

Changing Text Element Width

Although text wraps within the column width, you can change the text block's width. Switch to the pointer tool and drag any corner of the block of text to be wider or thinner, and longer or shorter.

To make the text block wider than a column (e.g., for positioning a headline across text that spans two columns), use the pointer tool to click any corner of the new text block formed by the Paste command. Drag the new text until it becomes a wider but shorter text block and the headline fits on one line.

Master Pages

Put a page header and footer on the master page so that they are repeated with each page. Headers and footers can accommodate a page number that changes for each page. Set the number of columns and space between columns on the master pages, if you want the same column layout on all pages.

Save all designed elements in a separate publication file—you can copy them to another publication via the Clipboard and the Copy and Paste commands. Save elements on master pages if the elements are to be repeated on almost every page (except the pages for which you selected to Remove master items). Also save the column layout of each page without text and graphics, but with design elements, so that you can place new text and graphics without reinventing the design elements.

The Display master items option in the Page menu, which is usually turned on (a check mark is displayed next to it), means that PageMaker copies text and graphic items from the master pages to the selected page for displaying and printing. To turn off the display and printing of master items for a selected page, choose the option again (the check mark disappears).

PageMaker offers the ability to save a publication file as a *template* file, which can be used to define new publications simply by replacing the contents of the template file with new contents with the Place command. Use the Save as command with the Template option. When you open the template file, it automatically opens as a new, untitled document, leaving the original template file intact and untouched.

Style Sheets

Style sheet names define the text font, size, style (italic, bold, etc.), leading, paragraph spacing, tab settings, indents, and color. When you change a style sheet definition, all sections of text defined by that style sheet change automatically to adopt the new definition. Assign style sheet names to sections of text with the Style palette in the layout or Story Editor windows.

When you use style definitions in Microsoft Word, place the Word file with the Retain format option and the Convert quotes option turned on. Do not turn on the Read tags option because that option requires the use of tag names in the text. PageMaker can import and export Word files with defined styles; tags are not required.

When using other word processors or placing ASCII text from any source, tags can be useful. A tag name (a name surrounded by angle brackets, such as <subhead>) can be embedded into any text file in order to define a section of text that follows it (until another tag name, or the end of the file, is reached). PageMaker exports text with tag names embedded so that they can be placed into other PageMaker files and retain style sheet names. Tags are also useful as assignments of style sheet names with word processors that do not offer style sheets. You use the Read tags option with the Place command to have PageMaker interpret the tags as style sheet assignments, and you use the Export tags option with the Export command to create a text file with tag names for style sheet assignments.

At any time, you can edit a style sheet definition in PageMaker. When assigning style sheet names to the text, it helps to display the style palette. (To do so, press the Control and K keys, or select Style palette from the Windows menu.)

Changing a Layout

To increase the white space by one line at the current leading, type an extra carriage return (press the Enter or Return key) while using the text editing tool. For a different measure, highlight the line, choose the Type specs command from the Type menu, and change the leading to a larger point size.

To mix column layouts on one page, draw a line to separate the layouts, and (if necessary) change the number of columns with the Column guides option. Leave the same spacing between columns (or use less spacing, if the columns are very narrow). Start at the top or left-hand section of the page and position the text in that layout first. Then change the column layout again and continue placing text in that layout. The change does not affect the text that you already placed in the first layout.

If you want a line style that is not available in the Line pop-up menu, try creating a box that is only one line wide by overlapping the box's edges until they disappear from the display. While the box is still selected, choose a pattern from the Fill pop-up menu.

Rectangle and Line Tools

You can draw an entire chart or graph using PageMaker's line-drawing, rectangle-drawing, and oval-drawing tools with gray patterns and colors.

PageMaker's Snap-to-guides feature makes it easy to line up several distinct rectangles to form a bar chart. You can draw perfect circles by holding down the Shift key while dragging with the oval tool, or draw perfect squares by holding down the Shift key while dragging with the rectangle tool. To make very thin dotted lines, use the rectangle tool, select a parallel lines shade, and drag the rectangle inward until it is as thin as a line.

Keyboard Controls

Certain characters not available on the keyboard can be typed using a special combination of keys. In text, you can use the Control key with another key; in dialog box entries, you can use a special character ($\wedge$) to represent the Control key. The special characters are listed in Appendix C.

The left/right cursor movement keys move the insertion point by a single character or space. The up/down keys move the insertion point by a single line.

Holding down the Control key when pressing a left or right key moves the insertion point to the beginning of the next word or previous word. Pressing an up or down key and the Control key moves the point to the beginning of the next paragraph or the previous paragraph.

Pressing the Home or End key moves the insertion point to the beginning or the end of the current line (or the next line if the point is already at the beginning or the end of the current line). When the Control key and the Home or End keys are pressed, the point moves to the beginning of the next sentence or the previous sentence. You can also move up or down in the text block quickly by using the PageUp (PgUp) or PageDown (PgDn) keys. If the Control key is pressed along with the PageUp or PageDown key, the insertion point moves to the beginning or to the end of the text that has been placed.

The entire set of commands for moving the insertion point are listed in the *PageMaker Quick Reference Guide*.

Changing Type Size and Style

To quickly change the point size of text, select the desired text and then press the Control, Shift, and < (less than) keys at once to lower the point size (in 1-point increments). Press the Control, Shift, and > (greater than) keys to raise the point size (in 1-point increments).

The leading is not adjusted, so if you intend to raise the point size to be a size larger than the leading, change the leading first so that the larger characters are not clipped as they become too large to fit within the leading.

To quickly change leading, style, and other font attributes, as well as the point size of type, select the text tool. Double-click on a word to select the word, triple-click to select the line, or click an insertion point, and use Control-A (or Select All from the Edit menu) to select the entire file. To select a range of text, first click an insertion point at the start of the range. Either drag until you have selected the desired area, or hold down the Shift key and click a second insertion point at the end of the range.

After selecting your text, use shortcut drag-across menus in the Type menu (Font, Size, Leading, Type style), or press Control-T to activate the Type specs dialog box. You can also drag across for alignment and style sheet.

Press Control-M to bring up the Paragraph dialog box. Press Control-I to bring up the Indents/tabs dialog box.

You can also change the text style to normal (Shift, Control, and spacebar), bold (Shift, Control, and B), italic (Shift, Control, and I), Strikethrough (Shift, Control, and S), underline (Shift, Control, and U), and reverse (Shift, Control, and V) for the selected range of type.

Special Effects

To draw a drop shadow of a frame, copy the frame to the Clipboard and paste the copy back to the page. Move the copy to the shadow position, and change its shade to black.

To move all of the elements at once, hold down the Shift key to select the frame and the text without deselecting the already-selected black shadow. Release the Shift key and click in the center of the group until you see the double-arrow symbol, and drag the entire group. Finally, to move the black shadow behind the frame and text, deselect by clicking the pointer tool again. Select only the black shadow and use the Send to back command (Element menu).

To wrap text around a rectangular box, select the box and choose the Text wrap option (Element menu). Then select the rectangular text wrap (the middle icon), which automatically sets the text-flow icon. Text flows automatically around the box, leaving space between the text and the box as defined in the Text wrap dialog box.

To wrap text around an irregular shape, use the Text wrap option as just described, and then adjust the wrap boundary by dragging its points. Create more points in the wrap boundary for fine-tuning by clicking on the boundary.

To spread text, such as a headline, to fill a space on the page, you can stretch or condense the characters by changing their widths with the Set width command in the Type menu.

To spread a headline to fill a specific width without distorting the characters, first isolate the headline as a separate text block and move the headline into place, dragging it to be as wide as it should be. Then select Force justified as the paragraph style. The result is a justified, evenly spread headline.

Typographic Controls

PageMaker sets type by deciding how many words can be fit on one line. You can control the way type looks by adjusting certain factors, such as the amount of hyphenation, the way certain words are hyphenated, and the amount of spacing between words and between letters.

Em spaces (Control, Shift, and M for each space in text, or ^m in a dialog box) are fixed spaces that are the width of a capital "M" in the font chosen, and unlike regular spaces between words, they are not changed by PageMaker. En spaces (Control, Shift, and N for each space in text, or ^> in a dialog box) are fixed spaces that are the width of a capital "N" in the font chosen. Thin spaces (Control, Shift, and T for each space in text, or ^< in a dialog box) and fixed spaces (Control and Spacebar for each space in text, or ^s in a dialog box) can also be typed in PageMaker. Em, en, thin, and fixed spaces are all nonbreaking spaces that connect the characters to their left and right sides, and they never fall at the end of a line.

In the Spacing dialog box, you have a choice of methods for measuring leading: Proportional or Top of caps. The proportional method places the baseline two-thirds of the way down from the top of the slug. With the top-of-caps method, the baseline is placed after calculating the height of the tallest ascender (the vertical stroke of a lowercase "b" or "h") in the largest font on that particular line. With automatic leading, if you set the leading of one or more characters in a line to be larger than the line's leading amount, the entire line's leading is adjusted automatically.

Kerning
Automatic pair kerning is usually turned on for all of the text that is larger

than 12 points in size, but you can change this setting in the Paragraph dialog box. If used for text point sizes less than 12 points, pair kerning slows down text placement and text flow over pages. You can turn on automatic pair kerning for selected areas of the text, rather than kerning the entire text. The degree of pair kerning depends both on the printer and the font that you use.

To manually kern between two characters, click an insertion point the text tool between the two characters. Press Control and Backspace, or Control and minus (-) on the numeric keypad, to tighten space by 1/25th of an em space. If you need more precision, press Shift, Control, and minus (-) on the numeric keypad to tighten by 1/100th of an em space.

To increase the spacing by 1/25th of an em space, press Control, Shift, and Backspace, or Control and plus (+) on the numeric keypad. To increase the spacing by 1/100th of an em space, press Control, Shift, and plus (+) on the numeric keypad.

To manually kern a selection of text at once, select the text and use the same key combinations described above. You can remove all kerning from a selection of text by pressing Control, Shift, and zero (0).

With track kerning, the kerning amount depends on the point size of the font. With the Normal track you get less space between characters at high point sizes and more space between characters at low point sizes. The other tracks (Very loose, Very tight, Loose, and Tight) are generally used for special effects with titles. You can remove all track kerning from a selection by pressing Control, Shift, and Q.

Hyphenation and Justification

Justified text is automatically aligned to the left and right margins of a column. To justify text, PageMaker first adds spaces between words (within the specified word-spacing ranges), and then it adds spaces between characters (within the specified letter-spacing ranges). If it still can't justify the line, it expands word spacing as necessary to justify the line.

You can adjust the spacing in justified text by decreasing or increasing the space between words (word spacing), and the space between characters (letter spacing). First, use the text tool to select the desired text, and then click the Spacing button in the Paragraph dialog box to specify new settings for word spacing and letter spacing. Change the minimum and maximum word spacing value to get rid of the river of white effect that can occur with justified text.

For optimal spacing for justified text, leave hyphenation on and set the word spacing range at 50% for minimum, 100% for desired, and 200% for maximum. Leave the letter spacing at -5% for minimum, 0% for desired, and 25% for maximum. Remember that narrower ranges of word spacing cause more hyphenation to occur. Letter spacing, by comparison, should be as close to zero as possible, which is the font designer's optimal spacing.

A nonbreaking hyphen can be entered by typing Control, Shift, and - (dash) in text, or ^~ (tilde) in a dialog box. The opposite of a nonbreaking hyphen, a discretionary or "soft" hyphen (which only appears if it falls at the end of a line) can be entered by typing Control and - (dash) in text, or ^- (dash) in a dialog box.

Hyphenation can be automatic or manual (with discretionary hyphens typed in as you need them), using either a dictionary or an algorithm. The Manual plus algorithm option provides the most hyphenation.

To avoid having too many hyphens in a row, you can turn off hyphenation for a selection of text with the Hyphenation command in the Type menu. You can limit the number of consecutive hyphens, and change the hyphenation zone to allow more or less hyphenation. A larger zone causes the right margin to be more ragged; a smaller zone causes more hyphenation and a less ragged look.

If you turn hyphenation off for nonjustified text and the column width is narrow in relation to the font used, or if hyphenation is on but the hyphenation zone is large in relation to the column width, then text will be more ragged than usual.

Font Issues

PageMaker remembers the font you chose, even if your target printer does not print that font. PageMaker substitutes the closest font, and remembers the actual font when you switch to a target printer that can print it.

When you add a printer to your Windows system, be sure to add both the fonts supplied with the printer on disk, and the screen fonts that display representations of the printed fonts. Dot-matrix fonts display on the screen exactly as they print and may be useful for decorative purposes, but look more jagged at the edges than higher-resolution laser printer fonts. Add screen fonts to Windows by double-clicking the Control Panel's Font icon.

Adobe Type Manager (ATM) is supplied with PageMaker to display and print outline fonts without using additional screen bitmap fonts. ATM provides the essential scaling and display functions for outline fonts. It is far more convenient to have one outline for the font stored on disk rather than many bitmap versions representing different point sizes. The one outline can be scaled to any point size for display and printing. ATM provides the best quality with Adobe's Type 1 outline fonts. The ATM Installer lets you install optional PCL bitmap fonts for HP LaserJet (or compatible) printers, which improves printing performance with LaserJets.

PageMaker can stretch or enlarge a screen font to display it as a substitute for another font (or to use a point size you don't have). PageMaker can also use the Windows vector fonts, which are displayed quickly and can be used to display any size font. No matter which font PageMaker chooses, the line endings match the line length of the printed version. However, they do not look like the printed version.

These options are available in the Preferences dialog box (Edit menu). Click the Other button in the Preferences dialog box (Edit menu) to display the screen font options. Usually the "stretch text" and "vector text" options are set to 24 pixels, and the "greek text" option—to display a pattern rather than text—is set to below 9 pixels.

If you are using ATM and Type 1 fonts, you should change the threshold number for vector text to 127 pixels, and the greek text option to 6 pixels. ATM displays fonts correctly only when the text size is between the greek and vector size thresholds.

Although paint-type graphics programs and drawing programs let you select fonts for text, and these fonts are carried over into PageMaker when you place the image, the text may not look as good as when it is placed as text (or typed) into PageMaker. Text within a graphics file is reduced or enlarged with the image as you resize the image, but the fonts usually do not correspond directly to laser-printer fonts (unless they are PostScript fonts defined in an EPS file). You may get better quality by deleting the text from the graphics file before placing the graphics, and then retyping the text in PageMaker. You can use PageMaker to type the text for the axes labels in charts and graphs because PageMaker can rotate text in 90-degree increments.

If the publication file was created with a different target printer, the selection of a new target printer causes PageMaker to ask you for a confirmation: Should the entire publication be recomposed? Click OK to the recompose operation because PageMaker must use the target printer's font information to perform proper kerning, justification, and spacing.

The recompose operation may change the line lengths of some of the text, so look over your publication carefully. For this reason, always try to begin a publication with the right target printer in mind.

Printing

Changing the resolution (dots per inch) of the printer affects the appearance of graphics. The lower the resolution, the faster the publication file prints; but the graphics will be coarser and hairline rules may not print at all.

You can also create a PostScript print file of the pages, rather than print the pages. The PostScript file can then be transmitted to another computer over a modem and telephone line, or transferred by disk. The receiving computer (which could be at a typesetting service) does not have to run PageMaker in order to send the file to the printer or typesetter, as long as the printer or typesetter interprets PostScript.

To create an Encapsulated PostScript file, click the Setup button in the Print dialog box, then click the Options button in the Setup dialog box. Select the Encapsulated PostScript file option, and supply a name for the Encapsulated PostScript file. By clicking the Header button you can choose whether or not to include the header with the PostScript file, which is necessary for printing the page by itself.

To create overlay pages that contain the colored objects, choose the Print command, and select the Spot color overlays option. PageMaker automatically prints color registration marks (for lining up overlays) and the name of each color on the overlay, and prints a different overlay for each color. Use the Knockouts option to create a blank spot on the bottom (black) overlay where the colors overlap. Use the Crop marks option if the paper (or film, in the case of typesetters) is larger than the page size defined in PageMaker.

You can choose Page setup from the File menu to change the margin settings, but that may affect your layout and make changes that you may not want. To print the completed pages at a smaller size without changing the layout, scale the publication to less than 100% in the Print dialog box, selected from the File menu at print time (if your printer supports scaling).

Archive Files

You can use PageMaker publication files as archive files. PageMaker exports text as text-only files, optionally with style tag names embedded to retain style-sheet assignments. PageMaker also exports text as word processing files with full formatting and style-sheet information.

Use the Save as command periodically when building a publication, and again when the publication is completed. The Save as command compresses the publication file so that it occupies less disk space and loads faster.

To save disk space with TIFF image files, you can compress the files from the Place dialog box. PageMaker provides two levels of compression: moderate and maximum. The amount of actual compression varies according to the content and the type of TIFF file. To compress the files, use the Place command and select the file in the Place dialog box. For a moderately compressed TIFF file, hold down Control and Alt while clicking OK. For maximum compression, hold down Control, Shift, and Alt and click OK. To decompress a TIFF file, hold down Control and click OK.

Nothing can be more rewarding than to finish a book project, make a copy of all the publication files, use PageMaker to make a set of archive disks, and then make a safety copy of the archive disks and store them in another location. No matter what may happen, those publication files can be used again. Nothing brings us more satisfaction in book writing than the knowledge that when we want to go back to a book and make an updated version of it, we can start right where we left off on the PageMaker page.

Someday most of publishing will be electronic in its delivery (rather than paper), and when that day comes, your electronic PageMaker publications will be ready for the new medium.

APPENDIX A
Word Processing Programs

PageMaker can import text from word processing programs, spreadsheet programs, and database programs as well as from other PageMaker 4 publication files. PageMaker uses a filter to prepare the text or data for importing, and in some cases for exporting to a word processor file. The filters for importing and exporting are installed when you first set up PageMaker as described in Chapter 2. You can at any time install or delete filters by running the Aldus Setup program. You can display a list of the installed filters by holding down the Control (Ctrl) key and choosing About PageMaker from the Help menu.

PageMaker expects external files to have specific file name extensions. If the file does not have a recognizable file name extension, PageMaker displays a dialog box so that you can select the appropriate filter for importing the file. The following are the expected file name extensions for word processing files:

Format	File name extensions
ASCII text-only files	sample.TXT
DCA files	sample.DCA or sample.RFT
DEC WPS-PLUS	sample.DX
HP AdvanceWrite	sample.AW

IBM DisplayWrite 3/4	sample.DCA or sample.RFT
Lotus Manuscript	sample.DCA
Lotus (Samna) Ami Professional	sample.SAM
Microsoft Rich Text Format	sample.RTF
Microsoft Windows Write	sample.WRI
Microsoft Word	sample.DOC or sample.RTF
MultiMate/Advantage IV	sample.DOC
Olivetti Olitext Plus	sample.OTX
PageMaker 4.0 Story Importer	sample.PM4 or sample.PT4
PC Write	sample.PCW
Reversible Form Text	sample.RFT
Samna Word	sample.SAM
WordPerfect 4.2	sample.WP
WordPerfect 5.0, 5.1	sample.WP5
WordStar 3.3-6.0	sample.WS
WordStar 2000	sample.DCA
XyWrite III Plus 3.53	sample.XY3

These word processing programs are fully supported—PageMaker recognizes character formats and fonts, indents, justification styles, and tab settings. Be sure to use tabs, rather than spaces, to line up columns of text in a word processor. In general, PageMaker will import as much character and paragraph formatting as possible while ignoring page-layout information, such as margin and column settings, which are more easily controlled from within PageMaker.

PageMaker treats a carriage return (formed by pressing the Enter or Return key) as the start of a new paragraph. Do not place carriage returns at the ends of each line, unless you want to force the lines to be separate paragraphs.

PageMaker imports style-sheet definitions from word processing programs that use style definitions, such as Microsoft Word and WordPerfect; however, you must have an import filter in order to import style definitions. You can also export style-sheet definitions back to Word with the Word export filter. After a style is imported, PageMaker displays an asterisk (*) next to the style name in the Styles palette for each imported style. You can change the definition of imported styles, just as you can change the definition of regular styles in PageMaker.

PageMaker can import style definitions in WordPerfect files, and if you hold down the Shift key when placing or importing such files, you are given the choice of not importing styles, importing styles as definitions only, or importing styles as paragraph-level attributes. In the latter case, PageMaker adds the style definitions to the Style palette and assigns the styles to paragraphs in the text (character-level and word-level styles are applied to entire paragraph styles as if they were paragraph styles). When you choose to import style definitions only, the styles are added to the palette but are not assigned to paragraphs.

In WordPerfect version 4.1 files, type styles (but not fonts and sizes), soft (discretionary) hyphens, indents, justification styles, tab settings, and some alignment commands are recognized by PageMaker. You must explicitly use the justify command if you want this command to be used by PageMaker, even though WordPerfect starts with justified text. The flush right and center alignment commands are recognized, and lines that end with them are treated as separate paragraphs. Tabs are converted (up to 20 per paragraph) using the pitch setting and according to the number of spaces between tab settings. PageMaker does not recognize WordPerfect's tab align feature. WordPerfect's type styles (normal, bold, underline, italic, superscript, and subscript) are used, but PageMaker uses its own default type specifications for font, size, leading, kerning, and spacing.

In Word for Windows files, PageMaker recognizes styles as well as specially-formatted tables, index entries, and TOC (table of contents) entries. When you hold down Shift while placing or importing such files, you can choose whether or not to import TOC entries, index entries, condensed or expanded spacing, page breaks before paragraphs, and tables. TOC and index entries are recognized and used by PageMaker for its index and table of contents generation. Spacing adjustments in Word are based on points rather than percentages of the font's size, so you are given the choice of importing this spacing information as set width information, changing the actual shape of the characters, or as manual kerning information, affecting the spacing between characters without changing their shapes. You can also choose to import the spacing information as tracking information (Normal, Tight, Loose, etc.). The page break information, used for every paragraph marked with "Page Break Before" in Word, can be treated as a page break or as a column break, or ignored entirely.

XyWrite III's character modes (but not fonts and sizes), indents, justification styles, and tab settings are recognized. PageMaker assumes that all measurements are ten units to the inch (10 pitch) and does not recognize fractional units in XyWrite's embedded commands. PageMaker also assumes that the left margin is zero units and the right margin is 78, and converts the left and right margin commands to left and right indents. XyWrite's character modes (normal, bold, underline, italic, superscript, and subscript) are used, but PageMaker uses its own default type specifications for font, size, leading, kerning, and spacing.

PageMaker 4 imports XyWrite III Plus files (with the .XY3 extension) with nearly all formatting characteristics.

Styles defined using the SS and US commands in XyWrite III Plus will appear in PageMaker's styles palette, but the text will not have the correct styles applied. (Use tags to define styles, as described below, or first create a matching style sheet in PageMaker with the same name as the style in XyWrite, and attach the styles to the text after placement in PageMaker.) PageMaker reduces the size of superscripts and subscripts to 7/12ths of the normal type size, and places them at 1/3rd of the selected point size above or below the baseline of normal text. For example, a superscript that occurs in a paragraph of 12-point text is changed to seven points and placed four points above the baseline. The indent paragraph command (IP) sets left and first-line indents that are retained in PageMaker. You can use the XyWrite III Plus filter to export text from PageMaker into the XyWrite III format.

WordStar 3.3's indents and type styles are recognized (double strike is converted to italics), as well as line styles, but not its variable tabs (except as the indent of the first line of a paragraph). PageMaker ignores justification, but recognizes fixed tabs.

DisplayWrite 3 (version 1.10) files saved as revisable form text (also known as DCA, or document content architecture) are recognized by PageMaker. Although bold text, superscripts, and subscripts are recognized, fonts are converted to PageMaker's default settings. PageMaker converts line spacing and lines-per-inch settings to leading, and uses tabs and first-line indents (in unjustified paragraphs), but not centered text.

Samna Word III's DCA files are recognized, but PageMaker ignores leader tabs, graphics, math functions, hanging indents, and bulleted paragraphs. PageMaker recognizes justification (but not centered text), regular and decimal tabs, type size, bold and underlined styles, and line spacing.

Volkswriter 3 (version 1) DCA files are recognized, but PageMaker ignores style sheets and embedded commands. First-line indents, up to 20 tab settings per paragraph (set in the first line), line spacing, and some type styles (subscript, superscript, and underline) are recognized by PageMaker.

WordStar 2000 (version 2) DCA files are recognized, including tabs, standard indents, nested paragraphs (without bullets—add bullets when using PageMaker), type styles (except italic), and font sizes (using the default PageMaker font).

If your word processing program does not use style sheets, you can still assign style-sheet names, or *tags*, to text by placing the style sheet names in the text surrounded by brackets (as in **<subhead 1>**). Such style tags must be placed at the beginning of a paragraph. Although you can't define the formatting settings for the style in the word processor, you can define it in PageMaker after placing the text with the Read tags option turned on. A paragraph that is not tagged adopts the formatting settings of the previous paragraph. You can also export a text file with tags by using the Export tags option in the Export dialog box.

PageMaker ignores the formatting of page numbers, headers, footers, columns, plus other word processor formatting that is not appropriate for PageMaker pages. If your word processor offers a variety of underlining styles, PageMaker changes them to a single underline.

The Export command in the File menu can be used to export a story or selection of text to an external file. PageMaker can export text in ASCII (text-only) files, DCA or RFT files, Microsoft's Rich Text Format (RTF) files, Microsoft Word files, Windows Write files, and WordPerfect 5.0 and 5.1 files.

ASCII: The Standard Character Set for Text

PageMaker reads text-only files, thanks to ASCII. ANSI (American National Standards Institute), the U.S. version of the European ISO (International Standards Organization), has developed ASCII (American Standard Code for Information Interchange). This character code represents a character set (text and symbols) that has been adopted by the ISO, and is known in Europe as the ISO character set.

IBM uses EBCDIC (Extended Binary-Coded Decimal Interchange Code) for their character set. This code standard represents most ASCII characters, but the 8-bit numerical values assigned by EBCDIC differ from the 8-bit numerical ASCII values. You can translate ASCII into EBCDIC, and vice versa, with the appropriate software. The IBM PC uses an ASCII character set, rather than the EBCDIC character set used on the large IBM computers.

PageMaker 4 offers an ASCII text filter with several options for importing ASCII-only text. You can choose to remove "extra carriage returns" from the end of every line, or from between paragraphs, or both. If you choose to remove them from every line, you can still have PageMaker recognize paragraph endings if paragraphs are originally separated by two consecutive carriage returns. If you choose to remove them from between paragraphs, the filter deletes one carriage return wherever it finds two in a row, thus deleting the extra line between paragraphs. With either (or both) suboptions, you can choose to leave indents, tables, and lists as they are. PageMaker recognizes tables and lists if each line of text has one or more embedded tabs but does not start with a tab, or if each line of text is followed by a line starting with a space or a tab. In either case, the line must already end with a carriage return.

You can also replace one or more spaces with a tab, so that if your text has a table that is justified in columns using spaces, you can change those spaces to a single tab character that can be adjusted in PageMaker. You can specify a specific number of consecutive spaces, and when the filter sees that many spaces in a row (or more), it replaces all of them with a single tab character. Another option is to import the table using the monospaced Courier font, so that the columns are aligned the same way as in a monospaced word processor. With a monospaced font such as Courier, each character and space is aligned with a character and space on the previous monospaced line.

Note that if you choose the option to remove carriage returns from each line, be sure to also check the suboption to leave the carriage returns in for tables and lists.

Importing Spreadsheets and Databases

The following are the expected file name extensions for spreadsheet and database files:

Format	File name extensions
dBASE III+, IV	sample.DBF
Excel 2.1-3.0 spreadsheets	sample.XLS
Excel 2.1-3.0 charts	sample.XLC
Lotus 1-2-3 v1A	sample.WKS
Lotus 1-2-3 v2.0-2.2	sample.WK1
Lotus 1-2-3 v3.0	sample.WK3
Lotus 1-2-3 graphs	sample.PIC
Lotus Symphony 1.0	sample.WRK
Lotus Symphony 1.1-2.0	sample.WR1
Lotus Symphony graphs	sample.PIC
Quattro spreadsheets	sample.WK1, sample.WKS
Quattro graphs	sample.PIC
R:Base	sample.DBF

In many spreadsheet programs, such as Microsoft Excel, spreadsheets can have named cells, rows, and columns for easy reference. You can refer to, say, the "Total Expenses" row of an expenses spreadsheet. You can place any named range in the spreadsheet. The text of the spreadsheet is placed and assigned a style definition, which you can then change as you wish.

With Excel, you have the choice of placing the spreadsheet (or chart) as an in-line graphic image embedded in the text (with formatting as set in Excel), or as text (with formatting controlled by PageMaker). When placed as text, each row is placed as a separate paragraph. Styles are applied so that you can change the formatting by redefining the appropriate styles.

An alternative, if the spreadsheet is in a file that is not compatible with PageMaker's filters, or if you plan to change the formatting of the spreadsheet, you can save the spreadsheet in a text format, PageMaker can import the text of the spreadsheet. First, use the spreadsheet program to save the worksheet as a text file. If you create a table in a word processing program, use the same number of tabs to separate columns (do not use spaces), and use a carriage return (Enter or Return key) to end each row of the table. Usually this is the best method for handling simple tables with row elements that fit on one line.

Complex tables and tables with multiple lines per element can be built in a table editing program such as the Aldus Table Editor (supplied with PageMaker), or in Microsoft Word (using its Table feature).

You can place a dBASE or R:Base database file and select the fields of the database for importing into PageMaker. Two methods of placement are provided: directory format, in which each record is placed as a single paragraph with fields separated by tabs (as with spreadsheets), or catalog format, in which each field is a separate paragraph with a separate style definition.

Graphics Programs

PageMaker expects graphics files to have specific file name extensions:

Graphics Files	PageMaker Filename
Adobe Illustrator	sample.EPS
Aldus FreeHand	sample.EPS
Aldus Persuasion	sample.CGM or sample.WMF
Aldus Table Editor	sample.TBL or sample.WMF
Arts & Letters 3.01	sample.EPS (also CGM, TIF, WMF)
AutoCAD	sample.PLT (also ADI, EPS)
CGM graphics file format	sample.CGM
Corel Draw	sample.EPS (also PCX, PLT, TIF, WMF)
Encapsulated PostScript	sample.EPS
Excel charts and graphs	sample.XLC, sample.XLS (also WMF)
HP Graphics Gallery	sample.TIF
HP-GL plotter file format	sample.PLT
MacPaint	sample.PNT
Micrografx Designer/Draw Plus	sample.PIC (also CGM, WMF, TIF, PCX)

Lotus 1-2-3/Symphony	sample.PIC
Lotus Freelance	sample.EPS (also CGM, PIC, PLT, TIF)
Mirage	sample.IMA
PC Paint	sample.PIC
PC Paintbrush	sample.PCX, sample.TIF
Publisher's Paintbrush	sample.PCX
Tag Image File Format (TIFF)	sample.TIF
Videoshow (NAPLPS) format	sample.PIC
Windows Metafile	sample.WMF
Windows Paintbrush 2.0	sample.MSP
Windows Paintbrush 3.0	sample.BMP, sample.PCX

The common PC graphics formats are PCX (first used by PC Paintbrush), PIC (first used by PC Paint), Lotus PIC (used by Lotus products), Windows bitmap (BMP), and Windows Metafile (WMF). The common formats used on PCs *and other computers,* such as Macintoshes and Unix systems, include CGM (Computer Graphics Metafile), EPS (Encapsulated PostScript), and TIFF (Tag Image File Format).

TIFF (tag image file format) files can be produced by a variety of graphics programs, including Scan-Do (Hammerlab), HALO DPE (Media Cybernetics, through use of CUTTOTIF utility), Gallery (Hewlett-Packard), Picture Publisher (Micrografx/Astral Development), and PublishPac (Dest). Scanner manufacturers bundle software with the scanner that produces TIFF files.

Scanned images are paint-type graphics, displayed with less resolution than when they are printed. PageMaker prints scanned images at actual size and at reduced or expanded sizes very well if you use the automatic resizing feature (by holding down the Control key while resizing). Use the Image control command to adjust the lightness and contrast, as well as the screen angle and frequency for halftoning, for any TIFF image.

To use the built-in resizing feature that automatically selects the best sizes for printing with your target printer, hold down the Control key while resizing (dragging a corner of the image). Hold down the Shift key also if you want to resize the graphic proportionately.

PageMaker can compress and decompress TIFF image files with no loss in data. To compress a file, use the Place command and select the file in the Place dialog box. For a moderately compressed TIFF file, hold down Control and Alt while clicking OK. For maximum compression, hold down Control, Shift, and Alt and click OK. To decompress a TIFF file, hold down Control and click OK.

Draw-type graphics (also called object-oriented graphics and vector graphics) can be resized freely without distortion, and without the need for the automatic resizing used for paint-type (bit-map) graphics.

You can place color drawings with PageMaker, but PageMaker may substitute black for all colors, or a pattern that makes the drawing appear different on the screen than from the printer. It is best to use black-and-white graphics and to specify colors for the print shop to use when running the job.

PC Paint lets you create both color and black-and-white graphics, but PageMaker places only black-and-white graphics. Convert all color images to black-and-white with PC Paint to prepare files for PageMaker, or else PageMaker substitutes black for all colors.

PC Paintbrush, which also works with scanners to manipulate scanned images, can produce very large files. Change your graphics mode to monochrome for scanning and for faster response in general. When scanning, measure the area to scan. Using PC Paintbrush, type in the dimensions of the area or mark the dimensions with a mouse. A scanned image can be a very large file, so PageMaker reduces the image to a size that fits inside of your defined image area. Resize the image for your layout.

Microsoft Windows Paintbrush files can be placed directly onto PageMaker pages or else displayed in a window. You can cut or copy an image to the Clipboard, and paste the image onto a PageMaker page.

Lotus 1-2-3 and Symphony graphics should look exactly the same on the PageMaker page. When you use hatch and fill patterns, the programs store them as line segments. When they are resized, these patterns are more widely spaced than usual. Text placed from Lotus graphics is in a sans serif font, positioned according to information in the file (which could be wrong if it was set for a different target printer). In this case, remove the text from the graphics before placing, and add the text using PageMaker.

Autodesk AutoCAD plotter files, created by plotting a drawing with the ADI plotter driver (shipped with AutoCAD), are recognized by PageMaker. Drawings are straight line segments; circular objects may print with undesirable results. Hatch and fill patterns are stored as line segments. When resized, these patterns are more widely spaced than usual. Text is described in straight line segments, which also produces undesirable results. Use AutoCAD to create graphics without text, and add the text with PageMaker.

EPS graphics files can be used if your printer is a PostScript device, such as an Apple LaserWriter or Linotype typesetter. EPS files contain PostScript code, and the format is useful for transferring descriptions of very complex line-art graphics (such as technical illustrations and logos) to and from different types of computers. EPS files can carry screen information for displaying the graphic as well as for printing it, so you may see an image on the screen. If the EPS file does not contain that information, you will see a text header that describes the image, and a bounding box that marks the boundaries of the image. You can crop and resize the image freely, even though you may not be able to see it.

If the EPS graphic image contains bit-mapped fonts or binary image data, PageMaker can't place it. If you see the PostScript code (text), rather than the image or a bounding box, rename the file with a filename that contains eight or less characters followed by a period and the letters "EPS" (as in SAMPLE.EPS), and then try to place the file.

PageMaker requires that the PostScript code in EPS files be well-behaved in the use of certain operators, stacks, global dictionaries, and the graphics state. PageMaker strips out ill-behaved PostScript code. The manual clearly states which operators and conventions to use and how to use them, but this information is only of use to PostScript programmers. For such tasks, it is recommended that you read Appendix C of the *PostScript Language Reference Manual*. (See Appendix E of this book, which also contains the address for EPSF technical specifications, written for PostScript programmers.)

APPENDIX C
Special Characters

Popular special characters include the following:

Character	Command
Character	**Command**
Bullet	Ctrl Shift 8
Close double quote	Ctrl Shift]
Close single quote	Ctrl]
Copyright symbol	Ctrl Shift O (letter O)
Discretionary hyphen	Ctrl -
Em dash	Ctrl Shift =
Em space (nonbreaking space)	Ctrl Shift M
En dash	Ctrl =
En space (nonbreaking space)	Ctrl Shift N
Fixed space (nonbreaking space)	Ctrl Spacebar
Nonbreaking hyphen	Ctrl Shift -
Nonbreaking slash	Ctrl Shift /
Open double quote	Ctrl Shift [
Open single quote	Ctrl [
Page Number marker	Ctrl Shift 3
Paragraph marker	Ctrl Shift 7

Character	**Command**
Registered trademark symbol	Ctrl Shift G
Section marker	Ctrl Shift 6
Thin space (nonbreaking space)	Ctrl Shift T

Use these special character codes in your text file, or add them after you position the text in the PageMaker publication file. (You have to use the latter method if your word processor won't let you create or export the special characters. Read your word processor manual to determine whether this is the case.) The availability of special characters in PageMaker also depends on your printer. Read your printer manual to determine if your printer can print the special characters.

A nonbreaking space should be inserted when you do not want a line to break between two words. The size of the spaces range from an em space (equal to the point size), to a fixed space (a normal space), to an en space (1/2 the point size), and a thin space (1/4 the point size, or the width of a number).

APPENDIX D
Transferring Publication Files

One reason PageMaker is attractive to service bureaus is because it can save a publication file for use on either a PC-compatible computer or a Macintosh. Another feature attractive to almost any user is PageMaker's ability to import files from a variety of word processors (as described in Appendix A) and graphics programs (as described in Appendix B). You can use either the PC version or the Macintosh version of PageMaker to publish information derived from PC or Macintosh files.

You can also transfer PageMaker publication files to remote computers for further production work, printing, or typesetting. You can recompose the publication for the target printer at the remote site. Note, however, that if the printer is different, PageMaker may substitute a default font for printing, but the program remembers the original font choice in case you use the original printer again.

PageMaker is supplied with Adobe Type Manager (ATM) for Windows, which provides outline font scaling for display and printing with Type 1 fonts. The fonts supplied with PageMaker are high-quality fonts; if they are substituted for fonts in the document that are not available for your system, they will at least look professional in quality.

PageMaker remembers its target printer font selection information, but if you print a publication designed for another type of printer

PageMaker will try to print the best possible matching font and size. For the best results, change the target printer by using the Print command in the File menu.

If you transfer a publication file from the Macintosh version to the PC version of PageMaker, or vice-versa, special characters may appear different because some characters are not duplicated in both systems. PageMaker remembers the original character that you chose, so that if you transfer the publication back to the original computer, the file will contain the same characters as before (unless you specifically changed them).

To use a publication file created with an earlier version of PC PageMaker or with the Macintosh version of PageMaker, start PageMaker 4 and then open the publication file (you can't double-click a 3.0 publication file to run PageMaker 4). The conversion is automatic, and the original file is left intact while PageMaker 4 creates a new, untitled publication file. If the Macintosh publication was created with PageMaker 3.0, it must first be converted to PageMaker 4.0 on the Macintosh before you can open it in PageMaker 4.0 on the PC. The new files may recompose the text to be tighter, and therefore may change the line endings.

Converting Graphics

PageMaker publication files can be transferred to a Macintosh and used with the Macintosh version of PageMaker, and vice versa. All text and font information is preserved when you transfer the publication, but you may not get the results you expected if you don't use the same printer. For example, EPS (Encapsulated PostScript Format) graphics print only on PostScript printers.

PageMaker can transfer within a publication file all text, all PageMaker-created graphics and formatting, all master page items, all EPS graphics, all graphics contained within the publication file (not in external linked files), and all style sheet information.

Scanned images, paint-type graphics, PICT and draw-type graphics, tables, and any graphics stored in external files are best handled by first converting and transferring the graphics files separately, then using the Place command in PageMaker to place the converted graphics back on the page.

For example, if your graphics came from PC programs such as Lotus 1-2-3 (graphs), Micrografx Designer, Windows Paintbrush, or AutoCAD, you have to transfer these graphics separately and convert them to the Macintosh PICT file format, or use the EPS (Encapsulated PostScript) format as described in Appendix B. The TIFF format on the PC uses a PCX image for display purposes; in order to see the image in the Macintosh version of PageMaker, you must convert the file into a Macintosh-based TIFF file. You can place the PC-based TIFF file on the Macintosh page without having to see it (a gray box is displayed).

If you used the Macintosh version of PageMaker with Macintosh graphics, and you want to bring them over to the PC, you can transfer the publication files with PageMaker and MacPaint graphics, or place MacPaint files directly into the PC version of PageMaker. PICT graphics must be converted to another format, such as EPS or TIFF.

With scanned images, PageMaker transfers the low-resolution display version of the image, but not the actual scanned image. You must transfer the image file separately. Use TIFF (Tag Image File Format) for scanned images, which is universally recognized. Image files are usually linked to the PageMaker publication file, so store the image file in the same directory (or Macintosh folder) that contains the publication file.

After you have transferred and converted the graphics files into the appropriate format, use the PageMaker Place command to position the graphics in the receiving computer's publication file. By replacing the appropriately converted graphics, you gain the benefit of being able to use PageMaker's automatic scaling to resize paint-type graphics, with a selection of optimal printing sizes that will depend on the target printer connected to the receiving computer.

To convert paint-type graphics, you can use various programs, such as The Missing Link (PC Quik-Art, Inc.), which handles a variety of paint-type graphic file formats, including MacPaint, Windows Paintbrush, GEM Paint, PC Paint, PC Paintbrush, BLOAD (PIC files), Dr. Halo, EGA Paint, and Publisher's Paintbrush. Hotshot (SymSoft) is another excellent program that offers the ability to convert graphics files. The Macintosh version of Adobe PhotoShop can also convert TIFF files and save in either the PC or Macintosh version of TIFF and EPS.

If there is no way to convert a graphic from its native format to the Macintosh or PC format, a final alternative is to scan the graphic and save it as a TIFF (Tag Image File Format) file, or as an EPS (Encapsulated PostScript) file. TIFF and EPS files can be imported into any version of PageMaker. You can also create an EPS file by tracing over a MacPaint or PICT image using Aldus FreeHand for the Macintosh, a PostScript drawing program that creates an EPS representation of the artwork.

Transferring by Disk

You can use a variety of methods to transfer data to and from various PC-compatible computers. The easiest method is by exchanging floppy disks, and most computers have disk drives that accept PC-formatted 5 1/4-inch disks that hold 360 kilobytes (360K, or more than 360,000 characters). You can transfer information by copying files from one disk to another. You may be able to transfer files on PC AT-compatible disks, which can hold up to 1.2 megabytes (more than 1.2 million characters). Another method is to use portable hard disk cartridges, portable hard disks, or magnetic tape cartridges for larger files.

For Macintosh computers, you can purchase an optional 5 1/4-inch disk drive from Apple Computer for reading and writing PC-formatted 5 1/4-inch disks (360K each), or you may purchase a disk drive from Dayna Communications that can read and write both 360K PC disks and 1.2-megabyte AT disks. You can also transfer files from IBM Personal System's 3 1/2-inch disks (720 kilobytes each) to the Macintosh IIx, IIcx, or SE/30 (which includes at least one 3 1/2-inch SuperDrive floppy disk drive that reads PS/2 disks).

Transferring by Network

A popular method for managing the sharing of information among different types of computers is a *local area network* (LAN). A LAN can be comprised of different types of computers linked by twisted-pair or wide-band cable, with files available to some or all computers through the use of a *file server*—a computer with a hard disk containing the files that are shared. Some networks are controlled by the file server computer; others allow any computer on the network to act as a file server.

PageMaker publication files can be shared over these networks just as easily as other files can be shared over the networks, but you may not get high-quality output if you use a printer substantially different from the printer you chose in the Print dialog box. In addition, PageMaker requires that you leave graphics files in the folders (or directories) in which they were located when you placed them. The recommended method for organizing files on a network for production and printing is to copy any shared files into a local disk-storage device for use with PageMaker. Then print the publication from the same computer with which you placed those files onto PageMaker pages.

The AppleTalk-based networks from Apple Computer and Farallon are examples of networks that connect several Macintosh computers to each other, to one or more LaserWriters, and to PC ATs and compatible computers. Other choices include interface boxes, called *gateways*, that connect PC networks and other networks to AppleTalk (available from third-party vendors). Or, you can link PCs and Macintosh computers in an Ethernet network from 3Com Corporation, which can also be used to link PCs and Macintosh computers to minicomputers and mainframes. Novell's Netware also lets you connect PCs and Macintosh computers in the same network.

The software supplied with these products allows the transfer of PageMaker publication files (and other types of files) simply and easily from Macintosh computers to PCs, and vice versa. Novell, for example, lets you copy files by choosing a server, which appears on the PC as another disk drive and on the Macintosh as another disk. Another method is to use electronic mail software such as InBox (Symantec) to send publication files, text files, and graphics files as part of electronic mail messages to a user at another computer.

Transferring by Serial Cable or Modem

Direct connection over serial (RS-232C) cable, or modem link through a telephone line, is the least expensive way to connect a PC-compatible computer to a Macintosh. It is also the only way to transfer files to and from a Macintosh and a computer other than a PC.

With a serial cable connection or a modem-to-modem connection, you can use a communications or transfer program such Laplink (Travelling Software) or MacLink Plus (Dataviz). Either package includes a cable that plugs into an asynchronous port on the PC-compatible computer and into the modem port on the Macintosh, plus PC and Macintosh software to enable the machines to communicate.

Both LapLink and MacLink Plus provide a table of file formats on the PC and a matching table of Macintosh formats, so that you can transfer Lotus 1-2-3 files to Microsoft Excel, or vice versa. You can translate nearly every popular PC word-processing file format into the Macintosh version of Microsoft Word, or into the MacWrite file format. You can also translate database information from dBASE II and other structures to Macintosh database structures.

Essential to any file transfer method is the use of communication protocols. Protocols let you transfer information with the secure feeling that no errors will be placed into the data from noisy telephone lines or other electromagnetic interference. MacLink Plus and Laplink provide protocols for transfer, and communications programs usually offer one or more protocols. The best protocols for transferring PageMaker files from one computer to another are Xmodem, Kermit, X.PC, or MNP. In every case, you need to use the same protocol in the programs running on both computers.

You can use the Xmodem protocol to transfer files to PCs from Macintosh computers, to Macs from PCs, and from both types of computers to CP/M, Apple //, and other computers and back again, without loss of data integrity. Almost every communication program for the Macintosh and for PC-compatible computers offers the Xmodem protocol.

Transferring to a Typesetting Service

You can send PageMaker publication files to a typesetting service that uses PostScript typesetters and film recorders. Many services use PageMaker, and you can supply the publication file on disk, or transfer the publication file via cable or modem as described above.

Although the typesetting service may have a copy of PageMaker, the service may not have the exact fonts that you use. In such cases, you may be better off by preparing a PostScript file with the font information included, rather than providing the original PageMaker publication file. Some services require that you prepare a PostScript file rather than a publication file.

Be sure to select the appropriate output device (such as the Linotronic 300) in the Target printer's Setup dialog box *before* creating the PostScript file.

To create an Encapsulated PostScript file, click the Setup button in the Print dialog box, then click the Options button in the Setup dialog box. Select the Encapsulated PostScript file option, and supply a name for the Encapsulated PostScript file. By clicking the Header button you can choose whether or not to include the header with the PostScript file, which is necessary for printing the page by itself.

An alternative is to print to a disk file rather than to a printer, saving the instructions in a file. First, use the Windows Control Panel as described in Chapter 1 to configure your target printer to the "FILE" port. Next, select the printer connected to "FILE" when you use the Print dialog box.

When you finish, you can transfer the PostScript files to the typesetting service as you would transfer a publication file, by using a modem or a disk. In fact, because the PostScript file is a simple ASCII file, you can transfer it using almost any communications program or electronic mail program.

When using fonts that are not available at the service bureau, you may have to include temporary soft (downloadable) fonts with your print file. Be sure your soft fonts are listed in the WIN.INI file under the correct [printer,FILE] heading (usually [PostScript,FILE]). You can open the WIN.INI file by double-clicking it, or by using Aldus Setup to view it (from the View menu). Adobe Type Manager (ATM) automatically copies the soft fonts for Type 1 fonts to the WIN.INI section.

APPENDIX E
References

Books

Adobe Systems, Inc. *PostScript Language Reference Manual, PostScript Language Tutorial and Cookbook,* and *PostScript Applications* (3 volume set). Addison-Wesley Publishing Co.: Reading, MA, 1985.

Beale, Stephen, and Cavuoto, James. *The Scanner Book.* Micro Publishing Press: Torrance, CA, 1989.

Berryman, Greg. *Notes on Graphic Design and Visual Communication.* William Kaufmann, Inc.: Los Altos, CA, 1984.

Bove, Tony, and Rhodes, Cheryl. *PageMaker 4 Macintosh: the Basics.* John Wiley & Sons: New York, NY, 1990.

Bove, Tony, and Rhodes, Cheryl. *The Well-Connected Macintosh: An Overview of Desktop Communications.* Harcourt Brace Jovanovich: Cambridge, MA, 1987.

Bove, Tony; Rhodes, Cheryl; and Thomas, Wes. *The Art of Desktop Publishing,* 2nd Edition. Bantam Computer Books: New York, NY, 1987.

Felici, James, and Nace, Ted. *Desktop Publishing Skills*. Addison-Wesley Publishing Co.: Reading, MA, 1987.

Garcia, Mario R. *Contemporary Newspaper Design,* 2nd Edition. Prentice Hall: Englewood Cliffs, NJ, 1987.

Holt, Robert Lawrence. *How to Publish, Promote, and Sell Your Own Book*. St. Martin's Press: New York, NY, 1985.

International Paper Company. *Pocket Pal, A Graphics Arts Production Handbook*. International Paper Company: New York, NY, 1983. (Includes extensive glossary of graphic arts terms.)

Laing, John. *Do-It-Yourself Graphic Design*. Macmillan Publishing: New York, NY, 1984.

Lem, Dean Phillip. *Graphics Master 4*. Dean Lem Associates: Los Angeles, CA, 1985.

Nace, Ted and Gardner, Michael. *LaserJet Unlimited,* 2nd Edition. Peachpit Press: Berkeley, CA, 1989.

Parker, Roger C. *The Aldus Guide to Basic Design*. Aldus Corp.: Seattle, WA, 1987.

Poynter, Dan. *Publishing Short-Run Books,* 4th Edition. Para Publishing: Santa Barbara, CA, 1987.

Poynter, Dan. *The Self-Publishing Manual*. Para Publishing: Santa Barbara, CA, 1984.

Shibukawa, Ikuyoshi, and Takahashi, Yumi. *Designer's Guide to Color*, *Designer's Guide to Color 2*, and *Designer's Guide to Color 3*. Chronicle Books: San Francisco, CA, 1983, 1984, and 1986, respectively.

Solomon, Martin. *The Art of Typography*. Watson-Guptill Publications (a division of Billboard Publications): New York, NY, 1986.

Strunk, William, and White, E.B. *The Elements of Style*. Macmillan Publishing: New York, NY, 1972.

University of Chicago Press. *A Manual of Style*. University of Chicago Press: Chicago, IL, 1979.

Venolia, Jan. *Write Right!* Ten Speed Press: Berkeley, CA, 1982.

White, Jan V. *Designing for Magazines*. R.R. Bowker: New York, NY, 1982.

White, Jan V. *Editing by Design*. R.R. Bowker: New York, NY, 1982.

White, Jan V. *Graphic Idea Notebook*. R.R. Bowker: New York, NY, 1981.

White, Jan V. *Mastering Graphics*. R.R. Bowker: New York, NY, 1983.

White, Jan V. *Using Charts and Graphs*. R.R. Bowker: New York, NY, 1984.

Wilson, Adrian. *The Design of Books*. Gibbs M. Smith, Inc., Peregrine Smith Books: Salt Lake City, UT, 1974.

Magazines, Journals, and Newspapers

American Printer. 300 West Adams Street, Chicago, IL 60606. $35 per year.

Electronic Composition & Imaging. Youngblood Publishing Company, 200 Yorkland Boulevard, Willowdale, Ontario, Canada M2J 1R5. $45 per year in the United States, $25 in Canada.

Graphic Perspective. Ashley House, 176 Wicksteed Avenue, Toronto, Ontario, M4G 2B6 Canada. (416) 422-1446. $40 per year.

Graphics Arts Monthly and The Printing Industry. Technical Publishing, 875 Third Avenue, New York, NY 10022. (212) 605-9548. $50 per year.

Inside Print (formerly *Magazine Age*). MPE Inc., 125 Elm Street, New Canaan, CT 06840. (203) 972-0761. $36 per year.

PC Ziff-Davis Publishing Company, One Park Ave., New York, NY 10016. (800) 289-0429. $44.97 per year.

PC World. PCW Communications, 501 Second Street, San Francisco, CA 94107. (415) 546-7722. $29.90 per year.

Magazine Design and Production. Globecom Publishing Ltd., 4551 West 107th Street #343, Overland, KS 66207. $36 per year.

Printing Impressions. 401 North Broad Street, Philadelphia, PA 19108. $50 per year.

Printing Journal. 2401 Charleston Road, Mtn. View, CA 94943. $16 per year.

Publish. PC World Communications, 501 Second Street, San Francisco, CA 94107. (415) 546-7722. $39.90 per year.

Publisher's Weekly. R. R. Bowker, 249 West 17th Street, New York, NY 10028. $89 per year.

Small Press, the Magazine of Independent Publishing. R. R. Bowker, 249 West 17th Street, New York, NY 10028. $18 per year.

Step-By-Step Graphics. Dynamic Graphics, 6000 N Forest Park Drive, P.O. Box 1901, Peoria, IL 61656-1901. (800) 255-8800. $42 per year.

VERBUM, Journal of Personal Computer Aesthetics. P.O. Box 15439, San Diego, CA 92115. (619) 463-9977. MCI Mail: VERBUM. $28 per year.

Newsletters

Bove and Rhodes Inside Report on Desktop Publishing and Multimedia. Tony Bove and Cheryl Rhodes, P.O. Box 1289, Gualala, CA 95445. (707) 884-4413. MCI Mail: TBOVE. CompuServe: 70105, 722. $195 per year in the United States, $220 foreign and Canada.

Brilliant Ideas for Publishers. Creative Brilliance Associates, 4709 Sherwood Road, Box 4237, Madison WI 53711. (608) 271-6867. Free to publishers.

CAP (Computer Aided Publishing) Report. InfoVision Inc., 52 Dragon Court, Woburn, MA 01801. (617) 935-5186. $195 per year.

The Desktop Publisher. Aldus Corp., 616 First Avenue, Suite 400, Seattle, WA 98104. (206) 441-8666. Free to registered users of Aldus software.

microPublishing Report. 2004 Curtis Avenue #A, Redondo Beach, CA 90278. (213) 376-5724. $175 per year.

Quick Printer's Guide. Lambda Company, 3655 Frontier Avenue, Boulder, CO 80301. (303) 449-4827. $75 per year.

ReCAP. Boston Computer Society, Desktop Publishing User Group, One Center Plaza, Boston, MA 02108. (617) 367-8080. $28 per year.

Seybold Report on Publishing Systems. Seybold Publications, Box 644, Media, PA 19063. (215) 565-2480. $240 per year. *Seybold Report on Desktop Publishing.* $195 per year.

SWADTP. Southwest Association of Desktop Publishers, 1208 West Brooks, Norman, OK 73069. (405) 360-5554.

Writers Connection. Writers Connection, 1601 Saratoga-Sunnyvale Road, Suite 180, Cupertino, CA 95014. (408) 973-0227. $12 per year.

User Groups

Boston Computer Society, One Center Plaza, Boston, MA 02108. (617) 367-8080. $35 per year membership fee includes choice of two newsletters, including: *The Active Window; re:CAP, the publishing/computer-aided publishing newsletter*; and *Graphics News*; plus other newsletters available to members at $4 each per year.

National Association of Desktop Publishers, P.O. Box 508, Boston, MA 02215-9998. (617) 437-6472. $95 per year.

New England PageMaker Users Group, c/o WordWorks, 222 Richmond Street, Providence, RI 02903. (401) 274-0033. Also represented by MCM Associates, 22 1/2 Lee Street, Marblehead, MA 01945. (617) 639-1548.

SouthWest Association of DeskTop Publishers, 1208 West Brooks, Norman, OK 73069. (405) 360-5554, (405) 682-8541, and (405) 364-2751.

Technical References

Tag Image File Format (TIFF) was originally developed and placed in the public domain by Aldus Corporation, in cooperation with several scanner and printer manufacturers. It was designed as a format for digital data interchange, and it is independent of specific operating systems, filing systems, compilers, and processors. For a copy of the latest description of TIFF, and further information, contact Aldus.

For questions about PageMaker, FreeHand, Persuasion, and TIFF, address queries to: Aldus Corp., 411 First Avenue South, Seattle, WA 98104; or call (206) 622-5500.

For questions about Microsoft Word, address queries to: Microsoft Corp., 16011 NE 36th Way, Box 97017, Redmond, WA 98073-9717; or call (206) 882-8080.

Index